# *When Ducks*
## *Were Plenty*

# When Ducks Were Plenty
## The Golden Age of Duck Hunting

A Pictorial and Written Anthology of the Origins, History, Impact, and Prospects of
## The Grand Passage of Waterfowl
## in America

Describing the

Haunts, Habits, and Methods of Shooting All Manner of Wildfowl

in Their Diverse Locations,

## From the 1840s to about 1920

*Ed Muderlak*

Safari Press Inc.

P.O. Box 3095, Long Beach, CA 90803

Muderlak, Ed

Safari Press Inc.

2000, Long Beach, California

ISBN 1-57157-206-6

Library of Congress Catalog Card Number:  99-71026

10 9 8 7 6 5 4 3 2

Readers wishing to receive the Safari Press catalog, featuring many fine books on big-game hunting, wingshooting, and sporting firearms, should write to Safari Press Inc., P.O. Box 3095, Long Beach, CA 90803, USA.  Tel: (714) 894-9080 or visit our Web site at www.safaripress.com.

# Table of Contents

## Section II  1880 to 1900

## Section III  1900 to 1920

# Dedication

*For Sandy and Winn*

# Foreword
### Duck Shooting by "Gaucho"
### (pseudonym of Captain Arthur W. du Bray)

Duck shooting, with all the term implies, is of all shooting sports the most difficult, the most trying, and at the same time the most rewarding; it offers the greatest test of skill and marksmanship, of endurance to wet and cold, and of courage under the most trying conditions. A veritable man-killer if carried to the limit, it is to other game shooting as football is to cricket. To stand immovable in a blind on cold, raw, wet days, to paddle a boat for miles, to lie out in an open lake in a sink box, to pick up decoys in water that freezes the fingers, to shoot at birds speeding by like bullets and then to hit them: Few men can long stand these activities, and fewer still can excel at them. And yet this is simply duck shooting. Very often, even on the best duck grounds, wind or weather may change the flight so that after all the labor, exposure, hardship, and planning, the sportsman returns with an empty game sack.

However, the excitement and real pleasure of one good day soon dispels all feelings of fatigue, disappointment, and discomfort. When conditions are right, a bred-in-the-bone duck shooter will leave a comfortable bed and shooting box at any hour of the night to face a blinding, driving sheet of rain or sleet. He will wade out to his blind and stand there for hours, or will break through a thin coating of ice with his canoe and then paddle into the very teeth of a howling gale to some spot where his duck sense guides him. He may fire two hundred or more cartridges, or less than a dozen shots. He may upset his boat in deep water or flounder into an unknown hole in what he thought was shallow water; in either case he will be drenched to the skin. But he hopes and presses on, and, if of the right stuff, grins and bears it, trusting his luck will change. So it does, perhaps for the better, perhaps for the worse, for he may lose his way in a labyrinthine marsh on his return.

Duck shooting is one of the grandest sports, and the man who is a good shot here ranks the highest in proficiency, as no other shooting demands as much judgment, skill, and steadiness of aim. Crippled ducks offer food for marsh scavengers, but only stone-dead ducks swell the game bag. The great charm of duck hunting is its endless variety: of the many shots presented, the ever-varying speeds of flight, and the many different species composing the duck family. One must be able to shoot dead center from fifteen to sixty yards, in any wind, with unsteady footing, often in a bad light, in foul weather, and nearly always so heavily clothed that the old familiar gunstock never comes twice to the same place. Nevertheless, one good day compensates for many heartbreakers. "Faintheart never won fair lady": It takes a man of courage, with a constitution of iron and a masterly eye and hand, to make a successful duck shooter, and no kid-gloved dandy need attempt it.

## Editor's Note

"Gaucho," or Captain Arthur W. du Bray (1849–1928), was a consummate sportsman and prolific "letters to the editor" writer, best known to those who appreciate the "Old Reliable" Parker shotgun. Du Bray was an on-the-road salesman for Parker Brothers from 1890 until 1913, when he "retired" to San Francisco and continued on as the maker's agent until he died at age seventy-nine. I first met du Bray on the pages of an 1898 issue of *Shooting and Fishing*, while researching shotgun-related literature of the Parker era (1865 to 1940). Du Bray's long letters to editors and his articles about shotguns, hunting, and trapshooting were a gold mine of historic information—fact and opinion—and I relied on him heavily when I wrote *Parker Guns—The "Old Reliable"* (Safari Press 1997). My Parker research involved scanning and speedreading over two thousand pulp weekly newspapers of the 1870s to 1930s, hundreds of monthly magazines, and an extensive library of rare out-of-print gunning books. Not infrequently I found myself diverted from the task at hand, engrossed in an off-topic tale of good old-time waterfowling. Many of the stories were in the form of long letters to the editor by otherwise unpublished authors, such as Gaucho, telling of their most memorable waterfowling experience or shot of a lifetime.

As I strayed from Parker-related research to tales of old-time waterfowling, it became apparent that I had an anthology in the making. The shards of individual stories could be assembled into a cohesive and clear window to the past. Buried in the frail pulp pages of ancient hard-to-find sporting newspapers and magazines were stories too priceless to let languish unread.

There is some mystical element of duck shooting that lends itself to the well-told story. The trials and tribulations of waterfowling are diverse and often spiced with hardship and humor. Tales from the "grand passage" of 1850 through 1920 engage the reader with nostalgic charm, as in chapter 8, in which "An Old Sportsman" reminisces about how he and a teenage friend caught and trained a loon to be their decoy. This story, from the period just after the Civil War, has the same naive appeal as Robert Ruark's boyhood experiences in *The Old Man and the Boy*. Other tales of this era portray a time of unregulated shooting and an abundance of game.

My primary goal is to entertain and amuse duck hunters and would-be duck hunters with stories from the grand passage of wildfowl. I have tried to present an overview of the waterfowling literature of the time as found in books, sportsmen's newspapers, and outdoor magazines. The earliest sketch, "Rail Shooting" (chap. 6), is from Henry William Herbert's 1848 book, *Frank Forester's Field Sports*; the last story of old-time duck shooting, "No Spring Shooting On Barnegat Bay" (chap. 54), is from an article by M. H. Ittner in the 4 January 1919 issue of *The American Field*.

The chapters progress in rough chronological order to show the evolution of American wildfowling. I have added "Editor's Notes" to many of the pieces and have listed contributing authors in a bibliography for those interested in further reading. I have selected, assembled, and edited the anthology material to give readers a sense of changing times and attitudes, unencumbered by present-day revisionism.

For example, in chapter 1 "Gooseman" summarized the history of geese in California from the 1850s to 1913 in "When Wild Geese Were Plenty": "The people drove them off [to save their crops], then killed them to eat, and when San Francisco grew enough to consume large numbers of geese, market hunters ended the great goose war. Today [1913] geese are so reduced that it is necessary to protect them to ensure decent shooting."

The other chapters in this anthology tell of wildfowling from Maine to Washington state, Florida to Canada, and the eastern seaboard to the Great Lakes and North Dakota; and from the former abundance and variety of ducks, geese, and shore birds to the extinction of the passenger pigeon. There are tales of duck-tolling dogs and live decoys, sneak boats and sink boxes, punt guns and stalking horses, market hunters bagging hundreds of birds a day, and "sports" who cooked their lone coot "from a sense of duty." Through these tales, the reader will come to understand the need for federal legislation to protect and control the endangered.

The stories that follow are as much a part of our heritage as the westward expansion, the Indian wars, the Industrial Revolution, and surgery without anesthesia. Twenty-first-century political correctness doesn't apply to nineteenth-century circumstances. The stories chronicle a different place and time; our duck-shooting ancestors provided us with a window to the past through which we can see the golden age of wildfowling, when ducks were plenty.

# *Prologue*

## *Teal Story by Ed Muderlak*

Illinois has a special early teal season each mid-September, and my local chapter of Ducks Unlimited tends to schedule its annual fund-raiser smack dab in the middle of this season. Now any duck hunter worth a decoy weight will think up at least one tall tale of waterfowling prowess to impress the captive audience at his particular D.U. banquet table. I'm no exception, but I do like to tell a story with some semblance of fact. And so it was on the morn of the great D.U. bash of 1978, I stood for a brief moment on the threshold of storytelling immortality . . . and then the teal flew away.

Back in the late 1970s, I was working at the consumptive profession of "courthouse lawyer," while trying to keep up with the healthful and honest pursuits of hunting and fishing. Circuit court judges were then loath to ascend to the bench before 9:30 A.M., so the early teal season, daylight saving time, and membership in the Northern Illinois Coon and Fox Hunting Club allowed me the luxury of some puddle jumping on my way to work. I was always up and on my way well before dawn. My destination, the Coon Club grounds, consisted of about 120 acres of swamp, ponds, and timber at the confluence of the Sugar and Pecatonica Rivers near Shirland. I was then one of only two duck-hunting members of that hillbilly heaven. The other forty-eight good ol' boys saw no sport in anything but chasing small tree-climbing furballs at night with packs of blueticks and redbones. Thus I usually had the place to myself during daylight hours.

The Coon Club, conveniently located between home and office, was my personal puddle duck heaven. The layout was such that I could check all the ponds and potholes in about thirty minutes, morning and evening, to and from work. My Parker Trojan 20-bore permanently resided in my car trunk just in case a situation called for a dose of $7/_8$-ounce No. 6s.

At sunrise I'd unlock the gate at the clubgrounds and drive through the woods to a place behind a small rise, about a hundred yards from the first shallow pond. I carried coveralls to slip over my suit pants, and rubber boots to cover my wingtips. Next I'd load the Trojan and slip it into an old cloth scabbard for protection. Then I'd creep and crawl toward the first pond, pushing the gun ahead while keeping a big swamp oak between me and the line of sight of any web-footed sentries. When I got to the tree, I could kneel and look to see if my labors were to be rewarded.

As luck would have it that D.U. banquet morning, a dozen birds were sitting on the pond about thirty yards away—all teal! I slipped the 20-bore from its case, checked the safety, eased myself up to full standing position, stepped out from behind the tree, and said "Shoo!" Instantly the pond erupted with a loud sucking *whoosh* as the teal all jumped at once. For a moment they startled me almost as much as I had startled them. The Parker went to my shoulder as a reflex, and I don't consciously remember selecting a bird or pulling the front trigger. I felt the recoil and saw four—count 'em, four!—teal drop back onto the pond, with one cripple flopping his way to a mud bank. I'd like to say I had picked out a certain bluewing, led him just right, and made my shot, but truth be told, I had flock-shot them, plain and simple, and seemed to have hit a good part of the flock.

Initial disbelief gave way to the realization that I had just scored a "quadruple"! The story of four speedy bluewings downed with one paltry shot from a 20-gauge started to form in my mind. I considered how I might embellish the epic tale to one-up my tall-tale-telling friends at the dinner that evening. Then the cripple started to get too close to the tall grass, so I extended him an invitation he couldn't refuse with my second barrel. As I stood there with an empty gun in the self-same hands that had just committed mass murder on four teal with one shot, two of the "dead" birds got up and flew away.

Thus ended an otherwise great story of a double brace of teal bagged with one small dose of 20-gauge No. 6s. Two birds with two shots still qualifies as a double and not bad shooting with a small bore, but anything less than ten birds with one shot would have hardly warranted mention in the second half of the nineteenth century. As a counterpoint to my story of teal shooting, let me take you back to that golden age with a short article,

"Blue-winged Teal about Boston," by I. J. Prouty, taken from the 18 July 1895 issue of *Shooting and Fishing*:

> Early one September morning back in the 1860s, I bagged eighteen bluewings at one shot, out of a flock of twenty-eight that were along the edge of a slough. The little chaps bunch up like so many peep and give great chances. The remaining teal flew off and lit elsewhere about the marsh. The next morning at sunrise I went to the same slough and got eight more with both barrels. I shot the last two the next day and thus completely obliterated the flock. I advise any gunner who can't get a sitting shot to shoot the instant a teal jumps. Once fairly up, the bluewing is off with such astounding speed that most gunners find hard work in stopping him after his initial spring.

I can't even imagine dropping eighteen bluewings with one shot from my vintage Parker breechloader— and Prouty was using a muzzleloader! His story might seem a bit suspect by current standards, but in the context of the chapters that follow, Prouty's good luck was par for the course in the golden days of the muzzleloading fowling piece.

# *Introduction*

If seemingly boastful stories of old-time duck-shooting prowess can be believed, this book is nonfiction. In other words, it ain't braggin' if it's true. I gleaned the fifty-odd chapters of out-of-copyright material from weekly and monthly sports newspapers and magazines, and from rare out-of-print books of the era. My first job as editor was to ferret out the gems of duck-shooting content from a resource base of over 100 million words. Most of the pieces—particularly those from pulp weekly newspapers such as *Shooting and Fishing*, *The American Sportsman*, *Forest and Stream*, and *The American Field*—proved to be gems in the rough by today's standards of grammar and punctuation. Many of the chapters represent the entire lifetime literary work of one-time-only-published freelance writers, and the demands and deadlines of weekly publishing prevented in-depth editing.

Nineteenth-century writers often favored the 300-word, one-sentence, excessively punctuated paragraph. Never mind that a story is of the first magnitude, anachronistic word use and proliferating commas and semicolons can be tedious for readers accustomed to modern brevity. My challenge was to edit heavily and sometimes paraphrase the grammatically diverse raw material into a semblance of year-2000 prose, while preserving nuances of historic context and retaining, unembellished, the content and spice of the writer's original work—no easy job. However, should any of the long-deceased authors miraculously appear to review my edited version of their work, I believe most would agree that their once-in-a-lifetime waterfowling stories suffered little in the translation from "Victorian" English.

# Section I
## Before 1880

The sport of downing flying feathered game with a gun has its popular origins in the early 1800s, when caplock replaced flintlock as the state-of-the-art fowling piece. There were reported instances of wildfowling in the 1600s and 1700s—a picture titled "Shooting Flying" is in Blome's Gentleman's Recreation (1683)—but in general, the lock time of flint guns was too slow to be effective on flying birds. Also, the flint, frizzen, and priming pan were susceptible to the vagaries of weather, especially on wet and blustery days when waterfowl were on the move. Thus it remained for a Scots clergyman, Reverend Forsythe, to invent a percussion priming compound in 1807, and for others to encapsulate his "fulminate" in paper, and later in waterproof copper caps.

By the 1840s, the sport of wildfowling on the wing was well established in America, and the era of the caplock muzzleloader—the 1840s through the 1870s—coincided with an era of abundant game. Literate sportsmen such as Henry William Herbert (pen name "Frank Forester") helped popularize the sport with articles in nascent sporting newspapers such as the *Spirit of the Times*. Books by Forester, John Krider, Dr. Elisha Jarrett Lewis, John Bumstead, Joe Long, Adam H. Bogardus, and John Mortimer Murphy described mid-nineteenth-century wildfowling in depth. *When Ducks Were Plenty* begins with "Gooseman's" description of geese in 1850s California, when wild geese were plenty.

# When Wild Geese Were Plenty
## by "Gooseman"

I came to California in the early 1850s, married a woman whose father had a 50,000-acre grain ranch, and started as a gooseman. I guess you never heard that word. I had thought it was a joke, but mighty soon I found out my mistake. After the first rain, the green, succulent wheat in the Sacramento Valley began to spring up and attract hoards of geese. Then the old man had to hire an army of at least three hundred goosemen, and I enlisted. Years later when I became bookkeeper of the ranch, an item on the books amazed me: "20,000 cartridges for the season of 1868, and 250 Mexicans and Indians to shoot geese." You wouldn't believe half of my stories if I sat down and got to talking "goose" with you.

# When Ducks Were Plenty

Back in the days before the Civil War, I saw miles and miles of wheatland covered with geese so thick, I might have taken an oath that California was under a blanket of snow. The geese watched the men plant and then would have the seeds out before they started to sprout. Only the efforts of three hundred goosemen, night and day for weeks, saved some of the big wheat fields. Everybody turned out, not to shoot geese—Lord bless you, no!—but just to scare them off the green fields.

A ranch wouldn't have had a crop five minutes without goosemen. We went through as much ammunition in ten years as was used in some wars, but we were at war with geese. As soon as planting began, we went on duty. Thirty goosemen patrolled on four-hour shifts, relieved by subsequent shifts all day and night. We fired over them with all kinds of guns, anything that would make a noise, trying to drive them off. We couldn't kill them. There weren't enough people in the state to eat the geese that three hundred men could kill in a night, so the only thing to do was ride around yelling and shooting. But when the geese left one field, they just settled in another.

One rainy night in the 1860s, I was sitting on my horse and talking with three new goosemen. It was foggy, and we couldn't see a thing. Suddenly we heard the all-too-familiar *honk! honk! honk!* It grew louder, and the awful sounds were coupled with a flush of wings. A Mexican gooseman fell off his horse and got on his knees, scared stiff: He thought the end of the world had come. The clamor was so loud that our horses began to stampede, while out of the fog dropped about a million geese. It was like a snowstorm of twenty-pound flakes. The horses ran and bucked off some of the new men. When the geese saw us, it was Hades for a few moments. One man was hit so hard by a goose that he was knocked completely out of his saddle. Birds alit on most of the horses. They were so thick that when a big honker landed on the back of my horse, she let fly behind and killed another goose in midair.

The situation was discouraging and heartbreaking for the original grain farmers in Glenn and nearby counties. The big owners offered all kinds of money to anyone who could invent some scheme to scare away the geese. One Yank came out from Nantucket with an old watchman's rattle that his grandfather used in the Revolutionary War— to scare Indians, I reckon. When he gave it a whirl I thought fifty volts had hit me. The old man had a hundred made from the original model; he thought they would clean out the birds, but they only cleaned him out to the tune of a dollar apiece. The first night that we charged the geese while whirling those rattlers I shall never forget as long as I live. The snapping and clicking scared the horses nearly to death. Half of the mustangs ran away, and the new men—the tenderfeet—all got bucked off. Some of the horses weren't found for a week.

That same night we regrouped with about a hundred mounted goosemen in a line and advanced on the enemy. The outfit charged at full speed over the ranch with every man yelling and screaming and whirling a rattle that sounded like the quintessence of bottled thunder. It simply set the geese crazy. The birds rose in bunches like big puffs of smoke. I once saw the explosion of a Mississippi River steamer at New Orleans that filled the air with cottony clouds. For a few moments the sky over the ranch looked the same. To those of us who kept in the saddle it was great fun, and we did succeed in routing the geese. But they were back again the next day.

I then divided up the force. Every man had a detail and a line to march. His duty was to ride up and down, firing off his shotgun and whirling his watchman's rattle. The minute this stopped, however, out of nowhere would descend one or two thousand geese. After two weeks we began to suspect they were growing fond of the rattle and, by jingo, they certainly were!

One of the most successful things we tried was to fasten big pieces of red cloth to about twenty geese. This scared them to fits. The tied-up birds would follow the flock, frightening them all. But it only worked until they got used to it, and that was the trouble: They always got used to it. We dyed a hundred geese red, a hundred blue, and some with red necks and blue wings. The ornithologists were crazy about the "new" species. One old goose flew around for weeks with a boy's trousers on, but nothing worked in the long run. Despite all our efforts, with the salaries and board of the goosemen, cost of ammunition, and all the wear and tear of geese and horses in the wheat, you can bet that 50 percent of the crop profits went whooping away with the honkers.

The goose question was eventually resolved through the settlement of the countryside. At first the people drove them off, then killed them to eat, and when San Francisco grew enough to consume large numbers of geese, market hunters ended the great goose war. But it took years, and from 1853 to 1868 I saw miles of Tulare and San Joaquin Counties covered with snow-white and other varieties of geese. Today [1913] geese are so reduced that it is necessary to protect them to ensure decent shooting. The days of the great flocks of geese are gone, and the gooseman is out of a job.

# When Wild Geese Were Plenty

## Editor's Note

To put Gooseman's tale of excessive abundance of wildfowl in context, the 1850 census listed a total of 92,597 white and "free colored" persons residing within California's 155,980 square miles, or a population density of .59 inhabitant per square mile. Thus Gooseman was not exaggerating when he wrote: "We couldn't kill them. There weren't enough people in the state to eat the geese that three hundred men could kill in a night, so the only thing to do was ride around yelling and shooting."

Pseudonyms, or pen names such as Gaucho and Gooseman, seem to have been the vogue in the nineteenth century. Sport hunting was then considered a frivolous avocation in America, so gentlemen sportsmen often hid behind modest pen names to shield themselves from personal criticism. Best known of the professional American writers was Henry William Herbert and his *nom de plume* "Frank Forester." But many of the more literate amateur writers were lawyers, physicians, or clergyman who feared Victorian censure should they openly admit to engaging in sporting pastimes that smacked so much of idleness and pure enjoyment.

I have researched all of the pen names in this book to "A List of Pseudonyms" in *Guns and Shooting, a Selected Chronological Bibliography* by Ray Riling (1982). The various authors' real and pen names are both given if they appear on Riling's list or if I discovered their true identity through independent research. For example, I tracked down W. L. Colville (chap. 25) when he used "Dick Swiveller" as his *nom de fusil* (shooting name) at an 1890s live bird tournament reported in *Forest and Stream*. However, Gooseman and many other once- or seldom-published writers effectively preserved their anonymity by not being well known during their lifetime.

# When Ducks Were Plenty

Pen names for professionals (with the exception of Herbert) were never popular in America, as the writers were seeking name identification as an aid in selling themselves or their product. For example, John Krider (chap. 5) had a diversified sporting goods store, Captain A. H. Bogardus (chap. 15) was an exhibition crackshot and tournament live pigeon shooter, and Isaac McLellan (chap. 17) was an oft-published poet known to his contemporaries as the "poet of the rod and gun."

The use of pseudonyms seems to have lost favor as the Victorian era expired along with Queen Victoria. When Edward VII ascended to the British throne at his mother's death in 1901, one of his first pronouncements was, "Gentlemen, light up." This was not so much an invitation to smoke cigars in parlors and drawing rooms as it was a signal that shooting sports and other manly outdoor pastimes were no longer to be frowned upon. Meanwhile, on the west side of the big pond it became increasingly difficult for women to criticize their sport-hunting and trapshooting menfolk while they themselves were riding bicycles and playing tennis and on Sundays at that. Thus the use of pen names after the turn of the century seems limited mostly to contentious "gun cranks" and writers who wanted to tell their once-in-a-lifetime story of a large bag or spectacular shot without the real or imagined censure of friends and acquaintances.

# Bay Birds on the Orleans Marshes
## by E. T. Marliave

I had heard wonderful stories about the shooting on Cape Cod from an old gunner named Bates. He was in the habit of killing plover and yellowlegs in such rapid succession as to necessitate half-hour intermissions for the purpose of cooling his gun barrels. When I heard that his customary daily bag was a wagonload, I decided the cape was the place for me. I pumped the old gentleman for information on the best localities, accommodations, etc., and was informed that one Tim Higgins, of Orleans, maintained a hostelry for sportsmen; that he kept plenty of horses and wagons; furnished excellent provisions, both edible and bibulous; had an ice house for preserving game; and provided it all for one dollar per day! That settled it. A couple of friends, Jim H. and Sam B., and I decided on 15 August as the day to test the first flight of larger bay birds.

# *When Ducks Were Plenty*

I had either dreamed or read or heard somebody say that a live pigeon was an excellent decoy in the marshes, so, after repainting my stools and duly attending to other necessary preliminaries, I toured the Boston birdstores in search of a suitably colored member of the pigeon family. This, however, was no easy task. I was finally obliged to purchase a white bird, and, with the aid of a box of hair dye, my flutterer was soon converted into a tolerably good imitation of a black-breasted plover.

At last everything was ready and I set out alone, my friends agreeing to meet me at Higgins's the next day. I took the railroad to Sandwich and a stagecoach thence to Orleans. At my destination there were some fifteen gunners. In answer to my inquiries they informed me that the flight had not yet struck, but was expected any day.

After an excellent supper, I retired to bed early to dream of innumerable flocks of birds and "countless thousands slain." Several times during the night I consulted my time-piece and at three o'clock, just as I had sunk into a sound sleep, a loud knocking at the door was followed by the announcement, "Breakfast ready." I quickly dressed and headed to the dining room where I found that early though it was, some had already breakfasted and were gone. I stopped only to swallow a cup of coffee and proceeded to the stable, got my horse and wagon, put my traps and refreshments aboard, and started out. It was pitch dark with an easterly wind and every indication of rain.

Uphill and downhill I jogged for an hour. At day-break my steed struck the marsh, whereupon I heard the bitterns quacking loudly as they went to roost after their night's feast. I followed the beach for three miles until I came to a stand that seemed favorably placed. I secured the horse, set out the decoys, produced and

8

capped my pigeon, affixed to its leg about twenty-five yards of string, and set him down among his wooden companions while I went back to the wagon for the rest of my gear. When I returned to my decoys the bird was gone. Instinctively I cast my eyes skyward and beheld the pigeon and line shooting up into space with the straightness and velocity of an arrow until they were lost to sight.

I had nothing to do but hide myself in the stand and wait patiently, and had just gotten nicely settled when an old fellow made his appearance and wanted to know what I was doing in *his* stand. I thought my presence there with my gun was, of itself, sufficient indication of my purpose, but politely replied that I was from Boston, was one of Mr. Higgins's boarders, and was out for a little sport. Upon this the old ruffian exclaimed, "Damn old Higgins and all his city gunners who come down here tramping all over the marshes, scaring the birds so that us folks who live here can hardly get a shot at anything. My name is Lennell. I own this marsh. I built this stand, and I want you to git." I essayed to argue with the irate Mr. Lennell, but finding his language unparliamentary and his mood unpleasant, I pulled up and departed to a point a mile farther on. I built a stand and resolved that not even the entire tribe of Lennells should eject me. I lit my pipe and was soon again ready for business. But with the exception of a few peeps, on which I disdain to waste ammunition, no birds made their appearance. If this were not sufficiently aggravating, it commenced to rain and blow "great guns." Shivering and drenched, I sought shelter under the wagon. I still had high hopes for birds, but after an unrewarding vigil, I harnessed up and turned my face homeward, a sadder if not a wiser man.

Jim and Sam arrived that evening. All hands sat late playing cards, and I occasionally went to the window to

# *When Ducks Were Plenty*

check the weather. It rained all night, and we did not sally forth until five o'clock the next morning. The marshes were alive with birds, affording capital sport that I enjoyed with my companions. After a while I decided to take a position by myself on an island not too far distant. I took a shortcut across some flats and suddenly sank up to my middle in quicksand. I would have disappeared altogether had it not been for my gun and the basket of decoys I carried. With the greatest difficulty I managed to get out and made my way back to the stand. There the absence of sympathy over my disheveled condition was evident by such questions as, "Why didn't you go over to the island?" and "Where are your decoys?" Sure enough, where were they? In my fright I hadn't noticed their loss. I told them I was glad to get back alive, but they assured me that I had been in little danger as they had seen me struggling and would have extricated me with the help of the horse. The rascals laughed.

I put an end to further levity at my expense by stating that birds were abundant, and we were soon busily engaged in filling our bags. Then Jim shot a bird that fell about fifty yards distant, and he was going toward the spot when he disappeared with the celerity of a theatrical demon. Sam and I looked at each other in silent wonder until Sam said, "Let's go and see."

As we approached the spot we heard groans and muffled appeals for help. We quickened our pace and soon beheld the heroic James up to his neck in one of those delightful "honey pots" which nature seems to consider indispensable on all popular marshes. Our friend was clutching wildly at the overhanging grass in a futile attempt to pull himself out, and pleaded for our assistance.

"Sam," I said, "have the kindness to run and harness the horse."

# Bay Birds on the Orleans Marshes

*"Jim and Sam arrived that evening. All hands sat late playing cards and I occasionally went to the window to check the weather."—E. T. Marliave.*

"Oh, confound the horse," cried the unfortunate.

"No nonsense now! And pray tell, did you find the bird, or is he down there and you are trying to kick him out?" I said.

"He isn't looking for the bird," said Sam, "He's treading for quahaugs; can you feel any, Jim?"

After a few more remarks and a brief consultation, we extended helping hands to the afflicted, who was with difficulty "snaked" out in a most unenviable condition. Jim was covered from hat to boots with a thick, black, aromatic mud that caused us to suggest a trip to the beach. Acting upon our advice, Jim slowly departed to perform ablutions and was nearly devoured by greenhead flies while drying his apparel.

Birds continued flying until about noon, after which the flocks were less frequent. About four o'clock we started for home, but on coming to the creek intersecting the marsh we saw that the tide was unusually high. Although a species of corduroy road spanned the creek, we decided to wait for lower water. We had been cautioned before leaving the house not to depart from the "straight and narrow way." While we waited for the tide to ebb, a large flock of birds alighted on the other side of the creek. Jim and I waded across in water up to our waists, leaving Sam in charge of the wagon. The birds were so shy, however, that after much patient maneuvering we were obliged to give them up. We returned to find our horse and wagon half out of sight. The overconfident Samuel had started across the creek, but got too much to the right and slumped through with the horse up to his belly and the wagon to the hubs. The author of this fresh calamity was standing up, hatless, speechless, pale as a ghost, and scared half to death. It was two hours of vigorous tugging and pulling before we were able to extricate our transportation from this predicament.

Our misfortunes had been so numerous that we agreed to conceal them from Higgins to avoid additional aggravation. We rinsed off in silence, counted the bag, and took some consolation in our ten dozen birds as we headed for home.

# Tolling Ducks
## by Elisha Jarrett Lewis, M.D.

*tolling* as in ringing a bell to summon; to allure
or entice; especially to decoy game . . .
　　　　　　　　　　　—Dictionary entry

　　Some shooters employ a most curious method for
decoying canvasback ducks within gunshot. This process,
termed *tolling*, is practiced extensively on the flats of
the Chesapeake Bay, where great numbers of canvasbacks and redheads resort every autumn.  A mongrel
water dog or common cur is taught to run back and
forth after stones, sticks, or other missiles thrown from
side to side along the shore.  During a shooting excursion, the shooting party ensconces themselves with
heavy double-barreled duck guns and the trained dog
at break of day, behind one of the numerous blinds
contiguous to the feeding grounds.  As the morning

mists clear off, the ducks will be seen feeding on the shallows not less than several hundred yards from shore. The dog is put in motion by throwing stones from one side of the blind to the other. The ducks soon become curious, and feeling anxious to inform themselves as to this sudden singular phenomenon, raise their heads high and commence swimming toward shore. As long as the dog is kept in motion, the ducks will not slow their progress until within a few feet of the water's edge, and often will stand on the beach, staring in mute and silly astonishment at the playful motion of the animal. If well trained, the dog takes no notice whatever of the ducks, but continues his fascination until the quick report of the battery announces that his services are wanted in another quarter, and he immediately rushes into the water to arrest the flight of the maimed and wounded.

A sportsman is said to have discovered this mode of decoying ducks. As the sportsman sat concealed behind a blind patiently awaiting the near approach of canvasbacks, he observed that they suddenly lifted up their heads and moved toward shore. He naturally looked around to discover the cause and observed a young fox sporting on the riverbank. The ducks were eager to gaze upon Reynard and steered their course directly for shore. Be this as it may, the duck's peculiar fascination with the dog has long been known and used to advantage on the ponds of England.

The canvasback tolls better than any other duck and will not only be decoyed by the dog, but will often be drawn in by waving a fancy-colored handkerchief attached to the ramrod. I have seen a dog fail to attract their attention until bound around the loins with a white

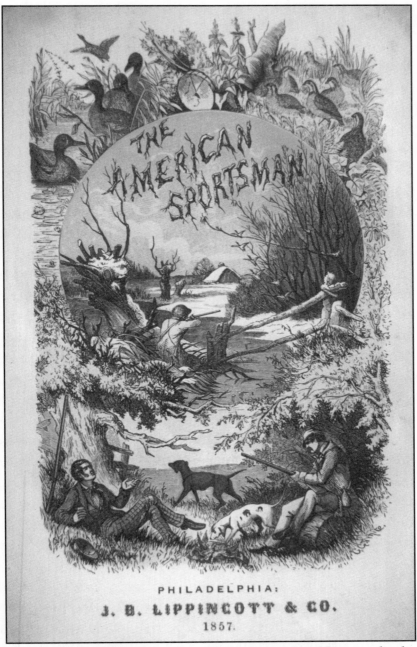

*Frontispiece of* The American Sportsman *(1857 second edition) by Elisha J. Lewis, M. D.*

# When Ducks Were Plenty

handkerchief; the handkerchiefed dog will then succeed perfectly well. These ducks, although cunning under ordinary circumstances, seem bewildered by these strategies. Several years ago I decoyed the same batch three times in an hour, each time slaying a large number. The proper and most destructive moment to shoot ducks that have been tolled is when they present their tails or sides to the gun.

The tolling season continues about three weeks from the first appearance of the ducks, as the birds soon become more cautious and are no longer deceived in this way. Some sportsmen assert that canvasbacks alone can be decoyed in this mode. But a number of other ducks feed with the canvasback, particularly the redheads and blackheads who partake of the top of the grass that the canvasback discards after eating the root. These less noble ducks, though they come in with the canvasbacks when tolled, do not seem to take any notice of the dog, but continue to swim along carelessly feeding, as if entrusting themselves entirely to the guidance of the other fowl.

Although tolling ducks is simple, few dogs possess sufficient industry and perseverance to arrive at any degree of perfection in the art. Most dogs tire and stop running just when the ducks get near shore but are still too far off to be reached by the guns. This spoils all, as the birds will swim or fly off if the motion of the animal is arrested for even a few moments.

This plan of killing ducks, though practiced by all the gentry as well as pot hunters who frequent the bayshore, is not altogether recognized as a sportsman-like way of bagging game, and is forbidden on the grounds in possession of some clubs. Against the utility of this regulation I will not venture an argument. The gentlemen composing these organizations no doubt have good reasons for their restriction. But I see neither impropriety nor anything unsportsmanlike in thus decoying wary fowl within gunshot, especially where all other modes of getting at them would surely fail. I have always found a great deal in the sport to admire. Tolling ducks is frequently attended with a high degree of pleasurable excitement, and there is a certain amusement in witnessing the playful antics of the dog operating so strangely upon his bewildered and silly victims, who so soon pay the forfeit of their idle curiosity in death. And playing the part of a sage, we might also draw a moral from the incident by demonstrating that foolish and idle curiosity often results in disastrous consequences to the parties concerned.

## *Editor's Note*

Dr. Lewis's book, *Hints to Sportsmen*, was first published in 1851, and republished in 1855 as *The American Sportsman*. A number of revised editions were published as late as 1906, and in 1967 the Abercrombie and Fitch Library reprinted the third (1863) edition.

John Bumstead wrote *On the Wing—A Book for Sportsmen* in 1869, and lifted verbatim Dr. Lewis's entire chapter on tolling ducks. At the time such "plagiarism" was customary when a work was considered seminal. As to the charge of plagiarism, the attitude toward instructional literature through the nineteenth century was quite different than we expect today. Authors lived in a considerably less literate culture than ours, and laws of copyright were not strictly applied. It was the custom to reuse written works, partly out of respect for the past, and partly out of a desire to link definitive prior writings with the present text, almost as a lawyer would cite legal precedent supporting a legal brief. Each new work drew authority from and quoted from its predecessors, added new ideas, sifted out obsolete notions, and then tacked another story onto what was seen as a shared house of knowledge. Authors considered long quotations of their work to be the ultimate compliment, perhaps, in part, because copyright litigation was expensive and the entire profits from a limited-interest-gunning book might not have covered court costs.

Dr. Lewis's description of tolling ducks is typical of the treatises on hunting and shooting that predominated in the pre-1870s sportsman's library. Mid-nineteenth-century books by Dr. Lewis, John Krider (chap. 5), Frank Forester (chap. 6), and John Bumstead (chap. 10) may seem overly explicit in the twenty-first century, but these authors were in the vanguard when hunting and literacy were almost mutually exclusive in America. According to the editors of the anthology, *Classics of the American Shooting Field* (1930):

> English shooting literature is richer than American, for the English were following field sports in a scientific way and writing about them when most of this country was a wilderness. Then, again, most of the shooting in England was and is done by men of the leisured upper classes, who had the time, inclination, and ability to write about it. Shooting and the preserving of the game were taken very seriously. In this country, on the other hand, until comparatively recent years a man who devoted much time to field

sports in a new land, where there was so much
constructive work of all sorts to be done, was
considered shiftless and a ne'er-do-well, and
most of the shooting was done by backwoodsmen
and market gunners.

While gun-toting Americans may deem themselves
the inheritors of Davy Crockett and Daniel Boone, if
the truth be told, shooting a muzzleloading gun was a
less-than-universal skill in the years preceding the Civil
War. One of the biggest military problems for both North
and South was the inability of conscripts to properly
load and fire a simple caplock musket. Thus it's not
surprising that the first post-Civil War shotgunning
book—Bumstead's *On the Wing*—was written on an almost
remedial level as a primer for the then emerging class
of proletarian sportsmen.

By the mid-1870s, most published gunwriters had
gravitated from the instructional treatise to the "Me and
Joe" genre of stories about abundant game and successful outings. Books about American wildfowling,
however, were surprisingly scarce before the turn of the
century. The published record of the grand passage
was, for the most part, on the pages of pulp weekly sporting
newspapers, written by amateurs who hoped to
memorialize their once-in-a-lifetime shot or best day of
waterfowling with a story in *The American Field*, *Forest
and Stream*, *Shooting and Fishing*, or Wilbur Parker's
*The American Sportsman* (not to be confused with Dr.
Lewis's book of the same title).

My publisher suggested that we omit Dr. Lewis's
anachronistic account of the lost art of duck tolling because
*The American Sportsman* was "not well written" by modern
standards. I agreed that the good doctor's book was

tedious reading, but pre-1870s descriptions of duck hunting are too scarce to let this one get away. The chapter, however, was heavily edited and carefully paraphrased to be more readable, with every effort being made to preserve the unique and historic content.

"HANG ON MAC, WE'LL GET HIM!"
SERIES C 30 Copyright 1910 by Oscar Erickson

# Tame Ducks as Decoys
### by "Cosmopolitan"

The Delaware River below Philadelphia offers a fruit-
ful field for sportsmen who can brave the inclement
weather of early spring. Sam Mason and I were in the
habit of paddling for ducks in the vicinity of Monas and
Chester Islands, with our skiff painted white and with
white covers over our corduroys. At a little distance it
required better eyes than a duck possesses to distinguish us from the many lumps of ice floating with the
tide. So complete was the illusion, especially when the
atmosphere was a trifle misty, that we frequently have
mistaken the boats of our friends, rigged out in the same
fashion, for lumps of ice.

One dull, gloomy day in February, when the ice was
running thick after a trifling thaw, we set out from the
boat landing early in the morning with the prospect of a

good day's sport. After an hour's paddling we were fairly in the channel, and, reclining in the bottom of the boat, we allowed her to drift at the will of the tide. Not far in front of us we saw a raft of twenty or thirty black ducks appearing to be asleep alongside a sheet of ice. They were huddled together so closely that a napkin might almost have covered them. Giving two or three strokes with my paddle and motioning my friend to be ready, we soon were among them. Strange as it may seem, not a duck moved. Sam actually reached over the gunwale, seized two of them by the neck, and lifted them into the skiff. This started the bunch and away they flew, but not without leaving behind seven of their number that fell to my two barrels. Doubtless we should have secured more, but Sam had both of his hands occupied in strangling his two victims, and such fluttering and quacking was never heard. We had a good laugh at this novel way of shooting ducks, and drifted on.

The day that opened so auspiciously proved a complete failure. Late in the afternoon we had only the nine ducks secured early in the morning and no prospects for more. We paddled on in a disagreeable mood. As we were about to enter the creek back of Monas Island, Sam called my attention to a bunch of fifteen or twenty ducks just ahead, not far from an ice cake. We brightened up and paddled slowly toward them, when, to our disappointment, we found the ice cake to be a boat and the ducks to be decoys. Then Sam suddenly exclaimed: "By George! Bill Hooper is fast asleep, and there are two mallards among his stools; here goes for them, anyhow." He cocked his gun and was ready to fire when the mallards dove, reappearing in a few minutes swimming contentedly among the stools. Sam tried again, and I tried, but it was no go, for as soon as the gun was fairly to the shoulder, the ducks were under the water. We sat and looked at each other, partook of an infallible remedy for bad luck, and tried once more without success.

"Talk about hell divers," said Sam, "Those mallards win the prize." We heard a chuckle, and Bill slowly rose in his boat, his ruddy face aglow with suppressed laughter. He said, "When you fellas get tired of trying to shoot my decoys, let me know and I'll take a drink with you." We silently passed him our flask. Upon inquiry we found the old fellow had actually taken a pair of ordinary barn-yard puddle ducks, resembling mallards, and trained them to act as decoys. They did their work well, for at the first sight of a bunch of wild ducks they would quack most energetically and generally succeeded in enticing their wilder brethren within gunshot. But as soon as a gun was raised, they would dive and remain under until the danger was over. I was so pleased at their perfor-mance that I asked old Bill if he would sell them, and he agreed for five dollars each. I tossed him the money, but he hesitated. Finally, the unlimited (to him) amount of whiskey represented by the gold pieces was too much for his nerves. He succumbed, and we took our live decoys. Many a time after this memorable day did my friend and I shoot over these ducks, and they never failed to draw whatever game was about. I have used live decoys in the sounds of North Carolina, and found they work as well as on the Delaware River, but I have never succeeded in training birds up to the same degree of intelligence of my Monas Island pets.

To use live birds as decoys, we attached to one leg a strap of leather, to which a cord was tied through an eyelet. At the end of the cord was a heavy weight that served as an anchor. When anchored among a lot of wooden stools, the decoys' actions so nearly resembled the motion of wild ducks feeding and playing in the water that it was no wonder their cousins were deceived. However, when using live decoys one must be careful not to anchor the birds in swift running currents, as they will be drawn under the water and drowned. I lost a fine pair of ducks this way in North Carolina.

After their work was over for the day, we placed our decoy ducks in a comfortable shelter and gave them a good feed. They had such great fondness for this treacherous sport that in the morning before starting out, the drake would frequently, of his own accord, hop into the basket in which we carried them to the skiff. We used these ducks three winters, and finally, when the Civil War broke out and stopped our sport, we gave them to our friendly host as a parting legacy when we left to join our regiment.

# "Sunk Box" Canvasbacks
## by John Krider

The canvasback stands proudly preeminent among waterfowl of the United States, for the elegance of its plumage, the exquisite flavor of its flesh, and the sport that it affords the shooter. Gentle reader, have you ever lain submerged in a battery on Devil's Island, or in an ambuscade in the narrows of Spesutia, and watched them pitching in their superb way among your decoys? Or bent to your oars on a blustering day to snatch them from the rough waters of the Chesapeake? Or studied the markings of their winter dress as they lay upon the thwart-board of the scow in pairs of fifty at a time? And finally, have you ever sailed, poled, or swept back to Havre de Grace by the light of the moon, dropped anchor, and gone on shore to dine upon them cooked *au naturel*? If so, you realize to the fullest extent the spell cast by *Anas valisneria*, the canvasback.

# When Ducks Were Plenty

Late in the fall of 1850, while partridge shooting in the neighborhood of the Chesapeake, I received an invitation from Mr. J. W. McCullough of Port Deposit, to accompany him on an excursion in a new scow that he had built and equipped especially to kill ducks in the Susquehanna and Upper Bay. She was wall-sided and flat-bottomed, forty feet long and nine feet beam. She carried a jib and a large fore-and-aft mainsail. A space barely sufficient for a tall man to lie at length was decked off forward. The cabin contained three or four bunks, a small stove, stooling guns, several bags of heavy shot, kegs of ducking powder, a quart coffeepot, and two large baskets of provender. This hardy market-hunter's cabin was pitched so as to be watertight and was entered by a small scuttle with a slide. Here McCullough cooked, ate, slept, kept tally of his game, manufactured heads and necks for decoys, cut his gun-wads, spun his yarns, drank his grog or coffee, and kept care outside from October until April, the severest season of the year.

*After a shot with the swivel gun.*

# "Sunk Box" Canvasbacks

The scow's rudder was set on a pivot so as to be readily unshipped in case of necessity, and could be used like the steering oar of a whale boat to bring her heavy bow through the wind. She had large leeboards that enabled her to lie very close to the wind in moderate weather, though her shape and shallow draft made sure she would make much leeway in a rough sea. Going large in fair weather she sailed and steered well, and, in fact, the scow was especially adapted for navigating the shoal waters of the Upper Bay.

The battery or "sunk box" rested amidships. Piled up in great heaps abaft on either side, but so as not to interfere with the motions of the rudder, were the decoys or wooden ducks. Each had its cord, with weight attached, wound round its body, the last turn taken round the neck in regular duck-shooter fashion. They had evidently seen much service from their bleached and weather-beaten looks. Some of them looked well peppered in the way of business, and particles of grass could be seen adhering to the anchors and cables of a few. The scow was furnished with raft poles and heavy oars or "sweeps," to be used in forcing her over the flats in a calm. Two large four-oared, flat-bottomed boats, called yawls, were towed astern.

At two o'clock on a cold, clear morning we set off from McCullough's hospitable abode. Traversing the single twisting, narrow street, we reached the scow at Wilmer's wharf, where we found the helmsman, Davis, and the boy waiting for us on board. The fastenings were cast off and, once clear of the rafts, we put up the jib. The wind was fresh from the nor'west, so we stood down along the shore where the white front of a dwelling occasionally loomed up above the town in the dim glimmer of starlight. It was our intention to set the battery on Devil's

Island, a sunken shoal lying nearly southwest from Havre de Grace, on the western side of the channel or swash, through the submerged flats. This shoal extends for eight miles or more from the mouth of the river to the island of Spesutia, and is the feeding ground on which tens of thousands of the choicest species of ducks are annually slaughtered by the market shooters of Havre de Grace. Below Spesutia the water is deeper, but from the island to Havre de Grace the shipping channel is but a mere swash. This area, rising slightly with the tide and thickly covered with celery grass, is especially suited for the operations of the floating batteries.

It was my good fortune to be accompanied on this excursion by Fred, an old friend from Philadelphia, whom I encountered at Port Deposit. After seeing the mainsail set and the craft fairly under way, steering for Havre de Grace, we retired to the cabin to wile away the time. We listened to the sporting experiences of the owner of the scow, and chatted over our adventures of the past. Passing Havre de Grace, we found many duck shooters already on the stir, and were successively hailed by Baird, Holly, and other famous shots who were preparing to drop down to their respective anchoring grounds.

Coming to at last, just as the moon rose, we dropped anchor on the shoal and waited impatiently until within half an hour of daybreak. Then, all else in readiness, we transferred the decoys into the yawls and launched the battery over the side. This last was done by our united strength as carefully as possible so as to avoid shipping water into the box. McCullough then stepped aboard, unfolded the floating wings, and turned up the guards. Several pigs of iron, sufficiently heavy to sink the frame of the battery to the water's edge, were placed on the bottom of the sunken box. A board covered with a blanket was then laid over the ballast, and, after receiving guns and ammunition, the occupant pushed off from the scow with his boat hook. We jumped into the yawl to tow the machine to the selected spot and assist in setting the stools. The box was then anchored stem and stern and, by the waning light of the moon, we proceeded to set the decoys.

McCullough, like most expert duck shooters, is fastidious, and we were careful to place the stools so that they would not touch each other. The trick is to avoid leaving a gap in any part of the rank and yet prevent, if possible, the decoys from falling foul. A few of the lightest were placed on the wings, and several heads of decoys were firmly affixed to wooden pins on the deck of the battery. The false ducks were not all imitations of canvasbacks; we had redheads, blackheads, and a few baldpates intermingled with the nobler variety. The outside duck at the tail of the rank was a veteran canvasback, facetiously called "the toller."

The rank was now complete and made to mimic life by the action of the ripples as each duck rode knowingly to its anchor. The frame of the box was set flush with the water's edge, prevented from filling by the floating wings fore, aft, and at the sides. The box was deep enough to hide the body of a man laid at length, and when sunk some eighteen inches below the surface, the shooter is perfectly invisible to passing ducks except from the air immediately overhead. The water was moderately smooth, so the guards were turned down flat with the deck. The yawls pulled back to the scow, and we immediately lifted her anchor. The shooter loaded his three guns, placed them in the box with their muzzles resting on its edge, and took a last look at his decoys. Then, with daylight breaking in the east, he laid himself flat on his back on the board and shut out every object and sound, save the pale dough sky and the slight rippling plash within an inch of his head. All eyes and ears, he waited patiently for his first dart.

We anchored about half a mile upwind from the shooter so as not to interfere with the flight, which, as a rule, works to windward; the ducks approach leeward of the shooter, at his feet. Soon we heard the faint report of McCullough's gun, although it was not sufficiently light to see either the ducks or the decoys from the scow.

The boy reported shot after shot while we ate our breakfast in the cabin. As we came out, Davis directed our attention to a large flock of canvasbacks that he swore, in his emphatic way, "were going into the pot." Glancing along the broad expanse of water on which the sun had just now risen, we plainly saw ducks sweeping swiftly up to the toller at the tail of the decoys. The foremost had hardly alighted when the dark figure of McCullough arose from the water as if by magic. We heard the successive discharges and saw the fall of each duck, the boy counting five down. The next instant the shooter was standing up, waving his cap, and jumping into the yawl with Ben Davis. Fred and I pulled away with might and main in the second yawl to secure the dead ducks.

Fifteen canvasbacks and three redheads were on the water, and two cripples were "shot over," as the phrase goes, with a small gun loaded with No. 8s. We then rowed straight for the battery, and McCullough insisted that I should take my turn. There was no time to argue matters with ducks on the fly, so, landing on one side of the deck, while he came off the other, I took my place with some

# "Sunk Box" Canvasbacks

trepidation. Years had intervened since I last had drawn trigger on wildfowl. The remembrance that my friend from Philadelphia was a capital duck shot by no means allayed this feeling. When the sound of oars had died away, I was alone with the decoys, which kept bobbing their heads as if they were swallowing duckweed with the greatest possible gusto.

I soon regained my wonted nerve and made up my mind to mischief. The next moment I was saluted by the whistling of wings and the patter of feet as ducks alighted near the battery. Seizing the small gun, I sat up in the box and knocked over one canvasback swimming along the stools and another as it rose. I quickly took up the second gun and fired ineffectively at two others making off. After charging the pieces, I cast a glance at the dead birds to ascertain the direction of their drift and then sank back out of sight, without as much as looking at the scow. I was certain that had I the presence of mind to govern my actions, all four ducks would have been at that moment floating dead on the tide. In fact, in the heat of the moment, I had committed a great blunder by shooting at the ducks in the water when I should have drawn first trigger on those yet upon the wing, just as they dropped their sterns to alight. Then I should have used the second gun on the others as they jumped. Hindsight! Had Fred been here, I thought, he surely would have had four ducks down. But, *n'importe*, they would come again.

At least ten minutes of anxious expectation elapsed before I had another shot. To recover my coolness I watched the motion of a redhead decoy near the battery. A comical-looking, hard-a-weather old fella he was, with the nail of his bill shot off and his head turned over his back. He kept veering and bowing, now looking me right in the eye over the edge of his wing as we topped a small surge, and then disappearing from sight again—when, all at once, a small flock of blackheads appeared and set their wings to alight right over him. Shooting more coolly this time, I managed to kill three out of seven and cripple down a fourth without even using the second gun. The survivors flew off so swiftly that they were far to leeward by the time I had turned. After this it was pretty shooting for about an hour until Davis came out to relieve me. Fred preferred to take his turn in the afternoon, as the swell was sinking fast with the wind, and in half an hour it bade fair to be calm.

Davis had fired not more than half a dozen shots, killing a canvasback at each discharge, before the water was smooth as a millpond. Our decoys and those of two other batteries in the distance loomed on the glassy flood as large as geese. The ducks ceased to stool, so we passed away the time until noon, chatting and examining the game that lay arranged in pairs on the thwart boards. Meanwhile, a report from Davis's gun told of the occasional single duck passing over his stools.

While we were at dinner, a circumstance at the battery almost caused Davis to avow himself a believer in predestination—at least regarding wildfowl shooting. Not having had a shot for some time, he was lying at his ease with his cap drawn over his eyes to defend them from the vertical rays of the sun, when a swan passed slowly over his decoys. Strangely, every gun in the battery missed fire, and the noble bird continued its course down the bay unharmed.

"I had drawed for his neck," said the unfortunate swan-shooter, "and was as sure of him as I was of my supper, but the Walker caps are not worth the copper they are made of anymore. I suppose the d--- bird would

# "Sunk Box" Canvasbacks

have gone free even if I had fired the biggest swivel gun on the Potomac at his head."

The wind soon freshened, and the bay was all animation again, the ducks flying in large flocks, the batteries cannonading, boats plying to and fro, and Fred shooting in a style not to be surpassed. The puffs of smoke rising from the water's edge reminded me strongly of the hurried glimpse of a white spout that a sailor sometimes gets when he turns his head for a moment while pulling to windward in chase of a sperm whale. The sight of a dark figure suddenly standing apparently on the water a half-mile off, and then as suddenly sinking again, bore some resemblance to a whale's head thrust vertically out of the sea, as seen from the masthead on a clear day.

Fred continued in the box during the whole afternoon and did not miss a single duck. At sundown we pushed off from the scow to "take up." While securing the decoys, a persistent canvasback darted twice between the boats and the battery, and, returning a third time, was killed by our city friend who was still in the box. I have often observed this sort of fatal infatuation in the most wary and shy of the feathered race, especially while being tolled by a well-trained dog.

Taking up some two hundred decoys on a cold, blustery evening is rather tedious and benumbing work to a novice. While one person manages the oars, the others pick up each decoy singly so as not to entangle it with its fellows, and, after winding the cord around its body and removing any weeds from the weight, stow it in the bow or stern of the yawl. In the meantime, the man in the box lays aside his guns and secures the few decoys near the wings, turns up the guards, and, as soon as the stools are all in the boat, weighs the anchors of the battery and is towed down to the scow. The contents of the boats and the box are then passed on board, and lastly the battery itself, after which sail is made for home.

On reaching Havre de Grace, we went into Bairds' Hotel, where the duck shooters of the place are in the habit of congregating to talk over the exploits of the day. These men, both fishers and fowlers, are engaged during the spring and part of the summer in the extensive fisheries of the Potomac and Susquehanna, returning to their more congenial occupations in the autumn. They are generally well informed on all matters connected with their business, and some of them realize handsome profits from their hearty and exciting pursuits. They are almost universally expert shots. It is as common for a man reared on either shore to shoot well as it is for a dog in the same sections to swim and dive like an otter. In fact, many of the poorer inhabitants train their large dogs not only to retrieve ducks but also to assist in bringing in driftwood that comes down the stream with "a fresh." Some are said to supply themselves with winter fuel this way.

The next morning we anchored the battery on the eastern shore between Havre de Grace and Port, off Stump's Mill. The wind was easterly and the weather cold and stormy. A great many ducks were on the fly down the river. My ears were constantly saluted with the *whew! whew!* of the widgeon, the harsh cry of the south-southerly, the whistling wings of the goldeneye, and the sharp *quack!* of the butterball. I was kept constantly on the alert by knocking over canvasbacks and redheads until near noon. Then the wind increased to half a gale, the battery went adrift, the scow dragged her anchor, the yawls were off to the rescue, and for a while we were, as sailors say, "caught in a heap." Giving up the search for the dead ducks, Davis and I pulled might and main for the battery, while Fred and the boy lifted the scow's anchor, hoisted the jib, and ran closer to shore. On approaching the box, we found McCullough standing knee deep in water, having thrown overboard all his iron after driving down through the decoys. The battery had been brought up, but the waves were making a clean breech over the box, and the stools were in a confused state of entanglement and disarray. Some had been detached from their weights and were floating off toward the lee shore, tumbling about on the waves as if in joy of their escape; others were foul of the anchors under the battery. Meanwhile, the wind blew stiffly in gusts from the opposite shore, and the river grew rougher every moment.

McCullough, appearing to stand on the water while actively plying his boat hook to grapple for the anchors, reminded me of the picture of Washington crossing the Delaware. Working hard, it was some time before we secured all the decoys and shipped the battery. Then, after taking a bumper of good old bourbon all round, we stood over toward port, beating scow-fashion, broadside as often as bow on. We heard afterward that Baird and several other shooters had drifted completely across the swash in their batteries that morning. No serious accident happened, and, so far as we are informed, no case of drowning ever occurred in the batteries on the Chesapeake. However, there was the sinking of an old yawl, loaded to the water's edge with stones as a substitute for a battery. She was struck by a sudden flaw of wind and sank, drowning her occupant, who, for some unexplained cause, went down with his ship in eight or nine feet of water.

# When Ducks Were Plenty

Ducks were formerly very abundant on the western shore between Port Deposit and Havre de Grace and great numbers are still killed from blinds and batteries between the bridge and Stump's Point at the mouth of Furnace Creek. The digging of the tidewater canal, however, drove the ducks off the flats and marshes of the western shore. Below Havre de Grace on the western side of the swash near Donahue's Battery is good canvasback and redhead ground. About a half-mile east from the battery, Mr. Charles Boyd of Havre de Grace killed 163 canvasbacks on 10 November 1852, and in the spring of 1850, the same famous duck-shooter killed 271 canvasbacks and redheads off the mouth of Northeast River. On the same day that Boyd killed his canvasbacks near Donahue's Battery, Mr. John Holly, another expert duck shot, killed 119 of the same species on Devil's Island, and it is said that several thousand ducks were brought into the town that day by the different parties engaged in shooting on the flats.

The next night we sailed for the narrows of Spesutia, where we had some good shooting from the battery and from points. While harboring in one of the creeks of the narrows at night, we heard the distant booming of the swivel guns of poachers who "boat" the sleeping flocks by moonlight. This mode of killing ducks still has a spice of adventure in it, and is far more defensible than the old, cold-blooded practice of strangling diver ducks in the meshes of gill nets as they dive for food on the shoals. Although wildfowl are market game, taking them in gill nets without the slightest sport seems to violate a sense of fair play. Perhaps someday sportsmen will work to ban this practice.

# "Sunk Box" Canvasbacks

## Editor's Note

John Krider was a gunmaker and dealer in all kinds of fishing tackle and shooting equipment. Krider's Sportsmen's Depot was established in Philadelphia in 1826, and was filled with cutlery, tackle, guns of all kinds, and a large array of miscellaneous goods from dog collars to compasses. After twenty-seven years in the field sports business, Krider, with the help of H. Milnor Knapp as editor, put together a book of *Krider's Sporting Anecdotes* (1853) that mixed business with pleasure. According to the preface, "In offering these unpretending pages, it is simply the wish of the

SPORTSMEN'S DEPOT.

## JOHN KRIDER,
Corner Second and Walnut Streets, Philadelphia,
IMPORTER, MANUFACTURER, AND DEALER IN
BREECH AND MUZZLE LOADING
# SHOT-GUNS, RIFLES, AND PISTOLS.

PIN-FIRE GUNS ALTERED TO CENTRAL FIRE.

Particular attention paid to Loading Cartridges for Breech-loading Guns, at lowest market prices.

Has always on hand all the different makes of
## BREECH-LOADING SHELLS.
*Guns Bored for Close Shooting.*

*Bogardus's Patent Rough Glass Balls and Glass-Ball Traps,*
AND
## FISHING TACKLE OF ALL KINDS.

*From* Field, Cover, and Trap Shooting *(1878 revised edition) by Adam H. Bogardus.*

author and his editor to draw the public's attention more particularly to American field sports, and the reader will soon find that avoiding the tedium of a regular treatise or manual, we speak right on, with the hope to interest and amuse. If successful in this, our point is gained." But Krider had higher hopes than to simply to "interest and amuse." For example, the chapter "Canada Goose" had Krider giving advice: "To those who have leisure and a desire to engage in paddle-shooting, we say go to Krider's and select one of his splendid double ducking guns. . . . " Notwithstanding the commercial spin, a first edition of *Krider's Sporting Anecdotes* is a prize acquisition for a gunroom library, and the 1966 Abercrombie and Fitch reprint can suffice for those interested in reading rather than collecting.

# Rail Shooting

### by "Frank Forester"
### (pseudonym of Henry William Herbert)

From the middle of August until the frosts of winter, the curious and excellent little rail may be pursued in the localities that he frequents, by those who care for the sport. Rail are not comparable to game that are followed with dogs in the field, nor is the rail very sporting in its habits or is much skill required to shoot him. He is, however, delicious to eat. He abounds on the reedy mud flats of those rivers that he frequents, and his season is one when there is little or no other occupation for the sportsman. So, between the epicurean desire for his flesh, the absence of more agreeable and exciting sport, and the easiness of his pursuit—which to young hands and bad shots is a recommendation—the rail is very eagerly sought. During those periods of the tide which permit his pursuit, a stranger on the Delaware, sixty miles below or thirty above Philadelphia, might well believe that two armies were engaged in a brisk skirmish, so incessant is the rattle of small arms firing at rail.

It is the habit of this little bird to skulk and run among the reeds and water oats of the flats that he inhabits, and owing to the peculiar form of his long flat-sided, wedge-like body, with legs situated far behind and wings closely compressed, he can pass with such ease and celerity among the close stalks of the water plants that the sharpest dogs cannot compel him to take wing. He is so thoroughly aware of the advantage he possesses and of the perils of rising before the gun, that it is utterly useless to attempt beating for him with dogs on foot, nor is it worthwhile to try walking or kicking him up from his lurking places when the tide is down.

But as soon as the tide has risen high enough to allow a boat to be forced through the partially submerged, partially floating grass, the rail becomes unable to run for want of solid substance on which to tread, and is unable to swim in the dense vegetation. He has no choice but to float reluctantly, and usually does not take wing until the bow of the boat is close upon him. His flight is then slow and heavy, with legs hanging down and wings heavily flapping, and he rarely flies farther than forty yards. Thus the rail is exceedingly easy to kill—so much so that as soon as the tyro has mastered the slight difficulty of getting accustomed to the motion of the boat and has what a sailor calls his "sea legs," he can cover a bird on the wing with the slowest conceivable swing, pull the most inexpert trigger, and scarcely fail to bag many of these birds in succession.

# Rail Shooting

The boat used is a long, light skiff, built flat to draw as little water as possible and sharp to force its way through the heavy tangle of water plants. The shooter stands erect in the bow of the skiff, balancing himself in the rocking eggshell, while the pole man stands behind him propelling the vessel with his long punt pole, the more rapidly the better, through the weeds and grass.

The pole man's duty is to steer and urge the boat with his punt pole, to mark the dead birds and collect them, and get the advantage of all other boats for his shooter. Marking is by no means an easy task, as the vast expanse of level green herbage affords no point or marks by which to identity the spot where the bird has fallen. Moreover, the reeds and grass are so thick and so similar in color to the plumage of the rail that, unless marked with the most perfect accuracy, it is almost useless to look for a wounded bird. So many boats, moreover, are darting about in all directions with the rival pole men driving their skiffs with all attainable velocity, and the emulous shooters banging away at the thick-rising birds without much caring whether some other sportsman is within range and line of shot, that not a moment must be lost bagging the dead birds. Crippled rail are almost impossible to bag, so quickly do they die and so cunningly do they skulk.

The great onus and excellence of the sport depends on the pole man, or pusher. With two equally good shots, a difference of nearly half the bag is with the gun that has the better assistant. The skill at marking dead birds, rapidity of bagging them, and adroitness at pushing that some of these men attain is truly remarkable. They are accustomed to the society of gentlemen, usually have a good stock of sporting anecdotes, and are generally very conversable and discreet fellows with whom a few hours can be spent, not only without tedium but with some profit. (John Horn of Bristol, Pennsylvania, is the best pusher I ever encountered, and many a good day's sport and fun have I enjoyed in his company and under his guidance on the broad and tranquil Delaware.)

Time for beginning this sport depends on the depth of the water on the particular flat where you are about to try your fortune; you must commence the moment the rising tide will permit your boat to run over and through the reeds. Your sport will continue as long as the birds rise before you, which will generally be until about the first quarter of the ebb. But as the water falls, the rail become less willing to take wing. The largest number of rail can be flushed during similar portions of the rising and falling tide.

I should also give a few hints as to the accou-

*"Pushin' for rail" by unknown. Courtesy of Kevin McCormack.*

terments and equipage on which—with the merits of your pole man and the celerity of your shooting—the amount of your bag will depend. The shooter should stand in the tottering and fragile skiff with feet planted firmly a little way apart and the left foot somewhat advanced. Do not brace your legs or stiffen your knees, but rather bend them a little to humor the motion of the boat. It does not much matter, except so far as you dread a

# Rail Shooting

ducking, whether you chance to get overboard or not, for the sport is pursued in the shallowest of water, and drowning is out of the question. As the weather is generally warm during rail season, a light shooting jacket and a straw hat are appropriate dress. Your shortest and lightest gun is the best tool for the sport, and a large landing net on a long pole is a convenient appendage that will save your pole man much time in bringing your dead birds to bag.

For ease in gun loading, use no shot bag, and put the charger of your powder horn down to its minimum. The rail is so easily killed, and the range of his flight so short, that only half the ordinary charge of powder and three-quarters of an ounce of No. 9 shot are necessary. With the recklessness I've seen displayed in this sport, large charges and heavy shot would be of real danger in the popular areas above Philadelphia on the Delaware. For flock-shooting at reed birds, carry a second heavier gun with an ordinary load of No. 8s. Sometimes teal or other wild duck will pass while you travel to or from your ground, and for a chance at these it is well to reserve a barrel, if not a gun, loaded with Ely's cartridges of Nos. 3 or 4 shot.

You will find it well to have a square wooden box with two compartments, one capable of containing eight to ten pounds of shot and the other a *quantum suff* of wadding. A small tin scoop set at three-quarters of an ounce capacity, lying in the shot, will save much trouble and half the time in loading. This box and your powder horn will lie on the bench or thwart in front of you, and your copper caps will be in your waistcoat pocket. Being thus provided aforehand, you will get three shots for every two of a rival who lugs his flask out of his pocket and charges with a pouch after every shot.

# When Ducks Were Plenty

Finally, take your time and be deliberate. With rail you can afford to be slow, for he shall rise within ten feet of you ninety-nine times of a hundred, and you will miss him only by getting flustered or by tumbling overboard. Although rail shooting scarcely deserves to be rated as a sport or honored with a place among the nobler kinds of wildfowling, it is a pretty pastime; and when birds are abundant and rise well, the rapid succession of shots creates much excitement, which is often compounded by competition with rival boats and gunners. There is also the stimulating apprehension of being peppered soundly by a stray charge of shot, followed by variations of vituperation and recrimination.

The rail is, as I observed before, capital eating. He is to be cooked and served exactly as the snipe, with no sauce or condiment whatever, but in his own gravy caught upon a slice of crisp buttered toast, with a sprinkle of salt. Like all water birds, he is to be eaten fresh, the sooner after killing the better. Twenty-four hours dead and he is not only ancient but fishlike. He should be laid at rest in red wine, as an unquiet ghost in a red sea. Peace to him! He shall sit lightly on your stomach.

### Editor's Note

Henry William Herbert was born in London on 7 April 1807. His father, the Hon. and Rev. William Herbert, was the third son of an earl, so the future "Frank Forester" was shirttail nobility. Henry, as the son

FRANK FORESTER.

# Rail Shooting

of an author and scholar, had the benefit of a literate home life, and family circumstances were such that he was educated at Eton and Cambridge. But the junior Herbert had the unfortunate knack of spending more than his income, and was bankrupt soon after coming of age. With prospects dim in England, he emigrated to America in November 1831, and made the acquaintance of Col. Porter, editor of America's then-preeminent sporting newspaper, *The Spirit of the Times.*

H. W. Herbert established himself as a novelist in his own name by 1840, and used the *nom de plume* Frank Forester for his more controversial writings in the *American Turf Register* and *The Spirit of the Times.* His first Frank Forester book, *The Warwick Woodlands* (1845), was an instant success, and it was apparent that his writings as Forester had more appeal than those of H. W. Herbert. *The Warwick Woodlands* was soon followed by *My Shooting Box* (1846), and in 1848, *Field Sports of the United States and British Provinces of North America* (the source for this chapter).

Herbert was a literary genius. He could knock out an H. W. Herbert novel and simultaneously write a seminal work of sporting nonfiction as Frank Forester and, all the while, still send off monthly articles under both names to half a dozen magazines. But our hero had a darker side, which included more than just his profligate spending. Herbert once fought a duel after a trifling dispute with a lawyer named Valentine. The legal luminary lost a button from his waistband, and Herbert, according to his biographer, was "shot near one of his ankles." Another duel was to have taken place in Canada for legal reasons, but a snowstorm intervened. One of the seconds for Herbert's antagonist reproached him later in New York. The irate

Herbert fired twice, but the shots went into the door as his accuser exited in haste.

Another scandal proved Herbert's undoing in his later years. In 1839 he accepted an invitation to be groomsman for a friend who was to marry the daughter of the mayor of Bangor, Maine. Herbert traveled from New York to Maine with the expectant bridegroom, but it was Henry William who married the bride. The first Mrs. Herbert died in 1846, just as Frank Forester became a household word.

The Newark, New Jersey, and New York City newspapers announced the marriage of Henry William Herbert and Adela R. Budlong as having taken place on 16 February 1858. Apparently the groom's reputation had not preceded him with the new Mrs. Herbert, but her friends soon told her of his unstable character. His bride packed her bags and went home to mother. He went off the deep end after she left. Upon receiving a letter stating that she wasn't coming back, he announced that he would commit suicide on the same day of the month that they were married—the sixteenth. Herbert was late for his last appointment: He fatally shot himself at two o'clock in the morning on 17 May 1858.

# With Powder Flask and Shot Pouch

## by Joseph R. Kendall

I should state my qualifications for presuming to write my shooting recollections of the good old days. When about thirteen years old, I was given a small double-barreled shotgun—a muzzleloader of course, for this was long before the days of breechloaders—and it made me a happy boy. Those were the days of powder flasks, shot pouches, and waterproof caps. My family passed every summer in Swampscott, Massachusetts, near Phillips' Beach and Farmer's Pond. There my elder brother showed me how to load and fire my new gun. I have no recollection of the result of that first day, but my memory of the second day is perfectly clear—and still humiliating.

# *When Ducks Were Plenty*

I went alone to the pond and tried my hand at "peeps" as they flew by, singly or by twos or threes. After several shots, not a peep had I to show. In a field bordering the pond, a man was mowing with a scythe. He was about one hundred yards from me, and every time he heard the report of my gun he would turn his head to see the result—satisfactory to the birds, but not satisfactory to me. Finally, a flock of a dozen or more peeps flew by, and I cracked away at them. Not a bird fell. This was more than the mower could stand, so he said in a loud voice, "Didn't you kill any then?"

"No," I replied weakly.

"Well," said he, "I will tell you what I will do. I will stand off at forty yards, and for a penny a shot you can shoot at my back all day." This broke my heart, and peepless I went home. The experience, however, did not deter me from going again.

During the next few seasons after my first trying experience with the peeps, I shot many yellowlegs and brownbacks (dowitchers) on Farmer's Pond. There were other large birds, of course—willets, great-marbled and Hudsonian godwits, golden plovers, long-billed and Hudsonian curlews, and jacks—but they were not often present in numbers.

In the winter of 1862–63, I was with my regiment in New Bern, North Carolina. When we were not away on some expedition, and when camp routine did not require my presence, I would sometimes row up the Neuse River two miles to where it narrowed, set out my decoys, and occupy a blind for a few hours of shooting. The ducks were mostly bluebill widgeon, with some canvasbacks, ringnecks, and others. Many a nice dinner we had as a result, providing a welcome change from our ordinary rations.

# With Powder Flask and Shot Pouch

In the mid-1860s, I was living on a sea-island plantation near Beaufort, South Carolina. In the spring, jack curlew, willets, black-bellied plover, redback sandpiper, and other shorebirds were plenty. I had good shooting as there were no laws against it then; no one realized how soon their numbers would be diminished. My decoys were the skins of large shore birds properly cured and stuffed with cotton. I made no attempt to stand them up as though alive; rather, I cut crotched sticks like the letter Y, including some extra long sticks to be used where the water was up to a foot deep, and placed each decoy across two sticks. A few of these makeshift decoys were better than many of the ordinary wooden or tin decoys, and the birds came to them readily.

Shorebird shooting can be a pleasant day's diversion in the warm months before the arrival of the larger wildfowl, but when ducks and geese are in season, I give them my full attention. Having been told that many ducks were on the Combahee River—a shooting ground heretofore unknown to me—I decided to try my hand there. I left on 27 November 1865, and my outfit was unique: two pairs of wheels with a plank platform and a dory resting on them, two mules and a driver, my guns and baggage stowed in the dory, and myself on horseback. This caravan made for a comfortable and satisfactory way of traveling the twenty miles of sandy roads from Beaufort to my destination. It was about ten miles across Port Royal Island to the ferry, then six miles to Gardner's Corners, and four miles more to the house where I was to stay.

At the point where I was to shoot, the water in the Combahee River is fresh, but it ebbs and flows several feet according to the ocean tides. The river, as I remember it, is more than a mile across, with rice fields on the low ground on each side. When under cultivation, the water was kept from the fields by a system of dikes; but after the close of the Civil War, many of the dikes were out of repair, allowing the river water free ingress. This was lucky for me, for I had my best shooting from blinds in the flooded rice fields. As I was on new gunning ground, I had to learn by experience where to go, what to do, and how to do it. In the daytime, American widgeon (baldpates), pintails, green-winged teal, shoveller ducks, and bluebill widgeon occupied the fields five miles upriver. The mallards and white-front, or laughing, geese resided five miles downstream and flew to the upper rice fields to feed at night. After three times trying the fields downstream, I gave it up as too uncertain, and afterward always went to the upper fields.

My forty decoys were wooden, of first-class shapes and finish and painted quite artistically and accurately. The water in the rice fields was from a few inches to a foot in depth, and the non-diving ducks fed by immersing their heads and necks. The baldpates, graceful and handsome, were the most numerous, and called with soft, sibilant whistles of three notes, musical and sweet. The pintails, also handsome birds, were shy, but their flight was remarkably steady—no fancy style for them. Pintails were more likely than baldpates to circle the field too high to be within gunshot. The beautiful little green-wing teal were a delightful study. They are lightning-fast, and the moment they catch sight of any motion by the gunner, the flock will split to pieces like the fiery stars of a bursting rocket. Lucky is the shooter who gets one bird with the first barrel, and unless he is as fast as the teal, the rest will be out of range before he can shoot with the second barrel.

# With Powder Flask and Shot Pouch

The house where I stayed was known as the Lowndes Place. A fine but dilapidated mansion, it had been abandoned during the war, then occupied by Uncle Sam. The two officers there made my stay very pleasant. I think I was welcome for the change I made in their rations. During the ten days of my stay, I tried the river and several different fields and any number of ways of "laying" for the ducks. I wanted to get acquainted with the ground as much as possible, for I intended to come again.

On return to my plantation home, I wrote to George Mackay in Boston, giving an account of the Combahee shooting, and invited him to visit me for another trip to the flooded rice fields. Of course he came. Another Boston boy, Douglas Frazer of Hilton Head, also joined us. As soon as our preparations were completed, we started early one morning from Beaufort and arrived at the Lowndes Place before sunset. The two officers were still there—Lieutenants Craig and Loomis—but not having known we were coming, they were not stocked with provisions. All they could give us for supper was a small bit of bacon and hoecake.

*Across the carry at last.*

# When Ducks Were Plenty

The next day we went to the fields upriver to set up blinds at Blake's Dike.  When we were approaching the first site, I told the boys to keep quiet, and I noiselessly grounded the nose of the float on the dike.  Cautiously George reconnoitered and reported a flock of teal within range.  I told him not to mind us but shoot, which he did, and we picked up sixteen birds.  I must apologize for this pot shot, but it was the only one made during our stay of three weeks.  Our excuse was hunger, due to the bacon and hoecake of the night before.

The next day, 29 January 1866, we were all at one field in three blinds.  George wrote up the record of the day:

> The fowl of all descriptions came very fast, mostly in large flocks, flying for the most part very high, so we succeeded in getting but few to our decoys.  The immense quantity of fowl here is truly astonishing, and it would pay any man who handles a gun to come a long way to see what I saw—and this my first day on the Combahee River.

Our last day was 15 February.  I awoke soon after midnight and heard a hard nor'wester tearing through the trees.  At half past one I dressed and got breakfast, and at three o'clock we left the house.  After three hours of rowing against the tide and in the teeth of the gale, taking turns at the oars, we arrived at Blake's.  We hauled the float over the dike, and soon were ready for ducks.  The decoys were placed in a landlocked pond.  We sat cross-legged and side by side on the bottom of the float with two guns apiece, and piled up long reedy grass behind us to make a shelter from the piercing wind.  The shooting was mostly at single birds or pairs, as the flocks separated when approaching the decoys.  The speed with which they would "climb upstairs," as George expressed it, was marvelous. We stopped shooting at four o'clock and reached home at nine, after four hours of rowing against a reversed current backed up by an unusually high tide.

On the last day alone we shot 132 ducks. In ten days of shooting we had amassed 191 baldpates, 68 shovellers, 54 pintails, 26 mallards, 22 bluebills, 9 ringneck ducks, 8 hooded mergansers, 6 ruddy ducks, 4 black ducks, 3 gadwalls, 3 buffleheads, 2 white-fronted laughing geese, 3 cormorants, 1 whistler goldeneye, and 100 green-winged teal, for a total of 500 wildfowl. Some readers will say, as others have said before, "The birds must have been thick." Duck gunners, however, know that something more is needed than a great quantity of fowl. We like to think our shooting had something to do with our success.

Next comes the proper question, "What did you do with so many?" In the first place, we breakfasted, lunched, and dined on ducks the whole time; second, we sent 70 to our friends in town with Douglas Frazer; third, we left 40 with the officers to keep them along; and fourth, we took 120 to my house near Beaufort for ourselves and friends. I have often been asked, "Did you ever get tired of them?" Not at all! I can truthfully say that I never enjoyed such eating in my life. Those rice-fed ducks were the best ever, and the baldpates led them all.

In the Lowndes house were several large open fireplaces for burning logs, and the fire in one of them was never allowed to go out. This meant an ever-present bank of live hardwood coals, making the best possible heat for roasting ducks—if one only had a tin kitchen. Not having one, however, I used a wooden cracker box instead, bored a hole in each end, and spitted the birds on an iron ramrod three at a time. About twenty minutes was required to cook them right, and while we were eating these, three more were put on the spit for our second course. Six were not too many for four boys, as our appetites were not feeble.

What is it that makes a duck shooter so willing and eager to work so hard, to get out of bed hours before daylight, to stand such biting winds and freezing weather, and to endure so many days of disappointing experiences? The passion for duck shooting must be born in him. If one could always bag plenty of fowl, the sport would soon lose its charm. But the very uncertainty of the day—breezy and snappy: a fair to good chance; calm and warm: a poor show—and the fact that it requires knowledge, experience, and skill to stop the fowl in their rapid flight, all contribute to make the lifelong enthusiast.

This was my last visit to Combahee, for in March following, I migrated to Boston, and have never again been at the plantation in winter. But now, forty-three years later, I can still see in my mind's eye the ducks decoyed to our rice-field blind at Blake's Dike, and I can almost taste the baldpates grilled over hardwood embers at the Lowndes place.

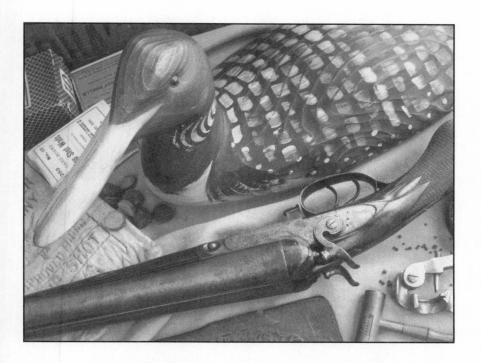

# Loon Used for Duck Decoy

## by "An Old Sportsman"

When we were boys about fifteen years old, my chum Douglas Walcott and I continually roamed around the ponds with our old percussion-cap guns over our shoulders, looking for a shot at a stray duck or two. To our delight, we occasionally succeeded.

I shall never forget a pair of loons that we hunted day after day all summer, often getting a shot at them, but never making a hit. The smart old birds would dive at the flash of a gun. We would see the shot strike all around where they were swimming, but they would be underwater ere the shot arrived. We worried

*Circa 1880s studio photograph of two earnest young hunters and their dog—just the sort of boys who would devote a whole summer to catching and training a loon.*

# Loon Used for Duck Decoy

a great deal over this, until one day we got lucky.  I
was in the boat and managed to work them in near
the shore.  Doug was in the bushes and fired, succeeding
in knocking one over, while the other disappeared with
a long dive.  I picked up the one he had killed and
laid him on the seat alongside me.  As I did so I saw
something protruding from his mouth.  I took hold of
it and pulled out a pickerel that measured thirteen
inches long.  We surmised that this loon had been in
the act of swallowing the fish, and could not bend his
neck quickly enough to dive under the water before
the shot struck him.

Having succeeded in getting one of them, we were
even more eager to get the other.  In chasing the loons,
we had often seen them dive, and though watching
closely, we sometimes could not see them come up.  The
pond was not large, so we could easily see the whole of
it at once.  The disappearing loons were a great
mystery, and we did some tall guessing on the subject,
but didn't solve the riddle until quite a while after
killing the first one.

In the middle of the pond was a little island formed
by hassocks and driftwood.  It was fifty or sixty feet in
diameter, with a spring hole in the center, about twelve
feet wide and filled with water as deep as the water
around the island.  In the fall and winter we would set
a few decoys there, as our blind was nearby on shore.
Often we would shoot a pair of black ducks or
broadbills that had settled in the spring hole.  One
day Doug was in the boat chasing the poor old loon.
As I stood on the edge of the island watching, something suddenly swam underwater directly toward me.
As it came to the bank it disappeared.  I turned around

and, to my surprise, Mr. Loon popped his head up in the center of the spring hole. As soon as he saw me, under he went, and in a few minutes he was well away in the pond and out of gunshot.

The mystery was explained, and now we had to make use of it. We decided to capture the old loon alive, and that, of course, was going to be no easy task. We racked our brains trying to devise some scheme by which we could have our own personal loon, and at last succeeded.

First we made a gate that could be thrust down into the water to cover the mouth of the tunnel after the loon had entered it. Then, with a strong net such as fishermen use in seine fishing, we covered the entire surface of the hole, fastening the edges securely. All being ready, Doug used the boat to chase the old fellow into a long dive. He soon obliged us, and when I saw the loon enter the tunnel, I dropped the gate. I looked over my shoulder, and there was our prize. As soon as he saw me, under he went, but finding no outlet he quickly surfaced. We had him dead to rights, but it was a difficult and delicate job to secure our captive without injuring him—or us. We conquered him at last, even though he gave us a hard fight. Our hands were bleeding, and Doug said that one of his eyes was "disjointed" by a blow from a wing. The great northern loon is a powerful bird.

We put him in a bag and carried him to my house, where we built a good-sized coop, and, after clipping his wings, placed him in his new home. We kept him there all winter and the following summer, feeding him and treating him so kindly that he became quite tame. He would follow us around like a little dog, begging us to feed him a few kernels of corn, of which he was very fond. Occasionally we would take him over to the island and put him in the hole. He remembered it quite well and would pass back and forth through the tunnel as we whistled from one side to the other, feeding him a kernel of corn each time he came through. He never wanted to leave there.

Our purpose was to use him as a decoy late in the fall, when the ducks began to fly. I well remember the first trial we gave him. We got on the island a little before sundown on Thanksgiving Day, and placed Billy, as we called him, in the hole. He swam around to his delight, continually diving and washing himself while we secreted ourselves nearby in the blind we had built early in the season. It was not long before Billy raised his long neck and gave one of those loud, mellow calls for which loons are noted. Soon we saw a flock of broadbills circle over-head. Billy flapped his wings and called again, and down they came into the water alongside him. After a while, Doug gave a whistle, and Billy dove down through the tunnel looking for his corn. When we saw him surface outside, we let both guns go. The ducks were bunched together, affording a slaughtering mark, and we hit seven out of ten. You never saw two happier boys.

We had Billy's services for two seasons, and he brought us many good bags of game. Believe it or not, if a duck was wounded he would seize it by the neck and bring it ashore. This all happened just after the Civil War, but it is as vivid in my mind as if it happened yesterday.

# When Ducks Were Plenty

## Editorial

### Do Sportsmen Need Decoy Cows?

It is expected that a decoy cow will soon be placed on the market by a western man who wants a patent for his invention. The imitation cow is described as being made of flexible material with a collapsible framework that may be folded into a small space when transported. When two men are within the device and desire to fire at game, the man who occupies the forward legs folds the head down by releasing a spring, while the rear man must shoot from beneath curtains or flaps. Directions for entering and getting out of the finished decoy will no doubt be furnished if it is ever sold. It may also be necessary to display warning signals or placards on the cow for the safety of the occupants. It is easy to imagine a farmer's anger on seeing a strange cow feeding in his wheat field. His first impulse would be to drive it away, and the methods to accomplish this could be painful to those enduring them. Suppose he set his dogs on the strange animal, or resorted to the old-fashioned and cruel but effective charge of salt? Then the patent-applied-for decoy's movements might not resemble the graceful stride of the bovine, but rather that of two men departing a painful situation in great haste.

—Shooting and Fishing, *16 September 1897*

*"Double-handed stalking horse at work." From Sir Ralph Payne-Gallwey's 1882 book,* The Fowler of Ireland.

# On the Kankakee
## by "Don"

It was the spring of 1867, and I had just returned to Chicago from a trip to the gold mines of Colorado, when I received a note from an old friend. He wanted me to join him in giving a warm reception to the large numbers of snipe and ducks scattered along the lowlands bordering the Kankakee River. My friend knew my keen love for field sports and that I was glad at any time to cast aside my law books for the more congenial company of gun and dog. Many a day we spent together on the broad prairies and entangled breaks, watching the runways with ready rifles while the mountains echoed with the music of our dogs.

I readily accepted his offer. In less than two hours I was on board an express train rapidly nearing the station where Harry was to meet me. When I got there I found him waiting, and a sharp half-hour's drive brought us to his neat cottage. A well-furnished tea table presided over by my friend's wife served as a hospitable reception and one that the chill spring air rendered very acceptable. That night, by a blazing fire, we talked over bygone days and speculated on the morrow. From the window Harry pointed out the snipe-shooting ground along the river, which glimmered like a broad silver belt beneath the full moon's light.

By seven o'clock the next morning we had finished breakfast and were ready to start. The dogs—his two black-and-tans and my red bitch—were in the highest condition and spirits, yet obedient to the slightest word, as if it were the last, rather than first, day of the season. We crossed two broad fields and came to as fine a piece of snipe ground as a sportsman could desire. The soil was soft and rich with promise of abundant food for the birds, and the reeds grew thick enough to afford splendid cover for either the longbills or skulking mallards.

The dogs had not beaten the bush for a hundred yards ere my red dog stood on a snipe that arose instantly. Harry riddled it with a charge of number eights, and at the report, up sprang a wild wisp of nearly a dozen birds. They gave sharp cries and twisted and dodged far out of shot, but suddenly turned and came directly toward us. We greeted them with both of my barrels and Harry's second, and three birds fluttered to the ground. For a time the snipe were very wild, and though we flushed large numbers, it was fully half an hour until we killed more birds. But as the sun rose higher in the heavens, the day

# On the Kankakee

proved to be unusually mild and soft. The snipe then changed their tactics and responded well to the dogs, affording us fine sport.

As we drew near the banks of the Kankakee River, up jumped a noble mallard drake with a loud quack. It dashed away like a bullet. Grabbing my gun, I fired on him and just had time to see him falling head downward when a sharp "Mark right!" from Harry called my attention to his mate. I turned quickly and cut her down, wing broken by a snap shot. While my dog was looking her up, the whistling of wings was heard overhead, and a line of teal sped by. Their diminutive forms looked even smaller for the speed they were moving. Harry had a good shot, and I saw both of his charges cut a lane through them. Three dropped with the first barrel, and two with the second. After a long search, I bagged my wounded bird, and we moved on. It seemed that every few moments we flushed snipes or ducks, and we gave a good account of ourselves until it was too dark to shoot. That night when we reached the house, we counted 123 snipe, 21 mallard, and 13 teal.

Welcome, indeed, was the supper that awaited us, and pleasant the hour we spent spinning yarns while reclining fireside in luxurious armchairs. More welcome still were the beds upon which we placed our weary forms. The triumphs and toils of the day were soon forgotten as we slipped into a peaceful and well-earned sleep.

During the night the weather changed. In the morning, cold gray clouds obscured the heavens, and the wind moaned round the house, foretelling a coming storm. But nothing would daunt us, and as soon as breakfast was over, we again donned velveteens and tramped the marshes until four o'clock. We were not as successful as the previous day, however, and our bag numbered only 89 snipes, 11 mallards, and 7 teal.

Thus ended my trip to the Kankakee. And though circumstances have prevented my going there since, I recall those days with a pleasure that often tempts me to set business aside and return once more to those broad marshes.

# How to Shoot Ducks
## by John Bumstead

Duck shooting is a very different sport from shooting upland birds. It is attended with so many hardships and uncertainties that unless the sportsman lives near the sea or some inland lake where ducks resort, it will hardly pay for him to leave the woods and fields to seek waterfowl instead of his usual inland game. The time for shooting wild duck and other waterfowl is also the season when woodcock, quail, and partridge are plenty; duck season, of course, coincides with the harvest season for all gamebirds. Waterfowl shooting is at best a tedious, wearisome business, and whoever pursues it must bear much disagreeable work. The duck shooter will often suffer from cold winds, storms, and wet feet, and sometimes he will go home empty-handed.

The best season for shooting wild ducks is in the fall, beginning in early October, and continuing through

December. If you live near a fresh pond or lake, you should prepare a shooting blind or brush house and visit it whenever you can, particularly on windy mornings and evenings. You would find it convenient to have your brush house close to the pond, made by driving four stakes into the ground in a square pattern and connecting them with strips of wood for support. Then cut some small trees and bushes, sharpen the ends, drive them into the ground, and fasten them to the bars. Make the house sufficiently high to stand in so that if you are up and on the lookout when the fowl are coming in, you can quietly drop down again without being seen. If well done, you will have a good cover that can easily be repaired when out of order. Put a quantity of dry hay on the floor to sit upon. The whole blind should look like a low cluster of trees and bushes and not resemble a hut.

If your pond is situated near salt water, you must visit it—day or night—when the tide is within two hours of being full. The tide drives the ducks from the low saltwater marshes to freshwater ponds to wash and preen themselves, leaving your activity in the blinds unnoticed. Set on the pond good wooden or living decoys. The latter are preferable if they can be had, as they will call the wild ducks to them. Be careful how you move about in your shooting stand when ducks are on the pond or are coming in. They are quick to notice any sudden movement; probably no other fowl of any kind can excel them in this. When ducks have come down to the decoys and are within range of the gun, find an open space in your brush house, draw back your gun, and put the muzzle to the hole, but not through it, lest your motions should be discovered. When you shoot, sight your gun down toward the water to avoid shooting over the sitting ducks.

# How to Shoot Ducks

If a number of ducks are on the pond, wait until they have come together so you can secure as many as possible, and endeavor to shoot at them while their sides and tails are toward you. It will be almost impossible to kill them when they first rise out of the water. I know of no fowl that rises from the water as quickly as the common black duck; where they get their tremendous force and velocity it is difficult to imagine. After having discharged both barrels at the ducks on the water, you must reload as quickly as possible while looking out for the lively cripples. Let the dead fowl lie until the others are secured. If the cripples get to shore they will soon hide themselves, and it will trouble you to find them, as they will work into the smallest imaginable holes. Should you, while searching for them, notice the tip of a feather sticking an inch or two out of the sedge, I would advise you to give it a pull, for you will probably find a good fat duck at the other end.

During October and November, wild duck shooting on our northern and western lakes is exceedingly fine sport, and so attractive that many sportsmen from New York and the New England states go annually to these lakes and shoot for the market. And a good business they make of it. Not only are they able to pay their expenses, but they generally derive considerable supplemental income, and, added to the pecuniary results, they acquire an enjoyment that cannot be expressed in dollars and cents.

## Editor's Note

John Bumstead's *On the Wing—A Book for Sportsmen* (1869) was the first post-Civil War book describing the use of a breechloading shotgun on small game and wildfowl. According to Ray Riling's *Guns and Shooting: A Selected Chronological Bibliography* (1982), *On the Wing — A Book for Sportsmen* (three editions: 1869, 1871, and 1875) was Bumstead's only book. He did, however, pursue his literary efforts on the pages of Wilbur Parker's newspaper, *The American Sportsman*, in the early 1870s, and was sufficiently well known in sporting circles to be called upon to endorse the beginnings of a conservation movement in Massachusetts — more on this in chapter 12.

# Wild Pigeon Shooting—A Memory
## by Jacob Pentz

The cool crisp days of late August stir my memories of days long past. Years and years ago, on just such an August morning, I stood upon a little square plateau at the very top of a knoll in Fairfield County, Connecticut. Rain had fallen the day before, but the sky cleared toward evening, and the sun went down half-hidden in a mass of dull blue clouds just above the western horizon. The summit of the hill commanded an unobstructed view eastward for many miles. I had stuck in the ground a square of freshly cut cedar trees of small size, standing from six to eight feet in height. The enclosure was under six feet square

*(Picture:  Passenger pigeons, extinct since 1914, R.I.P.)*

inside, and the thickness of the trees made for an impenetrable thicket to the not-too-observant eye.

The declining sun of evening was followed by fresh night winds out of the northwest, indicating that summer had gone and autumn's chill was close at hand. With sunrise would come the wild pigeons, flock after flock, one flying above the horizon to the eastward as the one before it passed over the hill. They would cut the air with a rustle of swift-moving pinions that I can hear as plainly while penning these lines as I heard them then.

Little sleep had come to me that long night. Scarcely had the light of dawn greeted my eye ere I stood in that green thicket with a pair of tame pigeons in a little basket. One was blindfolded by a chamois leather hood covering its head and eyes. It was the work of a moment to tie the legs of this bird together with a bit of cord and then to fasten the other end to a little green covered platform just outside my blind. I also tied the other pigeon's legs, but the cord was a long one. Guns and ammunition were close at hand. Then came a period of anxious waiting when each moment seemed to be an hour.

As the sun peeped above the line of blue hills in the east, a dark speck arose on the horizon. It grew in size as it moved westward; another followed the first, and then others, dozens of them, all moving westward, but on different lines. I then had an anxious thought: Will they come near enough to stool to my decoy? As if in answer, a big flock, hundreds of them, flew straight for my hill. I tossed the long-corded pigeon in the air; it felt its wings and rose to the length of its cord.

The nearest flock saw the decoy and with a whirl turned toward it. Inside the cedar screen, peering nervously, I stooped and held the short string tethering

# Wild Pigeon Shooting—A Memory

the bird on the green platform. What a moment of anxiety, of fear, of hope! I pulled the cord. The blindfolded bird, feeling its support disappearing from underneath it, fluttered its wings madly. Another period of suspense followed, but luck was with me, and the wild birds altered their course and flew toward the struggling pigeon. With a swoop and a curve they stooled to the tethered bird as wild ducks to a decoy

*Uncle Jake*

and alit on every branch of every nearby small tree and bush. They were so beautiful as they struggled for space to perch; it seemed a pity to shoot them. The iridescent colors of their necks flashed in the gleam of the rising sun; the dove-colored breasts were tinged to a ruby flame, and the blue of their backs shone as azure as the clearest sky. Every movement was a grace. Their eyes, red as rubies, told of their desire to rest and feed.

I grasped the gun. Was it butchery? Of course it was. Yet, in the 1860s, who ever stayed his hand when the flight was on? Out belched fire and shot from my double barrel, raking along the roosted pigeons. The earth was covered with the dead and dying. I was gluttonous indeed, but how unconsciously so! It seemed the thing to do at the time, yet the wild pigeon exists now [1896] only in the memory of the older generation, and with remembrance comes a pang of sorrow.

# When Ducks Were Plenty

## Editor's Note

Jacob "Uncle Jake" Pentz was perhaps the best-known shooting-sports journalist of the 1880s and 1890s. He was on the editorial staff of *Shooting and Fishing* and had charge of the trapshooting department. Pentz was on the handicap committee when the Grand American Handicap was held with live birds, and he served as referee at many of the tournaments he attended. He died Christmas Eve 1900, and according to a memorial in *Shooting and Fishing*, "His writing was peculiar in that it often was in the form of a personal letter to some congenial spirit rather than dry statements of facts. He was painstaking to an unusual extent, and never willingly repeated a statement he could not credit." Such posthumous recognition helped me separate the wheat from the chaff when I researched *Parker Guns: The "Old Reliable."* I felt confident that I could give great weight to any fact or opinion espoused by Jacob Pentz.

# Wilbur F. Parker, Conservationist
## by Ed Muderlak

Wilbur Fisk Parker (1839–1876) was the oldest son of Charles Parker, founder of The Charles Parker Company and Parker Brothers, makers of the famous "Old Reliable" Parker shotgun. Charles Parker's company in West Meriden, Connecticut, made everything from buttons to railroad wheels, coffee grinders, and steam engines by the 1850s. During the Civil War, his company manufactured government contract muskets for the Union army. After the war, Parker's gun works had on staff roughly three hundred soon-to-be-unemployed gun mechanics experienced in making long guns. Not surprisingly, postwar production shifted from military arms to breechloading shotguns for the civilian market. During the 1860s,

*(Picture: Destry Hofard's Illinois River punt gun and Wilbur F. Parker's* The American Sportsman, *both circa 1875.)*

# When Ducks Were Plenty

Parker Brothers produced the only truly workable American-made breechloading double-barrel shotgun, and the Parker was America's "best gun" through the end of production in the 1940s.

Wilbur was in charge of the gun works until his untimely death on Christmas day 1876, at age thirty-seven. According to a contemporary account by Jacob Pentz, editor of *Shooting and Fishing* (and author of chap. 11), "If ever there was an enthusiast in all that regards American guns or the capabilities of American mechanics, that man was Wilbur F. Parker. He most certainly led the way in the work of making guns in this country, and his development of the manufacture has been something to be talked about." Wilbur contributed much to the sport of game killing after the Civil War by increasing the firepower of breechloaders and associated self-contained ammunition. But there is another side to Wilbur Fisk Parker that has heretofore been little known, and, never to my knowledge, publicized: He was on the cutting edge of the game conservation and anti-pollution movement in the United States. Here is his story:

Through the 1860s, sportsmen's newspapers were mostly of general interest, with stories on boxing, billiards, horseracing, and theater interspersed with a few sketches on hunting and fishing. Wilbur Parker, with some help from Parker Brothers, founded *The American Sportsman* in October 1871; a monthly sixteen-page pulp newspaper dedicated exclusively to hunting, shooting, fishing, and natural history. Leading scientists, experts, and sportsmen of the day contributed articles. By October 1873, the monthly paper had become a weekly and Wilbur Parker was listed as "Editor and Proprietor" on the masthead.

# Wilbur F. Parker, Conservationist

*The American Sportsman* was the first such newspaper to specialize in shooting and fishing, so the name was changed in 1875 to *Rod and Gun* to reflect the narrow editorial focus. Wilbur's paper was his vehicle for promoting sportsmen's clubs and the conservation movement in the United States.

*Forest and Stream* was established in 1873, and acquired *Rod and Gun* after Wilbur took ill in 1876. The name of the combined sportsmen's weekly newspaper was then changed to *Forest and Stream—Rod and Gun.* After the turn of the century, *Forest and Stream* went to a monthly magazine format and was acquired by *Field and Stream* magazine in 1930. Thus the *Field and Stream* of today's newsstands, published by *Times-Mirror,* can be traced directly back to Wilbur Parker's *American Sportsman* of the early 1870s. Likewise, the organized conservation efforts of various present-day sportsmen's clubs and associations can trace their origins back to Wilbur Parker's vision of state and local clubs unified as members of a national organization, just as he editorialized on the pages of *The American Sportsman.*

To put Wilbur Parker's efforts on behalf of sportsmanship and conservation in a proper time frame and context, it should be noted that in the early 1870s, the eastern states were relatively densely populated and cosmopolitan. Meanwhile, Cincinnati was on the frontier, and central Illinois was still mostly prairie. In the west, passenger pigeons flocked by the millions, buffalo herds were immense, and Custer had not yet had his "last stand" in the Battle of the Little Bighorn.

Wilbur Parker and certain other influential New England sportsmen saw the deleterious effects of market hunting in the coastal corridor from Baltimore to Boston. *The*

# When Ducks Were Plenty

*American Sportsman* was Wilbur's editorial soapbox from which he promoted the formation of a network of sportsmen's clubs and associations on a state-by-state basis, and a national sportsman's association to coordinate local efforts. The Hartford (Connecticut) Fish and Game Club and the Massachusetts Sportsmen's Association were formed in 1875, with the idea that like-minded gentlemen sportsmen could act in concert to protect wild game and fish from the depredations of non-gentlemen sportsmen, market hunters, game hogs, and others who would violate what were then considered appropriate self-imposed personal limits and closed seasons—somewhat moderate goals by today's standards. The following excerpt from the 27 February 1875 issue of *The American Sportsman* explained the situation:

> Hartford, Connecticut—At a large and enthusiastic meeting of influential citizens to organize a club for the protection of fish and game, Mr. Wilbur F. Parker, editor of *The American Sportsman*, was called for and received with applause. He gave a brief synopsis of what his experience had been, and the necessity for such organizations if we expect to have good shooting and fishing. He considers the game and fish of the country as a source of national wealth that all could enjoy, if protected by proper legislation. His remarks were well received, after which the gentlemen present signed the constitution, and the Hartford club is fairly underway, with over fifty good, reliable members.

A week later in Boston, the Massachusetts Sportsmen's Association was formed with the idea of sending delegates to a national convention to be held in Cleveland, Ohio, 8 June 1875. A letter from John Bumstead of Boston (author of chap. 10) was read to the club:

> I have received and read your call for a state sportsmen's association for the protection of birds and fishes in this commonwealth. If such an association shall be formed, and carries out for the true purposes of the call as named, and not in form only, then I will say that you have my hearty approval and cooperation. We, who are the sportsmen of this state, should feel it especially our paramount duty to protect the fish and game birds of this commonwealth, if we desire in the future to cast our lines for the former, or ever intend to pull the trigger on the latter.

The club formed a committee to draft a Massachusetts game law, and Wilbur F. Parker addressed the club, setting forth reasons why there should be a national club for the protection of game and the pleasures of sportsmen. His remarks were brief but to the point:

> Even sportsmen who practice sporting as an art, who disdain to kill a sitting bird or catch trout or salmon except with the fly, are not particular about a closed season. Why should they be? If they spare the birds, the pothunters will not. But it is an amusing contradiction to hear gentlemen sportsmen at Delmonico's declaiming against the iniquity of violating the laws of season, and yet enjoying their trout or woodcock without inquiry as to the month or the day of the month. Thus I approach the subject of a national sportsmen's association. You may

ask me what the national association can do
that a state association cannot do?  Much!

In the first place we must remember that
the idea of preserving game is new to many.
We have no power yet of passing a central
national law on the subject, because we would
arouse prejudices and get into conflict with
the state jurisdictions.  The state may be quite
willing to make such laws as an association
may ask, and yet, with the best intentions,
the provisions of one locality may be inapplicable
to another, and close seasons in adjoining
states not being reciprocally adjusted, a
loophole is left for escape.

There is another consideration in reference
to this national association.  It constitutes
a central point from which action can be
directed on Congress.  There must be a day
when the pollution of our streams will have
to be considered.  The exertions of state or
local fish commissioners will be of small
account if acids, salts, and manufacturing
and city sewage are to be run into the
streams to kill off the supplies as fast as
they are brought to the water.  In that case,
a national association would have its value
and would give harmonious and one-minded
support to the efforts of gentlemen who were
acting not for a particular locality, but for
the whole nation.

Wilbur F. Parker would die on Christmas Day 1876,
and thus would not see his ideas come to fruition.
Ironically, the very pollution of which he warned in
1875 closed the last remnants of Charles Parker's
company a century later; oil saturation and polluted
groundwater under the manufacturing facilities in

# Wilbur F. Parker, Conservationist

Meriden, Connecticut, resulted in public interest lawsuits brought in federal court. (The company was no longer owned by Charles Parker's descendants during the lawsuits, and began manufacturing its products in Mexico in 1984.)

Notwithstanding Wilbur Parker's untimely death, the first steps toward a network of local sportsmen's clubs affiliated with a national sportsmen's organization were taken in the mid-1870s. One by one the local sportsmen's clubs convinced their state legislatures to pass licensing laws to curb or exclude nonresident market hunters. Laws were soon passed to prohibit the taking of game during the breeding season, and eventually to regulate spring shooting. Limits came later. Licensing

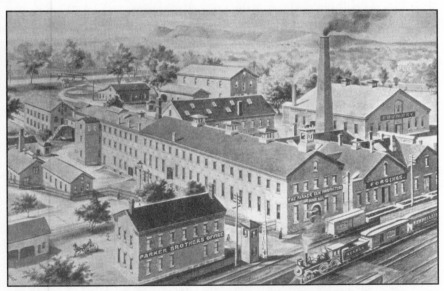

*Parker Brothers manufactory at West Meriden, Connecticut. At the time (circa 1870) this division of Charles Parker's company made everything from printing presses to drop-forging equipment, railroad wheels to buttons, and the soon-to-be-famous Parker Brothers breechloading shotgun.*

of nonresidents ultimately led to licensing of residents, even on a county by county basis, and the process was not without controversy and friction. The efforts of the sportsmen's clubs were duly noted by market hunters and their commission agents, who sought blatant retaliation, according to the 20 February 1875 issue of *The American Sportsman*:

> The market men, aggravated by enforce-
> ment of the game law by the shooting clubs,

*Who do you suppose shot the ducks?*

# Wilbur F. Parker, Conservationist

are endeavoring to induce the Humane Society to put a stop to trapshooting. Thus far the society has refused to act, and its president, Mr. J. C. Dow, says it is very doubtful if, under the existing law, it could do anything if it tried.

It should be noted that in the 1870s, the core interest of most clubs was trapshooting, which entailed springing live pigeons from traps. Alternative targets such as glass balls and the "Gyro Pigeon" were not particularly challenging, and George Ligowsky's clay pigeon had not yet been invented. A follow-up article in the 6 March 1875 issue of *The American Sportsman* said that "the market men are more quiet now, as so little game is to be had and their pockets are less affected by the law. They say, however, that they will see that the legislature makes it illegal to shoot at any time either tame pigeons or snowbirds." Market men were then still in the business of supplying wild pigeons to their antagonists, the sportsmen's clubs. Thus began the sometimes symbiotic love-hate relationship between professional market hunters and gentlemen sportsmen. Ultimately the market men and sport hunters reconciled after the selling of game was outlawed, and the professionals soon found it was more lucrative to guide hunters than to make a living by the gun alone.

Meanwhile, the sportsmen's clubs were on the ascendancy, and increasingly had the ear of state and federal legislators. Wilbur Parker's vision of local and state clubs affiliated with a national association "from which action can be directed on Congress . . ." came to partial fruition in 1900: Passage of the Lacey Act prohibited interstate commerce in game taken in violation of state laws. Finally, after numerous false starts and constitutional litigation, the Migratory Bird Treaty Act of 1918 shifted protection and control of all migratory wildfowl to the federal government. Thus ended what could be called the golden age of shotgunning—from the 1840s to 1920—when shooting was essentially unregulated.

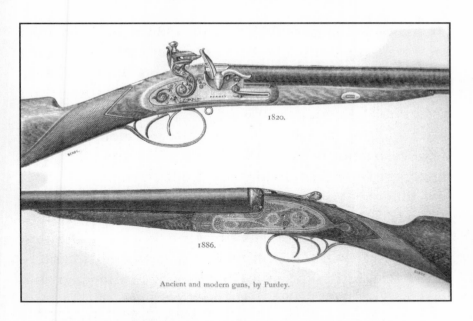

Ancient and modern guns, by Purdey.

# Muzzleloader or Breechloader?

## by Joseph W. Long

The following work endeavors to lay before the public, in as concise form as possible, full and trustworthy explanations of the various practical methods of hunting wildfowl in the inland portions of our country. Wildfowling as an art is but little understood by the great majority of sportsmen. It is attended with too much fatigue, hardship, and bad weather to be practiced to the point of expertise. However, before treating the various methods employed in the actual pursuit of wildfowl, I shall first proceed to the concurrent subject of guns.

On the comparative merits of breech- and muzzleloaders, I am willing to acknowledge the general superiority of the new invention; nevertheless, the muzzleloader possesses several decided advantages over the breechloader. The breechloader can be quickly reloaded when in the field or boat, and this capability alone is to compensate for many otherwise serious objections. No matter how smart a man may be with a muzzleloader, he will often lose many shooting opportunities by not being ready-loaded. Meanwhile, for a patron of the breechloader such occurrences are rare, provided he has plenty of loaded cartridges handy. However, the carrying and reloading of a sufficient number of metallic shells, or the transportation and room required for their paper substitutes, is the most serious drawback to the use of a breechloader. I formed this

*"The carrying and re-loading of a sufficient number of metallic shells or the transportation and room required for their paper substitutes, is the most serious drawback to the use of a breechloader. I formed this conclusion whilst sitting up at night loading shells and listening to the snoring of my fellow hunters, votaries of the muzzleloader; having eaten their supper, they had simply washed their guns, refilled their pouches and flasks, and rolled up in their blankets to 'woo tired nature's sweet restorer.'"—Joseph W. Long.*

conclusion whilst sitting up at night loading shells and listening to the snoring of my fellow hunters, votaries of the muzzleloader; having eaten their supper, they had simply washed their guns, refilled their pouches and flasks, and rolled up in their blankets to "woo tired nature's sweet restorer."

On pleasant days, when shooting my breechloader from a boat, I usually reload my brass shells as fast as possible between shots. I carry an ammunition box and loading tools with me for this purpose. But on stormy days or when shooting away from my boat, I have to refill my shells at night—often when I should be sleeping—or else forego shooting the next morning. Here, again, the muzzleloader has the preference. Also, man risks fewer long, wild shots with a muzzleloader, and consequently wastes less ammunition. He has less bulk and weight to carry in shells and loading tools. For boat-shooting, if he uses two muzzleloaders he can kill more game the season through than with one breechloader, as he will frequently have opportunities to shoot both guns into the same flock of ducks before they get out of reach.

To give the reader an idea of the good work that may be done with a muzzleloader, I subjoin a memorandum of shooting done by my friend Mr. Fred Kimble of Peoria, Illinois. During the spring of 1872, he used only a single-barreled 9-gauge muzzleloading gun. Not over three ducks were killed by any one shot, and nearly all singly. Fred's total for seventeen days of shooting was 1,365 ducks and 5 brant. His ammunition gave out almost every day. Not expecting to find such a large amount of game, his party carried too little powder and shot. The storekeeper at the little town nearby would order only a keg or so of powder at a time, and then would not sell it all to one person at any price, for fear of offending others. We can only surmise what Fred's score would have been, had he sufficient ammunition.

Now, even though I have so far favored the muzzleloader, do not consider me an old fogy. I intend to give the claims of the breechloader an equal showing. First, breechloaders have the advantage of rapidity in loading, which means that in wildfowl shooting, cripples may be more readily secured. Second, the ease and quickness of exchanging loads allows for shooting geese or swans while awaiting ducks. Third, their cleaning is easy. Fourth, they are less liable to misfire. And fifth, they are safe: There is no chance of getting two loads into one barrel, no need to have head or hands over the muzzle, and no need to leave the gun uncapped and loaded when not in use.

For the majority of uses, the breechloader is the superior weapon for novice or gentlemen sportsmen. However, for the poor market duck-hunter, if he can afford but one gun, I would advocate the muzzleloader. He will find it much less trouble to take care of and less work to keep loaded. He may kill a few more ducks with a breechloader, but they will cost him enough to make up the difference both in labor and ammunition. For boat-shooting, where it can be afforded, I would advise the use of both muzzle- and breechloaders. One or the other may be used as the occasion demands, and the special advantages of each can be secured.

For duck-shooting with a breechloader, I recommend metal shells, which are stronger than paper. Paper shells are liable to get wet and thereby spoiled, and require too much room if much shooting is expected. The disadvantages associated with paper shells in reloading, though insignificant to some, are not to be overlooked by the proper sportsman.

In addition to the breech- or muzzleloader decision, the reader will also have to make up his mind as to the dimensions that suit him best. For flight shooting, no larger than an 8-bore should be used, and a 10-bore is sufficient. For a breechloader, never use larger than a 10-bore, as the cartridges for an 8-bore are too bulky and require too much room for transportation. The 10-bore, if properly loaded, will kill nearly as far as the 8-bore, and generally the smaller gun will balance and point with more accuracy. My first breechloader was built by Tonks of Boston in 1871, and I now use a 10-bore made by Parker Brothers.

## *Editor's Note*

Joe Long's discourse on the relative merits of muzzleloaders and breechloaders was taken from the 1874 first edition of his book, *American Wild-Fowl Shooting*. By the second "revised" edition in 1879, however, the breechloader was so well established that even the most down-and-out market hunters had opted for the increased firepower of the new gun. Both editions of Long's book were dedicated "To my friend Fred Kimble of Peoria, Illinois, a crack duck-shot and an honest man." Kimble made a name for himself with his prowess at duck shooting and in the live pigeon ring, and was mentioned in writing by his contemporaries, including Captain du Bray, Edwin Hedderly, and Charles Askins (the Elder). William Chester Hazelton ascended to the leadership of the Fred Kimble fan club after the turn of the century. Hazelton published seventeen books on bird hunting between 1914 and 1944, including *Fred Kimble, Master Duck Shot of the World* (1923), from which the next chapter is taken.

# Among the Geese and Sandhill Cranes in North Dakota

### by Fred Kimble
### (Comment by Captain Arthur W. du Bray)

My Parker double gun handled large shot well; I could put a charge of No. 1 or No. 2 shot into a 30-inch circle at 40 yards. To test it further, I took a trip to North Dakota to shoot No. 1 shot at geese and sandhill cranes.

Twelve miles north of Dawson, North Dakota, I stopped at a farmer's house. A colony of New York farmers had settled upon a tract of land just south of the Manitoba line, and had planted it all in wheat. This field was the first feeding ground in the line of flight of the geese and cranes on their way south. The colony was called the New York settlement, and my stopping place was the nearest house to the railroad. All the other farmers had to pass the house on the way to and from town.

One afternoon, shooting from a pit in a stubble field, I killed 46 Canada geese and 37 sandhill cranes by sundown. Five of the largest geese weighed 16½ pounds each, while the lot averaged 11 pounds apiece. The cranes ran about 6½ pounds each. The total weight of the game shot inside of three hours was over 700 pounds. It filled our wagon box.

I had had an unusual experience that day. While I was waiting in my pit before the flight began in the late afternoon, a man ran across the field toward me from the direction of the nearest house, a little shack about a mile away. He was coatless and hatless. When within shouting distance he cried, "Say, you feller! I want you to git outen my field. Them's my geese what comes here, and I want to do my own shootin'."

I invited him over to the blind and told him that if he got his gun, I would have a pit ready for him by the time he got back. I told him he could shoot over my decoys, as it was lonesome business shooting alone, anyway. (The farmer who had brought me to my pit had taken the team off a quarter mile or more, to be out of sight of the game.)

He said he had no shells. On finding that his gun was a 10-bore, I offered to furnish him with all the shells he could shoot. He said his gun was "broke," so I offered to let him shoot my gun half of the time. I suggested that I could dig another pit alongside mine. But he then admitted that he couldn't shoot on the fly.

"Now, my good friend," I said, "how do you expect to kill geese, and what good will they do you, if your gun is broken and you have no ammunition, and you could not hit a goose if you tried? Hadn't you better let me kill some for you and take them over to your house this evening? I will be glad to do it." At this he appeared less hostile. He said he had been out in that country two years and had not yet had a goose to eat. If I got any, and could spare one, he would be much obliged.

He started back to the house and had only gone a short distance when a flock of geese came in sight. He saw me kill a pair, waved his hand at me, and kept on his way. It was only three o'clock, and the flight was now on. I could kill both geese and cranes at sixty-five yards, and had no trouble in killing pairs at sixty yards when straight overhead.

The flight ceased at sundown, and I beckoned to my man to bring the wagon. It took us until after dark to pick up the game, load it in the wagon, and fill up the pit, something I never failed to do before leaving a field. We then drove to the farmer's house. I left Mr. Stinchcomb (the man with the team) out on the road while I carried six big, fat geese to the front door. My friend was in good humor and allowed that two of the geese would be plenty, but I insisted that he take all six. The nights were cold, and I told him that by hanging them in the shade, they would keep two weeks. I also told him that when he passed Stinchcomb's house and saw game hanging up, he should help himself to all he could use, and that the man out on the road with the team was Mr. Stinchcomb.

Then he called out, "Hello, Stinch, is that you? Say, Stinch, if you will fetch this feller and his traps out to my place, he kin stay with me all fall, and it won't cost him a darned cent." But I knew when I was well off, and stayed with Stinchcomb. The farmers of that New York settlement had all the game they could use while I was on the job, and I had a fine time.

# When Ducks Were Plenty

The old Parker gun and I decided it was time to go home after a solid month of shooting geese and cranes. When we arrived back at Dawson on the railroad, I found that reports on my shooting had been brought in daily by the farmers; to hear them tell it, a goose couldn't fly high enough to get out of reach of that old gun. What it had done was the talk of the town. The farmers got first pick of the game, and that not used by them was shipped to Minneapolis and Chicago. The trip had been successful for everyone concerned; it was as fine a trip as I ever had in all my career.

## Recent Duck Shooting by Fred Kimble
### (Comment by Captain Arthur W. du Bray)

The last time I heard of Mr. Kimble's duck shooting *par excellence* was at a famous duck club near Los Angeles. A noted duck shot who had witnessed Mr. Kimble told me he had never in his life seen such extraordinary shooting, for no lone duck ever got away. When two or more ducks appeared, there was always a pair dead in the air. He left no

*Captain Arthur W. du Bray, sales agent for Parker's "Old Reliable" shotgun, must have met Kimble prior to joining Parker Brothers in December 1890, as he mentioned "my good friend Fred Kimble, of Peoria, Ill." in Leffingwell's 1890 book,* Shooting on Upland, Marsh, and Stream.

cripples, just riddled lumps of meat and feathers, and shot singles and doubles alike with such marvelous regularity and precision that it became monotonous to watch.

Men who are accustomed to shooting up north— often in rocking boats, breaking ice to reach the shooting ground, with numb hands and stiff joints—experience a revelation when they come to balmy California. Shooting in California is so much easier than in the middle and Atlantic states that it was child's play to a seasoned veteran such as Mr. Kimble.

### Editor's Note

Fred Kimble: Master Duck Shot of the World, by various authors including Captain du Bray and Fred Kimble,

*From the August 1936 issue of* The American Rifleman. *Fred Kimble's claim to fame was mostly that he outlived all of his contemporaries. Kimble was a local (Peoria, Illinois) crack duck shot in the 1870s, but he achieved his fame retroactively in the 1930s with a series of articles in* The American Rifleman, Sports Afield, *and* Outdoor Life, *where he claimed credit for exaggerated shooting accomplishments and various inventions, including choke boring. Kimble's story of 1880s "Goose Shooting in North Dakota," published in Hazelton's 1923 book,* Fred Kimble, Master Duck Shot of the World, *is probably factual. But his claim to have invented choke boring is pure invention, as much so as if Kimble had claimed to have invented sliced bread.*

# *When Ducks Were Plenty*

was published by William Chester Hazelton in Chicago in 1923, with only two hundred copies printed. This 53-page book commands four-figure prices in today's collectors' market, so I am deeply indebted to Carol Barnes at Gunnerman Books for her help in procuring the two sketches used in this chapter. Hazelton was a professional linotype operator, as well as author and publisher of seventeen books on bird hunting and duck shooting on the Illinois River and other wildfowling regions. Besides his own hunting reminiscences, Hazelton induced some of the best-known sports writers of his day to contribute their own duck-shooting tales to his small (53 to 168 pages) self-published books. Hazelton's hard-to-find books have struck a responsive chord with collectors specializing in duck-shooting topics. A good start for readers interested in Hazelton is his self-published *Supreme Duck Shooting Stories* (1936), available in reprint by Gunnerman Press (1989). Despite their imperfections, Hazelton's little books are treasured by collectors.

# Canada Geese on Thin Ice

## by Adam H. Bogardus

The best shooting at Canada geese is in the fall, when the young ones arrive from the far northern regions where they had been born. Their arrival is not looked for in Illinois until after a stiff frost, usually about the first of November. The corn is just then being cut, and the winter wheat is well out of the ground. The wild geese graze upon the young wheat, sometimes to the nub. When corn has been shucked and left in the fields, they will also consume that. In some wet places, I have known them to eat a third of the crop.

Canada geese are cunning and secretive. They choose their sleeping places in large, wet marshes near open water. When ice covers the marshes and ponds, the geese will roost on that, and they generally keep far from settlements, preferring to roost in places that are almost inaccessible. A few flocks still roost on the Salt Creek and Sangamon River bottoms near my home at Petersburg on the Illinois prairie. These bottoms are more than a mile wide in some places, and the bottoms of the

*Captain Adam H. Bogardus, "Champion Wing Shot of the World." Badges: (top) Championship of the World, won 7 August 1875 in England; (bottom left) "Lorillard"; (bottom right) "Champion of America." The rules governing these badges required the holder to answer any challenge within four months of a $250 forfeit placed with the editor of the* Spirit of the Times. *A live pigeon match to contest the badge would then be held, offering not less than $500 to the winner. For top guns like Bogardus, holding and defending various championships was a full-time job.*

# Canada Geese on Thin Ice

nearby Illinois and Mississippi Rivers are wider still, and considerably more extensive.

Some years ago [before 1870], I and three others found a small roost of Canada geese on the Sangamon River, just below the mouth of Salt Creek. There came a sudden frost and some snow, which iced over the river near the place the geese frequented. We surmised the geese would roost on the ice. In such cold weather, geese do not fly before nine or ten o'clock in the morning. At break of day we drove in a sleigh three miles to where they would be found. The river was low where we approached the bank, and we could hear a gaggle of geese chattering in the cold on the ice below. Heavy timber covered both banks, and we crept through the woods until we came within forty yards of our quarry. As we raised up to shoot, the Canadas started to fly. We discharged our eight barrels, killing ten. Our guns were muzzleloaders, but if they had been breechloaders we could have charged and shot again, as the geese seemed bewildered and did not fly straight away. Now began my bad luck.

The geese all fell dead on slush ice, which is weak and treacherous, even when thick. My companions were afraid to go after them, so I had to go, even though I was the heaviest man in the party. It is my habit not to let my gun out of my hands when I am shooting, so I carried it with me when I went out on the ice for the geese.

I brought seven birds to the bank, then went back on the ice for the other three. I was just stooping to pick up the last when I dropped through an air hole that had been covered with broken ice and snow. The river was twenty feet deep, and I would have drowned. However, by means of my gun in one hand and the three geese in the other, I got such a spread on the ice that I did not go clean under. Two of my companions were so confused by the suddenness of the occurrence and the danger of my situation that they did nothing. The other got an old ten-foot rail and shoved it toward me on the ice. The rail enabled me to struggle to the bank, gun, geese, and all. The cold was so intense that my clothes froze stiff the minute I was out of the water.

It was a long, cold three miles back to my house, and before we got there I felt like a solid six-foot chunk of ice. Once home, I put on dry clothes, wrapped myself in a blanket, took a seat by the fire, and drank half a pint of strong whiskey, neat. This put me in "good spirits," but when the blood began to circulate in my numbed parts, the pain was so intense that I finished the pint. Soon I was feeling no pain, and did not even take cold from the ducking.

## *Editor's Note*

Captain Adam H. Bogardus was born 17 September 1833, in Albany County, New York. In 1858 he moved to Elkhart, Illinois (near Springfield), on what was then the western frontier. Bogardus worked as a farmhand, carpenter, and part-time constable until the Civil War, when he served with the 68th and 145th Illinois infantry and achieved the rank of captain. After the war and until about 1881, he made his living as a market hunter on the prairies and marshland of Sangamon County. Elkhart was a stop on the railroad between Chicago and St. Louis, and Bogardus supplied the city markets with barrels of game packed in ice and sawdust.

In 1868, at the relatively late age of thirty-five, Captain Bogardus shot his first live pigeon match. He won the

# Canada Geese on Thin Ice

Elkhart $100 stakes with a score of forty-six; the next best score was forty. Although he lost his next match to Abe Kleinmann, the then champion pigeon shot of Illinois, he went on to become one of America's best-known and highly seeded professional shooters for the next fifteen years. In fact, many sweepstakes tournaments were advertised, "Open to the world except Bogardus, Carver, and Kleinmann." Captain Bogardus was injured in a hunting accident in 1873, and devoted his four-month recuperation to writing *Field, Cover, and Trap Shooting*, which was published in 1874. (This chapter was taken from the 1878 revised edition.)

By the mid-1870s, wild passenger pigeons were becoming increasingly difficult to procure for trap shooting, and various inanimate targets had come into use, including the Gyro Pigeon and glass balls. Bogardus set out to improve the glass ball targets and the catapult trap that launched them. In 1877, he patented an improved glass target, which had a rough, serrated exterior that made it less likely for shot to glance off the sphere. Bogardus also patented a "Ball-Thrower for Shooting Practice" in 1877, which was then generally conceded to be the most challenging trap on the market. However, George Ligowsky of Cincinnati, Ohio, introduced the clay pigeon trap in 1880, and glass ball shooting quickly became a thing of the past.

Glass ball targets are eagerly sought by shooting memorabilia collectors here and abroad, and Bogardus-patented balls are some of the most desirable. I have been told by several American collectors that certain glass target balls in good condition and of the right color can be priced from $2,500 to $5,000 each. In Scotland, a quantity of Bogardus balls have recently been recovered from the bottom of a lake. Apparently in the late 1870s a trap was set to throw the targets over the lake; those that were not shot fell in the water and sank to the bottom, there to reside for more than a century until dredged up by someone who recognized their value. A Bogardus ball was sold in Sotheby's 1997 Gleneagles gun auction in Scotland for £294 (about $450)—a bargain by United States standards.

Captain Bogardus traveled to England in 1878 and won the title World Champion Wing Shot, which he held for five years. In 1883, he published his last shooting challenge to the public in *The American Field*; after five weeks there were no takers, so he retired at age fifty as "Champion Wing Shot of the World." Meanwhile, he had begun a new career as an exhibition shooter with wild west shows and circuses. Bogardus moved from Elkhart to nearby Lincoln, Illinois, in 1893, and his last shooting performance is believed to have been in 1911, with the "Young Buffalo Wild West Show" in Peoria, Illinois, at age seventy-seven. The captain died in Lincoln on 23 March 1913, six months short of his eightieth birthday, and is buried in the cemetery at Elkhart.

# Wild Geese
## by John Mortimer Murphy

Wild geese are more abundant in the west in autumn, and in the southwest in winter, than in any other portion of the continent. They move in vast flocks comparable to snow storms. Their presence is a mixed blessing to farmers, as they often destroy large crops of winter cereals, and are so destructive in other ways that a relentless war is waged against them. Every means of destruction from shooting to poisoning is employed to lessen their numbers. They have been known to eat a third of the winter wheat in some regions adjoining the Missouri River. In California, they scarcely leave a blade of grain growing in quite a large area. It is estimated that they devoured crops valued at $200,000 in one county of California in 1878, and their depredations in other sections were equally great. Shooting so little affects their numbers that many farmers have given up in despair, and depend on grain soaked in strychnine to accomplish their purpose. But this method has its drawbacks, for geese that do not succumb at once to the poison may fly away and be shot by men who do not know what they have been eating, and as a result, persons who eat their flesh are frequently poisoned.

A mean way of destroying geese is practiced in some portions of the northwest. This is to soak corn in whiskey and scatter it in fields that they frequent. When they eat this they become helplessly intoxicated, and the men go among them and knock them on the heads with clubs. Market men often load cart after cart by this method, and send the geese to the city, where they meet with a ready sale.

The methods of wildfowl shooting practiced in the west range from elaborate to simple. Some farmers claim that they merely walk beside a trained horse, mule, or ox, and shoot away at the birds until they have killed all they want—and then send the animal to retrieve them! If one western wag is to be believed, he had a mule that flushed geese when told to do so, then brought them ashore if they fell into a river or lake.

The easiest method for shooting geese on the open plains is to approach them gradually under cover of a horse or ox, then open fire with a huge weapon known as a "scatter cannon." I have known men to kill two hundred geese in a day with a muzzleloader by stalking them in a field under cover of a well-trained horse. These men did not go directly to the birds, but approached them obliquely and very slowly, to trick them into supposing that no harm was intended. When the men got within shooting range, they opened fire with huge weapons loaded with BB shot, and frequently bagged from ten to thirty geese in one round. After the volley, the survivors would rise in the air and scream their annoyance at being disturbed. But after hovering for a few moments, they usually settled down again and resumed feeding. The geese eventually became suspicious of the horses. Market hunters have earned a hundred dollars a day and more by the "stalking horse" system. The birds are valued from fifty cents to a dollar each, and from ten to forty are bagged at every discharge of the big gun.

Geese generally feed on the plains and stubble fields during the day, especially in wet or murky weather, but in the evening they return to their nests beside bodies of water. Many geese are slaughtered on their roosting grounds on moonlit nights, as they will often stand a good deal of shooting before fleeing to safer quarters. This is particularly true if food is scarce or if the weather is cold and inclement.

"Fire hunting" is a favorite hunting method with some persons who prefer large bags to sport. These men build fires on the roosting grounds with the driest wood they can find, to produce as much glare as possible. When the

*Two speckled beauties.*

geese see the fires, they rise in vast clouds and honk their alarm, but instead of fleeing they hover over the treacherous beacons until the noise of the prolonged shooting scares them away. I know a man in Dakota who filled his wagon with birds in two hours by this method, and of another in Minnesota who killed three thousand in ten days. But such work is slaughter, not sport, and I refer to it simply to show how numerous the geese are in some portions of the country. Killing the birds in this manner is heavy labor and often the cause of disease, as the men are liable to catch severe colds or be seized with an attack of rheumatism that may cling for life.

A punt gun is not considered legitimate among gentlemen, as it is the weapon of the market hunter. But many men who disdain punting do not hesitate to kill geese and ducks from sneak boats. This system of destruction is so deadly that some western states prohibit the killing of wildfowl from any floating device—be it a sailboat, steamcutter, or sneak boat. The sneak boat used in western streams and lakes is a narrow, canoe-shaped craft, from ten to fourteen feet long, and so light in draught that it would almost float on the morning dew. The wildfowler lies on his back and sculls with a short oar that runs through a hole in the stern. The boat seems to the geese to be nothing more dangerous than a floating log. But they soon learn their mistake, for the man opens fire once he is in their midst. With two heavy-loaded guns, he may bag from ten to thirty geese out of every gaggle. Geese are worth from six to twelve dollars per dozen at wholesale, so it's easy to see that the business of killing them is a paying one.

Shooting geese over live decoys from a sink box or a blind is considered legitimate sport, as it gives the geese a chance. The sink box is simply a rude wooden coffin or

# Wild Geese

float, about six feet in length, in which the wildfowler lies while awaiting the arrival of the birds. It is buried in the ground even with the surface, generally near some spot which the geese frequent or pass over in their morning and evening flights, and where they are sure to see and hear the tame decoys. Sink-box shooting, however, is disagreeable work, as the weather is often severe enough to almost freeze the wildfowlers, and they dare not lift hand or foot for fear of scaring the birds away. They are sometimes so benumbed that they cannot handle their weapons, and become so stiff from lying in a cramped position that they can hardly move to emerge from their coffin.

Where the geese are numerous, some men make a living by guiding and letting boats and decoys to sportsmen who wish to have a day's wildfowling. These guides are generally gun aficionados, and know more about the habits of geese than all the closet naturalists I ever met. They usually keep what is called a "rig"—that is, a number of partially domesticated wild geese trained to act as decoys. These rigs can be found along the Atlantic coast from Long Island to Florida, but they are most numerous in Shinnecock Bay, the great wildfowler resort near New York City.

The decoys are either wing-tipped birds that have been cured, or the offspring of captives bred in confinement. During the summer they have a good deal of freedom in selecting their own food, for as soon as one of their wings is clipped they are allowed to roam wherever they wish. But during the shooting season they are fed regularly twice a day, and become so accustomed to their home that they return to it every night to be fed, no matter how far out on the bay they may have gone.

A good rig usually consists of fifteen to forty birds of both sexes. They are placed in coops and taken to the shooting grounds in a boat. The grounds usually consist of bars or spits of land that run into the sea, on which are placed the coffin-like sink boxes. The boxes are often trimmed with sedge to give them as natural an appearance as possible. The decoys are staked out on the bar at irregular intervals, each fastened to a post by means of a leather strap or "hopple" that goes around the leg. The best caller or "honker"—generally an old and "educated" gander—is placed away from the flock so that he may express his feelings of loneliness. A good honker of either sex is considered invaluable, for on it depends the success of the day. Those who possess such a prize would not sell it for two hundred dollars. A first-class caller will bring down skeins that might circle dozens of other decoys without paying them the least attention. When the honker sees a string of geese overhead, it commences to *cree-aunk! cree-aunk!* in the most vociferous manner. Its companions soon join in the cry, and the air then resounds with their cronking melody. Those in the sky usually answer them, but if they are coy, the decoys recommence their calling with redoubled vigor and seem to say: "Oh! Come down here; you'll have lots of fun and plenty to eat. Do pay us a visit. We're dying to see you."

When the wildfowlers bring down the visitors with a load of shot, the lures actually appear to enjoy it. They shake themselves, preen their feathers, and cackle their sense of satisfaction: Nothing seems to give them greater pleasure than to see the leaden hail dealing death to their kindred. Such is the condition to which man will reduce the most innocent creatures when he employs them for his own selfish purposes!

Next to the decoys, the most necessary accessory for a day's sport is a good "swimmer" of geese. The swimmer

# Wild Geese

is a man who sails up to birds on the water and attempts by careful maneuvering to drive them within call of the honkers. He tries to make them swim toward the blinds, if possible, as the chance of making a big bag is greater if the geese swim toward the decoys rather than if they are put on the wing. An able swimmer has instinctive talent for his business, and can deftly handle his craft.

This preliminary explanation having been given, let us see what a day in a blind brings us. A party takes their positions in their sink boxes with feet toward the decoys. Each man loads his two or three guns and impatiently awaits the birds. If the day is both cold and windy, he may see them moving about in vast flocks, yet not hear a note from them, as the storm drowns out their cries. But if the weather is comparatively mild, the honker is soon answered by the leaders of the wanderers. With luck, the wild geese wheel about and come directly to the deceiver.

"Here they come; lie low," is the command of the veteran of the party. This is promptly obeyed, and everybody tries to force himself lower as his heart beats with excitement. The skein sees the caller on the beach and descends with rushing wings. Soon both groups of geese commence chattering sociably to one another, expressing their delight at meeting. An anxious gunner partially lifts himself up to get a peek and a shot at the new arrivals, but is soon laid low by his leader who hisses, "Keep quiet until they get away from the stools."

The geese leave the decoys in a short time, and then comes the command: "Give them both barrels as they rise. Don't shoot them on the ground." Five men rise in their coffins and cock their guns. As soon as the geese see them they attempt to scramble away, but the steel tubes are too quick. Before the geese can get fairly on wing, ten dead and four wing-tipped birds fall to the ground or into the water.

As soon as the cripples have been shot over and picked up by the swimmer, the gunners return to their coffins and continue operations until late in the evening. This is exceedingly cold and silent work, but when the wildfowlers return home from a good day's work with a large number of geese, they soon forget their sufferings.

Shooting geese on an inland lake is totally different from the sink box method and is generally more interesting. I have heard enough tales about shooting geese to fill a volume, but I will relate an adventure of my own that happened in Wisconsin.

I was staying at a farmhouse situated in one of the most charming sections of the best wildfowl resorts of the state. While sitting near the fire early one evening, the farmer's son—a lad about fourteen years of age—entered and told me that a pond a short distance away was thronged with wildfowl. I seized the farmer's muzzleloader and started for the pond in hot haste, hoping to get a shot at the birds. The boy's tale proved true. Several species of ducks, from the stately mallard to the pretty blue-winged teal, and a large gaggle of snow geese were feeding in the shallow water and chattering contentedly to one another. Their activity and noise contrasted strongly with the silence of the forest, which was then arrayed in its most brilliant autumn colors.

Notwithstanding the beauty of the woods, I had "murderous thoughts," but the birds were too far away to allow me a shot with any assurance of success. While dodging along the shore in my efforts to get nearer, I found a small dugout canoe in the bushes. I pushed it into the water and took the scull in hand. Soon I was bearing down on the mass of feathers. The snow geese seemed to think

# Wild Geese

the craft was a floating bunch of sedge, for at first they only stared at it. But when they detected its true character, they rose "exalting on triumphant wings." Before they could get out of range, I cut a swath through their ranks, killing two and crippling two more. By the time I had secured these, every bird in the pond seemed to have fled. Yet I paddled on in hope of getting another shot.

I rounded a small cape and came suddenly upon two geese sailing about in the most indifferent manner. They attempted to rise, but as I was to the windward they had to come my way. When they were near enough, I blazed away and sent one into the water with a loud thud. Turning to fire at the other, I upset the boat and dove headfirst into an apparently unfathomable mass of reeds and mud. As soon as I had examined the oozy bottom, I returned to the surface and found my gun was gone. I dove and recovered it, but then saw my craft floating away at a leisurely pace. I swam after it as rapidly as one arm could propel me. When I overtook it, I was nearly fagged out, for my clothing and gun seemed an awful drag, and I could hardly use my legs, as my boots were full of water.

I scrambled into the stern of the boat and set about picking up the birds that had been lost. I then paddled ashore where I doffed my dripping garments, squeezed them as dry as I could, and washed the mud off my hands and face. I also ran a series of races with imaginary contestants until my blood was warmed up. Getting back into my wet clothing was a chore, and it was a long, cold walk back to the house with my trophies. On arriving there, I changed my clothing and soon felt as comfortable as ever. We feasted on roasted snow geese for several days afterward, and each meal seemed just compensation for my underwater adventure in the farmer's pond.

# When Ducks Were Plenty

## Editor's Note

*American Game-Bird Shooting* by John Mortimer Murphy is one of the best written and most interesting of the old-time shooting books in my gunroom library. Part of the impetus for assembling and writing *When Ducks Were Plenty* was my belief that there's nothing particularly timely about wildfowl shooting. In fact, century-old stories of large bags and unregulated shooting are considerably more interesting than present-day tales of scarce birds, Orwellian regulations, short seasons, small bag limits, etc., ad infinitum.

For readers who wish to possess scarce, out-of-print books, the gunroom library is built one title at a time. These books are somewhat like baseball: "You can't tell the players without a program." Thus, even the casual collector should have an annotated bibliography of shooting and hunting titles. Ray Riling's *Guns and Shooting: A Selected Chronological Bibliography* (1982) is a good first acquisition. Riling lists 2,747 titles on guns and shooting, from the years 1420 through 1950.

The next step for the would-be rare book collector is to get on the mailing lists of dealers who have commercial quantities of used and out-of-print shooting and hunting titles. Dealers with the larger book lists typically advertise in shotgun-oriented magazines. In my opinion, buying and selling old reading material is, at best, a break-even proposition, unless one is an established dealer with a regularly published significant list. A parting caveat: Beware of rare book dealers who make more money selling book lists than selling books.

# Caught in a Snowstorm
# on Barnegat Bay

### by Isaac McLellan

A few years ago [about 1870], the latter part of February was remarkably mild and springlike. Snow and ice had vanished from city square, village street, and country road. The prevailing southerly winds had softened the temperature into the blue and balmy weather of Indian summer. My shooting friend and I knew that with this genial weather, the icy bands that had fettered brook, bay, and river would be loosened, and the wildfowl would flock back toward open water. Visions of black duck, redhead, widgeon, whistler, and broadbill came to mind. We looked upward expecting to see the long, wedgelike columns of geese and their compact cohorts, the brant, winging toward their favorite resorts.

# When Ducks Were Plenty

The old ducking gun that had rested in our sanctum throughout the tedious winter now drew notice. It was forthwith stripped of its slipcase and gripped with a loving hand. This old muzzleloader had been true to eye and finger for several years, and had provided many a successful day's sport. It lacked the symmetrical beauty and perfect poise of a modern breechloader, and could not be loaded and prepared for action with the magical celerity of that superb gun. However, when charged and well aimed at a passing flock, the muzzleloader brought results. While it is true that you could load your breechloader in the time it takes simply to cap a muzzleloader, when fowl are scarce, what need of haste? With a muzzleloader, you have ample time to quiet your nerves and calm your excitement. I admit, though, that when fowl pass in swift succession, a breechloader is the preferred weapon.

The last week in February came and with it a message from our old host, Billy Chadwick. He kept a famous *hospitium*, or gun house, at upper Barnegat Bay, New Jersey—a hospice dear to sportsmen. Billy announced that the bay was entirely free from ice and that the wildfowl were beginning to collect in multitudes. These tidings thrilled my friend and me like an electric shock. Hazard powder, Eley caps, and horsehair wads were hastily purchased, and our two guns cleaned and oiled for service. We soon boarded a paddle-wheel ferry, and after that a Raritan locomotive, arriving at Farmingdale Station, New Jersey. Then a two-horse wagon conveyed us to Chadwick's Inn, some six miles from Point Pleasant at the head of the bay.

There stood the sportsman's retreat as of yore, with its weather-beaten, honest old face and its stooping,

# Caught in a Snowstorm on Barnegat Bay

shady piazza. There too stood Billy, smiling at us with cordial hospitality. We paused to gaze at the open ocean's gray and melancholy waste, tumultuous with its billowing waves, and then turned to view the wide expanse of the placid bay, for Billy's house stands midway between bay and ocean. We were welcomed to Billy's big barroom with its white, sanded floor and its blazing fire of wreck-wood roaring up the chimney. How pleasant and homey it seemed, and so full of the memories of sporting scenes and sporting friends. How often had those old walls echoed with the songs and laughter of fowlers, who collected on the broad hearth after the hard toils and triumphs of the day. With roaring laughter they would applaud the stories of our old chum, Frank Forester, to whom we owe our introduction to this gunning sanctuary.

We had arrived on a Saturday evening, and we honored the Sabbath, which maintained its serenity and promised us good sport for Monday's dawn. Billy and I passed Sunday on the lookout on the housetop, sweeping the bay with a powerful telescope and counting the fowl on the water. When we retired that night, not a breath of wind ruffled the sleeping face of the waters; but on awakening in the middle of the night, we realized that a heavy northeast gale was raging, and a smothering snowstorm was pelting the house. Here was a frosty end to our hopes of shooting. Dismayed, we went back to bed, and the next morning we crept at a late hour to the breakfast table. The house was veiled in a twilight shadow, for the storm had suspended a drifting, sifting curtain of snow across each window that the struggling morning light could scarcely penetrate.

# When Ducks Were Plenty

We found Billy and his good wife barricading the doors and windows against the besieging drifts, while keeping a sharp lookout on the coffee, steak, and buckwheat cakes that were smoking on the stove. As we entered, Billy explained, "This is a dreadful storm, the hardest of the winter, and it will spoil our sport for days to come. The bay will freeze up hard and fast, no boat can reach the points, and the fowl will go off to the south for open water."

We sat down to our meal, but before we had finished we were astonished to hear muffled footsteps. The door opened, and in stalked two figures, white as marble statues with the accumulated snow, and half dead and almost speechless with cold. We recognized through their snowy masks the faces of two well-known gunners from across the bay, Johnny H. and Johnny G.

"Where in tarnation did you drop from?" inquired Billy. "From the clouds or from the frozen regions?"

*Wildfowl shooting from a dinghy.*

# Caught in a Snowstorm on Barnegat Bay

"Sure enough," they said. "We spent last night at the frozen northwest point, and we feel right lucky to get here with our lives. Please give us something warm to thaw out our blood."

Billy hurried to his bar and produced two full tumblers of warm whiskey and water that the two sufferers absorbed with a gulp. We then noticed that Johnny G. had lost one of his mittens, and his right hand was as white and stiff as a lump of ice. We convinced him to plunge his frozen hand into a pail of water, but Johnny's hungry eye caught sight of breakfast on the stove. He was eager for food and tried to withdraw his hand from its cold bath, but we held it in place several minutes until it had recovered its normal color. Then both Johnnys sat down at the table and, like famished wolves, devoured the cakes faster than Mrs. Chadwick could furnish them. The rest of us sat by enjoying the scene and laughing at how rapidly the cakes vanished.

Not a word came out of either Johnny's mouth while they ate. Then, when each had filled his pipe, they told their story: Tempted by the pleasant weather, they had left their homes at Kettle Creek late Sunday evening. They went by skiff and landed at the northwest point. After carrying it into a meadow, they crawled inside the skiff, wrapped themselves in their blankets, and extended a canvas tarp over the hatch to keep them warm. They slumbered as only tired fowlers can sleep, and awoke at dawn. But such a dawn: The accumulated snows of the night pressed with a fifty-pound weight upon their persons, and when this was dislodged, they gazed upon a horrific scene. Snow was heaped above their boat and piled in drifts over the meadow; it filled the air with dancing flakes, and it shut out all view of the water. They knew that they would perish if they did not reach the gunning house a mile distant before ice blocked the creek. Instantly they launched their boat, and while one of them desperately worked the oars, the other stood forward to point the way. The snowstorm was so intense and the snowflakes so thick that they could scarcely see the creek beyond the boat. But both were hardy and experienced boatmen, both knew the windings of the creek, and both knew they were fighting for dear life.

Newcomers to the area would have been lost in such a perilous situation, but they struggled through it all. They finally beached their boat at a familiar point about a quarter-mile from the house. There they abandoned it and struggled and waded waist-deep in the drifts, floundering toward the scarcely discernible house until they blundered upon it. The hard exercise doubtless saved their lives by preventing them from freezing, and Johnny G. had not even been aware that his hand was frozen until he had it in the water pail.

They were now safe and happy in comfortable quarters, where they could enjoy plenty of good things to eat and drink, a big roaring fire, and a cozy bed. They soon forgot their hardships and made themselves at home. We kept a blazing fire of drift and wreck-wood going, and for several days we had a beguiling time with frequent games of euchre. Meanwhile, snow buried the shapeless sandy dunes of the beach, ice fringed the ocean shores, the waters of the bay congealed as hard as cement, and white snows shrouded the meadows.

Our two gunners were weather-bound, as they could not return to their homes without walking sixteen miles round the head of the bay. They had to wait for mild weather to thaw the ice so they could launch their boat. We asked

# Caught in a Snowstorm on Barnegat Bay

if they were worried about their wives and children left so long in a state of suspense. "Oh no," said Johnny G., "they are all right and won't bother about us." At last the snow began to disappear and the ice to melt. Soon the open water reappeared, and all the wide bay glistened and smiled in the light of morning. Our guests bade us farewell and departed. Soon the ducks returned to their haunts, and the wild geese began to *honk! honk!* overhead.

## Editor's Note

Isaac McLellan was known as the "poet of the rod and gun." McLellan was born in 1806 and died 21 August 1899 at age ninety-three. He was one class behind Longfellow and Hawthorne at Bowdoin College. According to his obituary in the September 1899 issue of *The Amateur Sportsman*, "More than forty years ago Mr. McLellan moved to New York, and after retiring from a career in journalism he wrote poetry in the form of collections of verses, many of which have been published in books that commanded a large sale. His best-known

# When Ducks Were Plenty

work was *Poems of the Rod and Gun* (1886). The poet passed
the latter half of his long life in Greenport, New York, living
much of the time in an unpretentious board house near
the sound, his gun and rod his most congenial company."

# Dangerous Ducking
### by Ed Muderlak

The last three chapters demonstrate that following wildfowl on the water (or seemingly frozen water) is not without risk. John Mortimer Murphy upset his dugout canoe on a Wisconsin pond, but recovered nicely and in good humor after "examining the oozy bottom and un-fathomable mass of weeds and mud." Lucky for Murphy that the Wisconsin weather in October was relatively mild, the pond calm and shallow, and that he was not far from a hot stove and dry clothes.

Johnny G. and Johnny H. had their close call on a Barnegat Bay point when caught in an unexpected February blizzard. Lucky for the two Johnnys that they were experienced locals and were within eyesight and achievable distance of Billy Chadwick's sportsmen's retreat. Would one Johnny have made it by himself? We'll never know.

# When Ducks Were Plenty

Captain Bogardus's life was a game of chance, be it in the pigeon ring shooting against the best (Doc Carver, Abe Klineman, Fred Kimble, and Al Bandle) or retrieving geese on slush ice when his three companions knew better than to gamble their lives for a few dead birds. Bogardus was lucky that he didn't drop all the way through the ice and get swept under by the current. He was also lucky that one companion kept his cool and was able to help him get to shore. And the soon-to-be-frozen-stiff goose hunter was doubly lucky that he could travel the three miles home by horse sled, rather than by foot.

One of the luckiest wildfowlers, however, has to be Harold Latham, according to a sketch in the 21 December 1905 issue of *Shooting and Fishing:*

> At the season when bays are packed with ice and strong currents and heavy winds prevail, the engagement of duck shooting is attended with many hardships and perils. This fact is attested by the experience of Harold Latham, an enthusiastic duck hunter, who narrowly escaped losing his life in Gardiner's Bay recently while hunting ducks. Through his enthusiasm in pursuing a flock of ducks he ventured farther from shore than the force of wind and his frail gunning sharpie would justify. When he attempted to return, the tide had changed, which, combined with the wind, effectively prevented his progress. After rowing frantically yet futilely for several minutes, he sprang overboard into the icy waters and swam ashore. Just as he reached the land he was overcome from his efforts and exposure and fell unconscious. He was found later by his father who carried him home. After the administration of restoratives, he recovered completely from his *adventure* [editor's emphasis]. His abandoned boat containing the

# Dangerous Ducking

clothing that he had removed before springing overboard was later found by the steamer *Manhanset* far offshore.

Notice the common theme that links Latham's story to several of the previous "Dangerous Ducking" episodes: "After the administration of restoratives, he recovered completely from his *adventure*." And notice the key word, "adventure"; the difference between a life or death ordeal and invigorating wildfowling adventure is simply attitude. More than one duck hunter has been known to exhibit a bad attitude on windless, sunny, warm days, only because the ducks weren't flying. The duck hunter's contrary view that cold, blustery, overcast, wet days are perfect for wild-fowl and wildfowlers alike perhaps finds its ultimate expression in near-death experiences of total immersion in icy cold water. Surviving the ordeal becomes adventure, especially in retrospect, while sitting in a Morris chair before the hearth, smoking a pipe, and partaking of the liquid cure.

Part of the duck hunter's attitude is a magnanimous and possibly masochistic sense of humor. The following is from the 27 March 1875 issue of *The American Sportsman*:

> Billy Barker, a Sacramento sportsman, found almost constant pastime in duck hunting and smoking. These two diversions seemed to be compatible, and, with a pipe in his mouth and a gun on his shoulder, he wore out many pairs of boots tramping through the woods and marsh. Once upon seeing a duck near the tules preparing to fly away, he hastily took aim. But the tobacco smoke obscured his sight, so he stuck the pipe in his pocket where his powder flask was. Four things went off in order: the bird, the gun, the flask, and Mr. Barker's leg.

# *When Ducks Were Plenty*

On a lighter note, and in the spirit of turnabout being fair play and "man bites dog" journalism, I have gleaned some blurbs from old sports newspapers. There are risks attendant to duck shooting—humorous in retrospect—that extend well beyond the usual expectation of spending large amounts of time and money to get cold and wet while possibly coming up empty. I don't vouch for the veracity of these stories, but if they were published, surely they must be true. Ha!

The following story of a hunter's thrilling experience comes from the *New York Evening Telegram*, and though considered almost beyond belief by the editors of *The American Field* (the 26 November 1904 issue), they republished the story ". . . for what it is worth":

> Abbott W. Nelson, a well-known local druggist and sportsman, has just returned from duck hunting in the Spenser Lake region, and tells a story of adventure which, from anyone of less unimpeachable veracity, would be set down as a very large bit of fiction.
>
> Nelson says that on Saturday last he started out early from camp to look for ducks before the others of the party were up, carrying nothing but a double-barrel shotgun and a few shells loaded with bird shot. While returning to camp he came face to face with a big bull moose that bellowed, pawed the ground, and charged. Nelson fired both barrels, then dropped the gun and shinnied up the nearest tree. The shot hit the nose of the moose and drove the animal crazy with rage. He spied Nelson up the tree, which increased his fury. Rearing on his hind legs, he pawed furiously with his fore feet. Nelson, in trying to climb higher, lost his hold and fell. The belt of his hunting coat caught him on a limb for a moment, but then the limb and all dropped directly in front of the moose.

# Dangerous Ducking

Nelson was entangled in the limb and believed certainly that his time had come. The moose lowered his head and charged. Both Nelson and the limb became tangled in the moose's antlers, and despite the animal's desperate attempts, he could not shake off the burden. The moose then bolted through the forest at top speed, occasionally trying to shake off Nelson and the tree limb. Nelson kept his face low on the neck of the moose, or he would have been badly lacerated by trunks of trees the moose passed in his flight. Nelson lost consciousness for a time—he does not know how long—but came to his senses when the moose plunged into the icy waters of Little Spencer Lake and swam across a small inlet. Nelson had great difficulty in keeping his head above water, and the moose was doubly troubled in this respect.

After they emerged, another moose appeared, and Nelson's moose charged it. The belt broke, and Nelson landed in a clump of bushes. The animals paid no attention to him, and he was too exhausted to move. He thinks the big fellows battled fully an hour until one of them dropped completely exhausted, so much so that Nelson, whose strength had returned, was able to get close enough to finish him with his hunting knife! Nelson got back to camp with innumerable cuts and scratches and his clothing in shreds.

The story about the duck hunter and the moose was also told in the 3 November 1904 issue of *Shooting and Fishing*. The article, titled "Fixed on Antlers, Saw Moose Fight—Nimrod from Maine Towed across Lake by Enraged Woodland Monarch," expanded on the story as follows:

Killed after a desperate battle, in which Abbott Nelson, of Skowhegan, Maine, almost lost his life, two giant moose, kings of the forest, are on exhibition at 10th Avenue and 13th Street, New York. The story of their capture is one of the most remarkable that has ever come out of the mountain vastness of Maine.

Nelson is employed by a New York pharmacy, and on 22 October 1904, while hunting ducks near the forks of the Kennebec, he met with his adventure. He was carried three miles through the woods on the horns of an infuriated moose, nearly drowned in a lake which the animal swam, and then swung on the woodland monarch's horns while it did battle with another moose.

Side by side the two big carcasses hang in the showroom surrounded by a curious throng, and the broken antler on which Nelson was caught and that supported him in his perilous perch on top of the moose's head is still locked with that of the moose to which it gave battle.

Nelson started from camp on Saturday afternoon armed with only a shotgun. On his way back a big bull moose barred the way. Nelson fired both barrels of his shotgun into the moose and then ran for the nearest tree . . . [etc., etc.] Should anyone doubt Nelson's story, we advise them to view the broken antler and be convinced!

Finally, Alfred Hitchcock's movie *The Birds* could well trace its central theme to the 18 December 1920 issue of *The American Field*. Mr. Murray was a likely candidate to "eat crow" if his story had proved false, while, on the other hand, he would have had plenty of crow to eat if his story were true:

Attacked by thousands of crows while duck hunting on the Missouri River near here, M. L. Murray of Salix [Iowa] killed and wounded more than five hundred of the angry birds in three hours of constant fighting, using about two hundred shells. The coming darkness gave him an opportunity to escape from the great flock, which probably would have killed or seriously injured him otherwise. Murray had started out on a duck hunt and, finding ducks scarce, shot at the first crow he saw. The fight started when the wounded bird cried for help, and soon hundreds of others came to its aid. As Murray continued to meet the advance with gunfire, the cries of the wounded became louder and more crows came. Soon the ground was covered with dead and wounded crows. His ammunition was exhausted, and the remaining birds attacked Murray, striking him with their beaks and wings. When darkness came, the hunter was able to retreat to a willow patch, and the crows, unable to advance upon him, returned to roost. Murray suffered only a few scratches.

I don't vouch for any of the preceding tall tales, but they fit a pattern: Ordeals become adventures given the almost masochistic attitude of duck hunters. As to the requirements of the sport, in the words of Captain du Bray, "One good day compensates for many heartbreakers. 'Faintheart never won fair lady.' It takes a man of courage, with a constitution of iron and a masterly eye and hand to make a successful duck shooter, and no kid-gloved dandy need attempt it." Amen.

# Duck Shooting in Illinois

### by L. B. Crooker

Frank Forester took his readers to the field with him.
Anyone who reads his *Warwick Woodlands*, although lying
upon a sofa Sunday afternoon, can almost see the birds
spring from cover and the hunter raise his gun.  The
reader "feels" the inspired sympathy between eye and
finger and weapon; he sees in his mind's eye the stricken
bird fall fluttering to the ground.  By merely reading
the account, he becomes part of the hunt.

I have often thought that I would try my hand at giving an account of a genuine Illinois duck hunt.  So then,
be it known that providence, when laying out this
mundane sphere, located a disgustingly wet and
muddy spot known as Winnebago Swamp about twenty

miles west of Mendota, Illinois.  This large tract has few charms, and consists mostly of sandhills and marshes. The region, however, entices mallards, pintails, Canada geese, and other wildfowl, and consequently I have meandered through this section for years, victimizing whatever game came my way.

About three weeks ago, just as everybody thought spring was putting on its agreeable mantle, I began to feel the shooting fever.  I got out "Old 10-Bore" and my shooting outfit, and decided to seek the cure.  I was alone in my glory when I boarded the train; a couple of hours brought me to Deer Grove, where lives Sam Hendricks, the quickest and best swamp shot in his neck of the woods.  When I arrived, I saw the swamp was full of ducks, but too full of water to be approachable.  The prospects for good shooting were slim.  However, it was too late to back out, so I struck out for Sam's and was heartily greeted by him when I arrived.

"What are the chances for meat?" said I.

"Too much water," replied Sam, "but I guess we can get a few.  We'll go out for an evening shoot anyway."

After attending to preliminaries, we drove our team along the edge of the swamp at the foot of the sandhills. The marsh was an almost uninterrupted sheet of water with the ground bare to its margin, affording no shelter and consequently no shooting, and a luckless hunt seemed likely.

"Never mind," said Sam, "we may get some field shooting," so we turned our horses toward the cornfield near Paddy's Island. At the top of a sandhill ridge, in the teeth of a sharp wind, there lay before us four extensive cornfields; and more to the purpose, two or three large flocks of wildfowl were circling around, looking for their evening meal of corn. We drove quietly down into the first field and then directed our teamster to go to a house and wait. I found a spot in the field while Sam walked in a lively manner for another.

As I reached the spot I had selected, I saw that I had to hide my rotund proportions, so I cut stalks with my jackknife and put up a blind. Having the disadvantage of being almost as tall lying down as when standing up, I flattened myself as best I could while a nice flock approached downwind: mallards, pintails, and brant mingled together in speedy confusion.

The flight of ducks swerved off, and then, as if they had reconsidered, turned and came directly toward me. At about sixty yards and with as many misgivings, five drachms of "villainous salt petre" exploded, and an ounce and a quarter of No. 6 shot hurtled toward the brant. One was hit, but quicker than a flash I saw that he might get away, so I pulled the other barrel at the same bird. Down he came with his pretty mottled breast upturned and his webbed feet beating a dying tattoo in the air.

I quickly gathered the brant, and then along came a pair of pintails— *crack! crack!* Both were dead in the air at once. Next a pair of mallards

*The evening return.*

dropped to my splendid Daly muzzleloader. I was ready to go to their funeral when I discovered an old mallard drake coming along, turning his head from right to left, looking out for trouble. *Crack!* The old greenhead folded his wings and dropped so fast that even if I had missed, the fall would have killed him. The ducks were thick and seriously interested in landing in my cornfield. I kept shooting while every now and then Sam's gun was heard in the adjoining field. I got pairs, singles, and so on, until the sun hid itself behind the sandhills and the shades of night put an end to our sport.

When I took an account of my downed birds, I found twenty-one ducks, all mallards and pintails, and one brant. Slinging them over my tired shoulders, I slowly walked toward the wagon, where I found Sam with twenty-one ducks and two prairie chickens. A short drive took us to Sam's hospitable fireside where the Missis had prepared a smoking hot meal, and afterward we lit our pipes and relived the day's events before retiring to "woo tired nature's sweet restorer."

The next day we went at it again, and I killed fifteen ducks and two geese, one of which weighed over thirteen pounds. Now I spend more time killing wildfowl on paper than in the field. But I wanted to give my account of a genuine Illinois duck hunt in the Winnebago Swamp near Mendota, in the spring of 1873.

### Editor's Note

Crooker described the Winnebago Swamp in the 16 May 1874 issue of *The American Sportsman*: "All along the borders of this swamp may be found sloughs letting into it, with any number of outside ponds, at all times affording good shooting. This is a desirable point for any shooting to be expected in Illinois, and well worth a visit from eastern sportsmen, *but its glory will soon depart, as every exertion that money and ingenuity can apply is being put forth to reclaim the land* [emphasis mine]."

Part of the "disgustingly wet and muddy spot known as the Winnebago Swamp," as described by L. B. Crooker, was purchased by the State of Illinois in the late 1930s, to be preserved as a game refuge and for public hunting. The 2,600-acre Green River State Wildlife Area consists mostly of sandhills and prairie, with about one-third wetlands and prairie potholes running through the center. There is currently no duck shooting allowed, but some old goose pits can still be seen scattered throughout the preserve. Most hunting in the Green River area is for ringneck pheasants, a game bird that did not exist in the United States when L. B. Crooker penned his article for the May 1873 issue of *The American Sportsman*.

# *"Piles" of Florida Ducks*
## *by John Mortimer Murphy*

The most pleasant duck-hunting day that I can recall was spent on the Indian River in Florida, where a party of us passed a portion of the winter. We left our ramshackle cabin before dawn on a delightful December morning. As we poled down the river, it gleamed like molten silver under the bright southern moon. After rowing about two miles, our cracker guide, who had brought two Chesapeake Bay dogs, planted several wooden decoys in front of our blind, then rowed up and down a contiguous creek to see if any ducks were near. On his return he reported that no birds were within a mile of us, so we crept into the blind and waited patiently for the approach of dawn and ducks.

When the faintest daylight appeared, two of us rowed the boat up a creek to conceal it in the shrubbery and prevent its being seen by the keen-eyed canards. While pulling heedlessly up the creek, we were startled by a tremendous churning and splashing, and were surprised to find ourselves in the midst of a huge bed of ducks that must have numbered several thousand. This unexpected meeting stupefied us for a moment, as we had not anticipated such good fortune. But even if we had known the ducks were there, I doubt if we could have seen them. The moon had sunk behind the forest, and the stream was tranquil as a millpond, giving back none of its reflections.

We recovered our wits, seized our guns, and fired all four barrels into the mass of feathers that whirled above us. A moment later we could hear the splashes of several ducks as they struck the water, and the frightened squawks of the crippled as they fluttered helplessly down the river. We set about picking up our birds and were aided considerably by one of the retrievers that had remained in the boat, seemingly asleep. He went to work without even being asked. Later we found that both dogs would rush into the water without any orders when they saw a duck fall, but if the shot was unsuccessful, they remained as still as if they were made of cast iron, and hardly blinked their feelings of disappointment.

Through the dog's exertions and our own, we managed to secure seven dead ducks and two cripples, but these were not all that we had brought down, judging by the splashes in the river and the opportunity we had for making a large bag. We concealed the boat, returned to the blind with our trophies, and received the congratulations of our friends for bringing them such early indications of good luck. The guide said we would have "piles of shooting" when the wind freshened at sunrise, and the ducks would come "booming" toward us. His prophesying was soon cut short by a loud whistling sound that emanated from a large dark cloud passing overhead at a high altitude. "Ducks by the million," explained the guide. "You'll have piles of shooting at daybreak."

That was the very thing for which we were so impatiently waiting, so when the dull gray light began to steal across the eastern horizon, our spirits soared. We discoursed enthusiastically about the balmy air and the luxuriance and color of the tropical scenery that surrounded us. As the

gray brightened into a steel-blue, and the blue into the roseate tints of dawn, the wind freshened and blew a fair gale from the ocean. "I'll tell you," said the cracker, "you'll have piles of shooting soon."

His prophecy proved correct, for the weak squawks of a team of approaching baldpates were heard, and then the ducks came sailing

*The first at the bridge.*

down toward the decoys. Just as they were momentarily hovering, preparing to settle, the contents of ten barrels were poured into their midst, and twenty-seven of them tumbled headlong into the stream and squawked or floundered about in the agonies of death. The remainder, seeing this catastrophe, turned, and with many a scream, winged back to the silent forest that stretched for miles beyond us.

Then the guide, who seemed to be staring at the clouds, sung out: "Mark ducks, here they come in piles." The first flock was composed of black ducks, and we expected to make a haul. However, just as we thought they would sink to our decoys, they wheeled about and fled, as if they had been suddenly imbued with the idea that the wooden images were gross frauds and dangerous acquaintances. The flocks behind them did not display such a suspicious nature, however, for they swept down to our decoys in the most familiar manner. Before many of them could settle, ten barrels again blazed forth almost simultaneously, and the shower of lead brought down thirty or forty mallards and canvasbacks. Several were only wounded, and, as they tried to flutter away, we had an opportunity to try our accuracy at shooting single birds. Before the last cripple was killed, another mass of ducks of several species swept toward us, producing a whistling roar like an approaching whirlwind. As they came fluttering and splashing about our decoys, we poured a heavy volley into the densest part, and a score or two of them gave their lives for their credulous natures.

When the remainder had fled, we launched our boat and commenced picking up the slain. The Chesapeake Bay dogs devoted all their attention to securing the wounded in the most admirable manner, for they often passed birds splashing wildly in their death struggles and instead chased those that were making efforts to escape. The ducks would dive when they saw the dogs approaching, but the dogs were wise to this stratagem, for they rose in the water and turned slowly in a circle to scan the surface. When a bird came up, they hastened to capture it or force

# "Piles" of Florida Ducks

it underwater. The chase continued in this manner until nearly all the cripples were secured, for the retrievers followed a duck until it died on the bottom through suffocation or was shot by a member of the party.

Some ducks have strong vital power, as evidenced by the failure of our party of five men to kill a duck that we all fired at simultaneously. We shot a bird down, but it had scarcely touched the water ere it began to swim away. This raised such a howl of indignation that Jem Smith jumped into a skiff and swore he would have that bird, as he did not want it reported that five wildfowlers could not kill a consumptive duck. He paddled after the fugitive, and on approaching it lifted his paddle to give it a whack, but the duck was under before the weapon touched the water. This prompted roars of laughter and a volume of suggestions. One of us told him to jump out of the boat and kick the durned duck to death; another wanted him to dive in after it; the third suggested that he throw salt on its tail; a fourth wanted him to pepper its nose and let it sneeze its head off. But before any of these suggestions could be carried out, the skiff and fowler disappeared suddenly, and we all speculated as to the cause. The consensus was that the duck had turned on Jem and dragged the skiff under. We searched for him along the shore and then went to a farmhouse a few rods from the lake. There we found our cold and wet companion, in his old slouch hat and a woman's calico dress, sitting near the fire.

"Where's the duck, Jem?" asked one of our party.

"Durn the duck," said Jem.

"Lost?"

"I expect she is. I ain't seen her since she went down the last time and took me with her."

# When Ducks Were Plenty

After a few hilarious comments at our friend's expense, he jumped up and threatened to shoot the next speaker, presumably with a squirt from his waterlogged gun. We all pretended to be afraid, and, discretion being the better part of duck hunting, we retreated to our blind. But the ducks had ceased "trading," and they settled in beds beyond our gun range or sought safety in the surrounding marshes. We managed to secure a few canvasbacks and redheads by tolling them toward the shore with a gaily-colored handkerchief tied to a stick and waved slowly over the blind, but the greater number were too cautious to approach within gunshot.

Our guide suggested we row back to his cabin for a hot lunch, so we loaded our morning's spoils—all 207 of them—in the skiff, collected Jem and his pile of wet clothing, and set out rowing for our headquarters in the warm midday Florida sun. An ordinary shot can kill from fifty to a hundred ducks in a day of flight shooting hereabouts, and if two heavy duck guns are used, a good shot can almost double the number.

# Sweeney's Snipe
## by Paul Pastnor

There's a two-fold sweetness in double pipes;
And a double barrel and double snipes
Give the sportsman a duplicate pleasure.
—Hood

We always spoke of his birds as "Sweeney's snipe," because Sweeney owned the marsh and the little hotel above it. Sweeney was a broad-shouldered, jovial-faced, Boston-born Irishman. He relished Cork culture, but his inherited brogue was softened by a certain Emersonian flavor. He trimmed his beard with the circumflex sweep of a down-east farmer, and wore corduroys and ate beans. On the whole, Sweeney made an admirable link between Tam O'Shanter and the Pilgrim fathers.

# When Ducks Were Plenty

Nearly every week during the fall and once or twice in the spring, a party of us would go down to look after Sweeney's snipe. It was an act of pure benevolence on our part, for the old man never paid any attention to the birds himself. He never set foot in the bog, or went out to see if there was a flight on, or tried to determine the occult effect of the October moon upon the movements of this mysterious bird. But Sweeney loved and respected his snipe, which brought him good revenue during the shooting season. He posted his marsh every few rods and kept everybody off who did not feel inclined to taste the hospitality of his hotel.

To the chosen few, however, who periodically visited him for the purpose of invading his marsh, Sweeney was cordiality himself. He had the biggest heart for dogs that ever beat under an innkeeper's waistcoat, and ill-deserving indeed must have been the cur who did not get as soft a bed and as well-lined a stomach during his stay at Sweeney's as his master himself. Cheering beverages were mine host's delight, and he provided free pipes and a villainous tobacco that no guest ventured to touch—more than once.

Such was the little hostelry at the head of the Marshfield meadows twenty-five years ago. I remember it in the good old days of the velveteens and muzzleloaders. Warmhearted, generous, jovial, courteous sportsmen of the "old school" visited by the score, every one of them magnificent specimens of manhood, and also superb shots. Sweeney at one time had entertained the great Herbert [Frank Forester] unawares, and never ceased to regret that the flight was so poor that week that his illustrious guest never came back.

Ten years ago, in October 1880, I made my last trip to Sweeney's. The rain was falling in torrents as I alighted from the cars and found his old "barge" awaiting me. The stable-boy, Billy, was clutching the ribbons, and there was no other passenger save myself. The rain thundered on the awning over my head as we drove into the darkness. But I rejoiced as I heard the wind soughing through the trees, for I knew it was just the sort of storm to bring snipe. On and on we bumped, over the ridge and down across the meadows, Billy standing up every few moments to peer into the inky gloom. We met no one, and presently the faint glimmer of lights through the storm told us that we were approaching the hotel. In a few minutes I clasped the hand of the jolly Irishman, and was ushered into the warm parlor. Here I found a gentleman, dressed in shooting costume, whom I did not know. Sweeney introduced him as Mr. Parkhurst of Hartford, Connecticut, and so began one of my warmest friendships.

I had supper and then enjoyed a cigar with Mr. Parkhurst, while we talked over the situation. He had been at Sweeney's two days already and had bagged but twelve birds in all. But he agreed with me that the storm then raging would probably bring birds in abundance. We arranged to go out together the next day, and were considerably amused to see that our dogs had already become fast friends. They lay before the stove with their heads on each other's haunches.

Morning dawned, still cloudy but cool, and with no rain falling. We sat down to breakfast at half past six o'clock, and my newly made acquaintance obligated me to him by serving some of his plump and delicious birds with our eggs and coffee. These birds had evidently been nesting for some time in Sweeney's marsh, for they were as fat as squabs. My friend said that they had lain so close that he had been obliged to kick some of them before his dogs pointed, which is rare with snipe unless they are overfed.

We started out soon after seven o'clock, each carrying one hundred shells loaded with three drams of powder and one ounce of No. 10 shot. We both wore hip boots, of course, as much of our work had to be done in water and mud halfway to the knee.

Sweeney's marsh covers about one hundred acres of bogland and reeds, lying on both sides of a sluggish creek. Near the head and center of the marsh, rude bridges have been built across the creek for the convenience of shooters. Mr. Parkhurst and I decided to work opposite sides of the creek, keeping abreast of each other and driving the birds back and forth. Accordingly, I crossed to the other bank, while my companion remained on the side nearest the hotel.

We had proceeded but a few yards when a large wisp of snipe rose wildly on Mr. Parkhurst's side and swung past me at a distance of about fifty yards. I brought

*The wounded snipe.*

# Sweeney's Snipe

down three with my two barrels, and the rest scattered and pitched at a considerable distance. I marked them down and shouted to Mr. Parkhurst that he had better cross the bridge and join me in working up the singles. He did so, and we walked, as nearly as we could tell, to the spot where most of the snipe had pitched down.

My companion's dog was the first to draw on a bird, which he did prettily, winding it a dozen yards away and working up the scent with his head in the air. Mr. Parkhurst stepped forward, and the bird rose with a harsh *scaipe!* flying low and twisting rapidly. My companion coolly held his fire until the snipe was about forty yards away and had ceased its zigzag darting; then he dropped it stone-dead in the reeds.

Parkhurst's dog was a non-retriever, so I sent my pointer to fetch the bird. However, he caught scent before reaching the patch of reeds, drew off to the right, and in a moment was rigid on the edge of a small pool of water. I asked Mr. Parkhurst to come up, in case there should be more than one bird. He did so, picking up his snipe on the way. We stepped up to the pointer, one on each side, and immediately a small wisp of four birds took wing from the reeds on the opposite side of the pool and flew helter-skelter in all directions. I missed one that skimmed off to the right, but bagged a straightway with my second barrel. Mr. Parkhurst fired two shots in rapid succession, and I turned to find that he had doubled on the two birds that flew to the left.

Without the assistance of my pointer, we would have been unable to find any of the birds we dropped, as we failed to mark them accurately. I asked my companion if he might have killed some birds on the previous days that he failed to find, and he admitted that it was no doubt so. He added that his dog had once been a capital retriever, but on one unfortunate occasion he trounced him for a hard mouth. As it turned out, the shot and not the dog had torn the birds, and the dog has refused to seek dead ever since. "I cannot blame him," said Mr. Parkhurst. "It serves me right. I shall continue to use Rex as a non-retriever until he dies, as a sort of penance."

We succeeded in finding three more single birds out of the wisp, all of which we bagged over points, and then began to work back toward the creek. Here we struck a treacherous piece of bog. The mud between the hummocks was well-nigh fathomless, and the hummocks themselves as unsteady as bits of froth on the top of a pudding. But we found fresh borings around the bases of the hummocks, and were soon rewarded for our balancing and plunging by seeing Rex draw a splendid point, backed by my dog, Helix, in beautiful form.

Jumping from tuft to tuft of the thick-rooted marsh grass, we approached within shooting distance and ordered the dogs on. Rex crawled head and shoulders over the hummocks where he had been pointing, and with a startling chorus of alarm, a larger wisp of birds than before rose from the mud. This time I was fortunate enough to secure a bird with each barrel. But my companion got ahead of me again by knocking one with his first barrel, and then, with his inimitable coolness, waiting until two birds crossed in their hurried flight and dropping them both with the same shell. I have seen many brilliant snipe shooters, but none who combine such rapid and sure execution with absolute coolness as Mr. Parkhurst. The snipe is a hard bird to assess after it has flushed, so it is a fine exhibition of nerve to see a man who can quickly calculate its flight path and bring it down.

# Sweeney's Snipe

This second wisp of birds towered high in the air, swung once or twice around us, looking like mere specks against the clouds, and then vanished in the distance. Mr. Parkhurst was fatigued, so I proposed that he sit down on a hummock and rest, while I returned to the bridge and came up opposite him. That way we could pursue our original plan of working along the creek on both sides. He willingly assented, and I began to work my way out of the bog. I was jumping carelessly from hummock to hummock when I was startled by a brace of birds flushing from almost underneath my feet. I tried to balance myself upon the hummock where I had just alighted, but in my excitement lost my balance and stepped off backward into the mud. Without trying to flounder out again, I fixed my eyes on the birds that were skimming away about six feet apart and dropped them both with a quick right and left. "Good!" cried my companion, "unless you are a fixture there for the rest of the day."

I began to fear that I was a fixture, for I had already sunk in the mud halfway to my knees, and, try as I would, I could not stir either of my ponderous boots. Finally I realized that I had better extricate myself from them first, so I grasped the hummock, drew my body over it, and worked until I had drawn both feet out of my boots. Then I turned and pulled the boots out of the mud. By this time Helix had brought me my birds, and, getting into my boots again, I soon made my way out of the bog to safety.

I crossed the bridge and walked down the opposite bank of the creek until I came abreast of Mr. Parkhurst. We then proceeded to work opposite banks. The best sport of the day now began. As soon as we came into the lower part of the marsh, where the reeds grew about hip-high, we found snipe in abundance: scattered singles, and birds lying in twos and threes. Evidently a large flight had arrived during the night. The birds were wild, but I had never seen them there in greater numbers, even in the "good old times." For an hour or more it was *bang! bang!* right and left for both of us; we paid little attention to each other. The walking was fairly good. The birds had to rise above the reeds to fly, so we had none of those deceptive low-skimmers that seemed to melt into the ground as they fled. Mr. Parkhurst was decidedly handicapped by having to retrieve his own birds, but when we came down to the second bridge and stopped to rest and compare notes, he had forty-six to my forty-one. It was rich sport, and we soon found that one hundred shells had melted down to a handful each.

As it was now past one o'clock and our shells were nearly gone, we worked our way back toward Sweeney's, picking up stragglers as we went. We planned to return to the lower part of the marsh after dinner. But before we reached the hotel, the already lowering sky thickened, and once at Sweeney's, a dismal rain set in that lasted the rest of the day and kept us chafing indoors. We were afraid that the storm might continue through the night, in which case many of the flight birds would probably have continued their journey southward. But about seven o'clock the storm sobbed itself out, and our hearts were at peace.

Next morning the sun rose on one of those glorious, cloudless October days that come after prolonged rain — days when the sky is so blue that it almost sparkles, the air is as clear as polished glass, and the whole world smiles like a child that just had its faced washed and has gone back to play again. We were early on the marsh and found the birds lying much better than they had the previous day; there were no wild flushes out of gunshot. When we struck a wisp of birds, they often arose in successive pairs and singles, giving us an opportunity for doubles that we highly appreciated. Other shooters appeared later that day, but we had the ground to ourselves most of the morning and made a large bag. In the afternoon the birds, having been frequently flushed and shot at, were wilder, and we did not have as good success. Parkhurst's bag for the day was eighty, and mine was seventy-two. We both left for Boston on the evening train, well satisfied with our two days of sport.

I do not know whether Sweeney is still in the land of the living, but his marsh must be there yet. One of these days I hope to visit again and refresh my memories of the place, even if I cannot duplicate old bags.

# *Wild Swans*

## *by John Mortimer Murphy*

Swans are more numerous west of the Rocky Mountains than in any other part of the world. So many swans alight at the mouth of the Columbia River in Oregon that the water seems to be reflecting cumulus clouds. Their trumpeting and whistling sounds are familiar to those who have camped on the wooded borders of well-watered prairies in October. They come in flocks from their arctic homes, seeking every available stream and tarn in search of food and shelter.

Market hunters of the Pacific coast usually shoot swans for their plumage alone. Swan down is used for trimming the garments of fashionable ladies, and is exported inconsiderable quantities by the Hudson Bay Company to France and Russia. Few sportsmen kill adult swans for

# *Wild Swans*

their flesh, as it is dry and tough. Cygnet meat is palatable, although inferior to the meat of young ducks and geese. A swan in full plumage sells as high as a dollar and a half when there is a good demand for the down, or when the bird is plump and tender. Swans are so common along the Columbia River, however, that I doubt if one there would bring more than fifty or seventy-five cents.

The best bag I ever made was on a sandbar in the Upper Columbia. This was occupied largely by swans, although geese and ducks literally covered the surrounding waters. I went to this place with a rancher who was a keen sportsman, a man whose idea of paradise was a lodge in the wilderness where he could hunt and fish whenever the desire seized him. We took up our position on the island at the romantic hour of half past four on a cold November morning. We waited anxiously for daylight and could hear the occasional *creeaunk!* of some sturdy gander, or the trumpet blast of a swan: sounds

that caused our blood to tingle and our hands to grasp the guns.

While anxiously awaiting the birds, we heard the shrill whistle of a steamer echo loudly in the woods and mountains,

*"White Swan Shot May 30, 1911, by Simon Gandy in Washington State, on an Indian Reservation." Photographic postcard from the author's collection, unusual in that it describes the event and names the person.*

and saw the white form of the craft down the river. We were anything but pleased at its appearance, but its scream caused the swans to rise en masse with a rush that augured well for sport. They came toward our sandbar as if they had no foe on earth. The swans were arranged in a queue. I aimed at the head of the first when it was about twenty yards away and brought it down with a heavy charge of No. 1 shot. Before the others could turn about, I bagged a second and scared the remainder so badly that they began to blow their trumpets as they hastened away. I picked up the dead birds with the aid of a boat, and gave my companion a look of mingled triumph and contempt that would have withered another man. He merely said, "I wouldn't have fired at the swans with a shotgun at that distance. If you had hit them in the eye with a rifle, you could have called it passable shooting."

"How could I see their eyes at that distance?"

"I could. I saw one wink back at the other when you lifted your gun, as much to say, 'Here's a joke. He's going to fire at us.'"

"They didn't find it a joke, though," I said. "Why didn't you fire at them?"

"Well, the fact is, my gun wasn't loaded. I'm going to make up for it the next time, so you needn't make a fuss. But we must stop our nonsense, for the first principle of wildfowling is 'no talking in the blind.'"

We waited at least twenty minutes before a large number of ducks came near again, and then we made up for lost time as we brought down three. We had no dog with us, so we had to do our own retrieving. This was such cold work that afterward we found it difficult to handle our weapons.

We seated ourselves on a fallen log to discuss the effect of the steamer on our day's sport. But before we could come to any decision on the matter, the steamer rounded a turn in the river and gave vent to such a piercing scream that she again flushed thousands of birds and sent them rushing toward us. Swans were mingled with the geese and ducks. We held our fire for the cygnets in the rear and bagged two of them. We gathered our trophies with the boat and then paddled round the lower part of

*Trumpeter swan.*

the island into an inlet. We had proceeded about half a mile up this ribbon of water when we saw an immense flock of ducks, swans, snow geese, and Canada geese bedded in the middle of the inlet, while cranes and herons lined the shore, and the woods resounded with their booming whoops. The cranes and herons announced our presence as we paddled rapidly toward the swans that we knew would be the last to take flight. Our approach soon decided their course, and they raised themselves partially out of the water and came flapping and splashing toward us, as they could not take wing without coming upwind in our direction. Before they could obtain momentum enough to rise, we blazed away, killing three and wounding two so severely that they could not escape.

We went ashore and anchored our boat with a large stone tied to the painter. We then prepared a cygnet for dinner. The cooking took an hour, as we had to bury it in the ashes. Having satisfied our cravings, we went to the boat but were thunderstruck to find it was gone.  We supposed at first that some prowlers had stolen it, but on glancing down the creek we saw it drifting slowly at least half a mile away.  We were at our wits' end as to what to do.  The only feasible plan was to swim after the craft, but that was more easily said than done, as the water was too cold to be borne for any length of time.

While we were helplessly debating our situation and considering the possibility of remaining until some passing steamer took us off, we saw a small canoe containing a solitary Indian floating down the creek.  When he came abreast of us we hailed him in such stentorian tones that their echoes may be hanging around there yet.  He came near shore, and we told him that we would pay well if he would recover our runaway boat.  He said he would do it for half a dollar.  The offer was accepted, and when he brought the craft back he was cheerfully paid.

The "son of the forest" warmed his hands at our fire, and we learned that he had been shooting on the upper arm of the inlet.  Ducks were so abundant there, he said, that he was able to kill nineteen brace in less than three hours with an old Hudson Bay musket.  When I saw the gun, I came to the conclusion that it could out-kick an Army mule, and subsequent events proved that I was not far from wrong.  The noble Indian had nothing to do for the remainder of the day, so we hired him as an assistant.  We then paddled upstream until we saw a flock of wildfowl riding the wavelets under the shelter of a huge crag, chattering pleasantly to one another.  The chances of bagging them from land were better than from the water, so my companion decided to bear down from leeward in the canoe, while the Indian and I concealed ourselves in the bushes onshore to shoot them as they flew past.

# Wild Swans

I was anxious to secure all the swans we could, and I asked the Indian to load his musket heavily with buckshot. He agreed as long as I would supply the ammunition, and I readily assented to his proposition. We took our position in a thicket close to the water and were not there long before the swans were sprung. The wind was blowing heavily, and they flew low and partially sideways. When they came within range of our guns, we blazed away. The Indian opened fire first, but the thundering report of his gun had hardly echoed from the hills before his scream accompanied it. The birds he shot were all pieces of legs and feathers and flesh flying about in the air. One glance proved that he had been extraordinarily liberal in the use of my powder and shot, and he paid for it dearly. But I ignored his plight, as I was too much absorbed in my own work.

When the swans came within fifteen yards, I banged away at their heads, killing one and wounding another so severely that it fell into the water not forty feet from the shore. I was under the impression that it was only winged, so I made a rush for it. But I stumbled down the bank and tumbled headlong into the ice-cold water. I arose in a hurry, puffing and blowing. My garments were wet, and I became desperate. Dashing farther out, I seized the bird by the neck and dragged it ashore, though not without receiving several blows from its uninjured wing. Shivering and wet as I was, I could not help laughing at the Indian who was making wry faces and rubbing his shoulder vigorously. To my query of what ailed him, he took the offending weapon in his hands and dashed it to the ground saying, "Him kick heap damn!"

When my pale-faced companion arrived on the scene, he decided we should hasten homeward, for fear

I might catch cold from my drenching. The proposition was agreeable, and we placed our trophies in the boat. The Indian joined us, as his arm was too sore to paddle his own canoe. We tied his craft behind ours and hoisted sail. In half an hour we reached my friend's ranch, but when I attempted to walk to the house, I found my clothes had frozen stiff. Once inside, I threw off my garments, bathed my body in cold water, and, after vigorous application of a rough towel, wrapped myself in a heavy blanket and retired to bed. There I took a generous quantity of soothing liquid, after which I closed my eyes and slept soundly until daylight.

When I awoke I felt as comfortable, both mentally and physically, as if there had been no mishap. The Indian had departed before I arose, so I could not tell how much he was injured, but my host told me that his arm was swollen and discolored. I recalled that the musket had kicked so hard that it drove him into the soft ground and knocked the moccasins off his feet. We had cygnets for dinner that day, and though the flesh was dry, it was palatable. But it took four days of seasoning to make the adults fit for the table, and even then they were not very dainty.

# Memories Are a Siren's Song
## by Frank H. Mulligan

Outside the wind howls and a storm rages—a bad night to be out. Inside the hearth fire burns brightly and radiates a cheery comfort. My old setter lies before the fireplace, head between his paws, content. His life shadow has grown long, and he has been pensioned off; younger dogs have come to take his place. I am reclining in a Morris chair with a freshly filled pipe, and drowsily dream of the days that have gone forever.

My thoughts go back to boyhood days and my boyhood dog, the pride of my life: an Irish water spaniel by King Slash. This dog was so thoroughly broken as a retriever that she would take in and put out decoys anywhere I wanted her to. With this dog came a gun, a veteran of the Civil War, bored to about 10-gauge. The name for this particular muzzleloader was "army

# When Ducks Were Plenty

musket," but we boys called it "Pazzas." I bought it from a camper with powder horn, shot flask, and cap box, all for $3.50. I had saved $2.50 by selling sacks from my father's barn, and when this particular bargain loomed up, I annoyed my mother until she gave me the other dollar. She said it would be the death of me surely, as soon as I got it in my possession.

What a strong heart a boy has. Think of getting up at 3:00 A.M., and, without any breakfast, hiking ten miles down the river, packing a musket as heavy as a crowbar; then returning home after 4:00 P.M., famished, with possibly one duck or rabbit to show for the day's efforts. My game bag was invariably light, but not for lack of game at which to shoot. Rather, the gun seemed to shoot everywhere except at the game.

I remember getting up once at 3:00 A.M., taking Pazzas from under my bed, calling the dog, and walking in the cold to some lakes about six miles from town. Just before daybreak I arrived and took position on a neck of land that separated two of the best duck lakes around. I made ready for the morning flight, loaded my gun, and adjusted the firing cap. I always believed the more powder I put in a gun the farther it would shoot, so I put in plenty of powder. My hands were so numb from the cold that when I pulled some newspaper from my pocket to use for wadding, I upset my shot bag and all the shot ran out, leaving me with but the one load.

I could hear singles and flocks of birds flying over in the dark. When it got light enough to see, I pointed Pazzas at the largest flock and shot into it, picking the leader as a target. An old-time duck hunter had taught me this technique. Gee! What a jolt that gun gave me when I fired. After the smoke had cleared I could see

154

six nice redheads down, and my dog was retrieving them as fast as she could.

This success made me keen for the sport, and I got busy reloading my gun. A large charge of powder the first time, with good results, called for an even larger one the second time. I put in about four fingers, with a large hunk of paper wadding on top. Then I rammed until the rod bounced out the end of the barrel. When I was ready for the shot, I found I had none. Undeterred, I looked around for a replacement. The first thing I found was some gravel, so, scraping up a handful, I poured it down the barrel. Someone had been repairing boats at this place, and several rusty nails and screws were strewn around. I picked these up and put them into the gun for good measure.

A large flock of canvasbacks were coming my way, so I crouched down. As the birds flew nearer, I hunkered down farther, and when they were over me, I was flat on my back on the soft and boggy ground. I took careful aim, as per the old duck hunter, and fired. There was a deafening roar and a singing of nails through the air. My head was bursting, my face hurt awfully, and my right shoulder felt as though it was sunk a foot in the mud. I rubbed my hand over my face and found it was bleeding. A great cloud of smoke floated away as I rose to my knees and looked at my gun. The stock was in splinters, and some of them were in my face. I looked around expecting to see most of the flock strewn about, but not a duck was in sight, either dead or alive. My dog was sitting a hundred yards away, watching me with a frightened look.

I gathered up my belongings and trudged wearily and painfully homeward. The entire right side of my face

# *When Ducks Were Plenty*

was black and blue, and my right eye was swollen shut. My dog kept her distance all the way home. When my mother saw me, the first thing she said was, "I told you that gun would be the death of you sure!" But oh, how proud I was of that bag of six ducks—worth a black eye, scared dog, and broken gun to boot. My wounds soon healed, my dog reestablished herself as a hunting companion, and I made a new stock for Pazzas out of a 2-by-8 pine board. But wait . . .

The hearth fire is burning low. I reach to stir the dying embers. A blond curly head in a "nightie," having heard me thrashing about as I reminisced, comes down the stairs and over to my chair, and, crawling upon the arm, she says, "Daddy, you'll be kicking about the light bill next."

# Section II
## 1880 to 1900

By the 1880s, hardly a muzzleloading fowling piece could be found except as a first gun in the hands of a young boy. Meanwhile, machine-made and hand-finished American shotguns of the highest quality were being turned out by Parker Brothers, L. C. Smith, Lefever, Colt, Winchester, and Remington. A multitude of gentlemen sportsmen had taken up wildfowling in earnest. Transportation and infrastructure had so improved after the Civil War that by the 1880s it was as easy—and probably less trouble—to travel from Boston to hunt in Illinois as it is now in 1999! The railroads solicited and accommodated sportsmen in every conceivable way, and duck boats, dogs, and shooting paraphernalia were a common sight in the baggage car. Some syndicates of well-to-do sportsmen even owned their own "shooting box" railway cars that were moved about the country to various prime hunting and fishing venues, while the members kicked back in absolute "golden age" luxury and comfort.

The "golden age," however, was only golden for those who had gold coin of the realm, as guns and travel were relatively expensive. A contemporary article in a late-1870s issue of *Forest and Stream* priced out a one-month hunting trip from Washington, D.C., to northern Iowa at $50 rail fare and $1.50 to $2.00 per day board, plus local transportation, guides, ammunition, and incidentals. Meanwhile, the stay-at-home farmer had little time for sport hunting, and the less well-heeled city resident would find that game was scarce within easy distance of the population centers. Compound these problems with ten-hour, six-day work weeks and Victorian moral restraints on Sabbath shooting, and it should be apparent that those who wrote about their greatest shot or most memorable duck-shooting experience were generally men of means, sometimes called "clubmen." Then, even more so than now, duck hunting was for the well-to-do.

The sportsmen of the golden age wanted their shooting just like it was in "the good old days." But the times they were a-changin'. The abundant wildfowl of prior years no longer existed except, perhaps, in localized concentrations accessible only to the most affluent members of private duck-shooting clubs. Smaller bags and the general scarcity of game prompted increasingly shrill calls for local, state, and even federal laws and restrictions on what essentially had been unregulated shooting. Thus the golden era ended at about the turn of the century, as the states and finally the federal government passed laws to ensure that ducks, geese, swans, herons, cranes, shorebirds, doves, and other migratory wildfowl would not go the way of the passenger pigeon.

# Old-Time Wildfowl Shooting
### by Charles Askins (the Elder)

At the time of which I write, the 1880s, I was a boy on a farm in Illinois, situated midway between the Mississippi and Okaw Rivers. Ducks, geese, swans, cranes, and all other waterfowl and waders "traded" back and forth between the two rivers, a distance of twenty-five miles. We lived close enough to the Mississippi to hear the steady *whamp, whamp* of the big 10-bore guns at break of day. South St. Louis was just across the river, and if any city had more duck hunters than St. Louis, the population must have been far greater. The ferries began running long before daybreak and were loaded with hunters. As to the bags, about this time one St. Louis duck hunter was supposed to have killed three hundred fifty ducks in one day's shooting on Creve

Coeur Lake, fifteen miles west of the city. Another man, shooting on the Sny, a backwater of the Illinois River, killed seventy-nine mallards at one shot from a punt gun on a moonlit night.

The incessant shooting on the Mississippi near St. Louis drove the ducks and geese toward the Okaw. Most of them flew high, but some flew within shooting range. Even before I could shoot a gun, I had a bow and arrows. I would stand in a little pasture and drive arrows up among the wildfowl all day long. If they were no more than two hundred feet high, I could reach them with an arrow. Right then I learned something about lead, for if the arrow wasn't directed forty or fifty feet in front of the birds, it would pass behind them. I never killed a bird, or even hit one, but I was always hopeful. The pintails would swerve and dodge as the arrows came among them, but the geese would go serenely on with never a waver.

By and by I was old enough to shoot a rifle. This made more of a commotion among the ducks, although I didn't kill any more of them than with my bow and arrows. My father owned three rifles: a Kentucky muzzleloader, a Henry rifle that had seen service in the Civil War, and an old Spencer of the same vintage. He wouldn't let me shoot the two breechloaders, because I would have used up all his ammunition, but I could shoot the muzzleloading rifle as long as I made my own bullets. Presently, seeing that I was wasting a lot of time with the old rifle, he traded a barrel of cider to a saloon keeper for a 16-bore shotgun. That little piece weighed only seven pounds and was held in great contempt by all the neighborhood duck hunters, but I killed some ducks with it, so it was a duck gun to me.

# Old-Time Wildfowl Shooting

In one corner of our pasture near a fencerow was a little pond on which teal sometimes alighted. I raised havoc with those small ducks. Of course I fired my first shot as they sat on the water and the second as the birds took wing, but never hit anything, partly because I had been warned never to cock both barrels at the same time. My brother, four years older than I, had tried that, and both barrels went off together, knocking him flat.

Down on the creek in a bit of a pond lived a wood duck drake. Every few days I'd go down for a shot at him as he flew out. After a dozen misses, through some freak of luck I killed him: my first duck on the wing. I was then about ten years old. Another morning I couldn't sleep for the noise of ducks flying over the house. My bedroom was in the garret, close under the roof. I grabbed my little sixteen and climbed out a window without awakening anybody. Just then, backlit by moonlight, a flock of some two hundred pintails came right over the yard no more than fifty feet above me. I shot into them, and a drake came down stone-dead. This woke up everyone in the neighborhood, and afterward even my folks believed I could hit them flying. That settled it: I was a wing shot and a duck hunter and, in my mind, soon to become a professional market shooter like everybody else.

Not far from the house was a large wet-weather pond in the middle of a hundred-acre wheat field. The wheat usually drowned in the wet spot, and grass and smartweed took its place. In the spring, pintails, locally called "sprigs," liked that pond, perhaps because nobody could get near them. One flock of the long-tailed ducks seemingly decoyed another, so that every passing bunch wheeled to alight on or around the pond. The pintails would drop in at daybreak or before, always coming from the west. They would make a circle according to their height, cup their wings, drop their feet, and slowly settle down.

After a few warm rains in late February, the wheat was tender and green. Flocks of pintails came into the pond, and their numbers increased from day to day. But nobody could get within shotgun range of them, and a

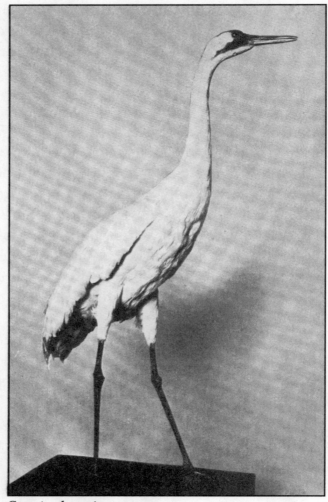

*Great whooping crane.*

# Old-Time Wildfowl Shooting

rifle could only be used with random results. Occasionally the exasperated owner of the field would get out and fire his rifle into the ducks, but he never killed any. Their numbers were so great that people came just to see them. It was estimated that a million ducks were feeding on that wheat field. I tried to get near enough for a shot with my little sixteen, and the ducks would let me approach within a hundred and fifty yards. Then they would stop feeding, raise their heads, and turn their snowy breasts toward me: fifty acres of ducks in the middle of a field, a solid patch of waterfowl, white as new-fallen snow! The first bird to take flight was a signal to all the others, and they would climb into the air with a roar of wings that could be heard a mile away. It was the greatest number of ducks that I have ever seen in a single body, even to this day.

My shooting chum, Albert, and I dug a pit near the pond and got into it before it was light. We got one shot and killed three birds, but the others seemed to know, and succeeding flocks circled high and passed. The frantic owner called in all his friends, and they surrounded the field. A few ducks were killed by the bombardment, but not many. Finally, the farmer put up scarecrows all about the field, and that was the end of our gigantic hoard of waterfowl. The ducks never came back, having perhaps coincidentally continued their migration northward.

One day my oldest brother, John, came home much excited, saying that there were some big white birds in the wheatfield pond—birds, according to him, that were as tall as he was. My brother-in-law, Fred, was in the house with his big 8-gauge, single-barrel muzzleloader. We set out for the pond, John taking my little sixteen, which left me only the old muzzleloading rifle. According to plan, John and Fred went around to take a position in the woods to the west, as the birds leaving the pond usually went in that direction. It was three hundred yards to the birds from where I stood behind a rail fence. I was to move in as close as I could and then fire at the great birds with my rifle.

We all knew about sandhill cranes, because they alighted in sight of the house every few days. These birds, though, were bigger and snowy white. Some of them stood erect and appeared as tall as a horse. However, most of them had their heads down busily pulling up wheat. Now and then they stalked about, taking long, stiff strides as if on stilts. That flock covered a couple of acres, and there must have been three to five hundred birds. We knew they were cranes, but didn't know what kind. Their cry was different from that of a sandhill—a deep, short, musical *whoop!*

It was a great show while it lasted, but I was too impatient. The big fellows looked as if they stood so densely that I couldn't shoot into them without hitting one. After waiting for John and Fred to get into position, I aimed into the densest mass and fired. Instantly the big white cranes sprang into the air and spread their wings, and although they had jumped high, their first wing beats were barely off the ground. Their progress was so slow that had I been among them, I might easily have sprinted and caught one on the wing. Not one remained on the ground, and a forlorn young duck hunter had failed again.

The huge white birds showed black tips on their wings as they slowly beat off in the direction of the hidden hunters. They were massed as closely as they could be and still fly. Alas, they never reached the timber where I knew the boys would be; a hundred and fifty yards from it they curved off to the south. They probably looked much closer to John and Fred, who fired without result. The big cranes never lost a wing beat, but continued to circle, then headed in my direction. They came directly over me, fifty feet high, winging with deliberate majesty, a wing beat every twenty feet and not making much noise, just a great, soft rush of air through extended pinions. I could see vivid red on their necks, and their black eyes looked down on me with supreme disdain. Each of those cranes looked a full six feet long. I aimed the empty rifle at them and could cover one without any trouble at all. And so I see them now, a full fifty years later: the largest flock of whooping cranes that I ever witnessed. The like will never again be seen by any man in the world.

## *Editor's Note*

According to Tom Stehn, "U.S. Whooping Crane Coordinator" at the Aranas National Wildlife Refuge in Austwell, Texas, the entire North American whooping crane population in April 1997 consisted of 354 wild and captive birds, up from 15 mature wild whoopers in 1941.

The would-be whooping crane shooter and author of this chapter, Charles Askins (the Elder), was born in 1860 and died in 1947. The source for this chapter was his article in the December 1934 issue of *The American Rifleman.* "Duck Guns and Duck Shooting in the Old Days" began, "At the time of which I write, *the 1880s,* I was a boy on a farm in Illinois . . ." Something's wrong. Either Colonel Askins had a prolonged childhood or the early onset of forgetfulness. But confusion seems to run in the Askins family.  For example, Askins Sr. begot Charles Askins Jr. in 1907, and both father and son wrote extensively about firearms and hunting.  Neither ever clarified his identity, and both had military titles, which only added to the confusion.

# Duck Shooting on Delaware Bay
### by "Dick Swiveller"
### (pseudonym of W. L. Colville)

The second week of November, long ago, I was snugly camped with my friend Barnard and three other companions in our duck blind on a point in Delaware Bay. The wind had piped around northeast by north, blowing an icy gale. Mingled with the blast was the roar of the surf as great combers galloped in, crested with foam. Meanwhile, the few sails in sight were making for a safe harbor to ride out the storm.

At nightfall the air was full of ducks flying high, with an occasional phalanx of wild geese, all seeking a temporary resting and feeding place en route to the land of sun. Among the ducks we noticed a few bunches of canvasback. This aristocrat among waterfowl is the most delicious duck at the table, and hence the most sought after. The wild celery, on which this duck feeds almost exclusively, imparts to its flesh an exquisite flavor.

At six o'clock the wind had increased so we looked for good and brisk work in the morning. Twenty-five yards from shore, in front of the blind, we had strung out over two hundred wood decoys. In the coops were thirty-odd live duck decoys and eleven domesticated wild geese, some of which were trained as decoys to be thrown into the air; these decoys returned to the beach for the corn scattered there, thus inviting the wild flock to alight on the water and follow them. The remainder of the stool geese were to be anchored in shallow water in front of the blind. These birds were invaluable in decoying bunches of geese. The wild birds, seeing their friends floating and feeding peacefully near shore, could hardly resist the temptation to join, and, once within the fatal twenty-five-yard limit, some of them would end their long journey here.

In the shanty all was snug and comfortable. Supper had been dispatched, pipes filled, and while under the soothing influence of "tobacca," we discussed the shoot that would begin at dawn. Yarns were spun of good days and bad days in past seasons; of the morning that three of those present killed fifty ducks and thirteen geese; and of the day the writer pushed the boat through the grass at high tide and Frank, sitting in the bow, let loose with the heavy double 8-gauge. He killed seventeen bluewing teal in one pot shot; our excuse for the lack of sportsmanship was the bad weather.

Outside the shanty the wind swept in from the ocean, rising at times to a howling blast. Just as we were getting ready to turn in for the night, we heard the

# Duck Shooting on Delaware Bay

shrill whistle of a bunch of curlew as they passed near, followed almost instantly by the hoarse *honk! honk! honk!* of a flock of geese that had settled in the water near us. All too soon it was morning.

I awoke and found Charlie cautiously waking the other two sleepers. It was dark outside and very cold. We hastily but noisily dressed in our warm shooting togs. Heavy underclothing and warm outer garments of dead grass color are essential. A cardigan jacket over a vest, and a shooting coat over that, admirably resist cool zephyrs.

The shanty door swung back on its well-oiled hinges, and we took our positions in the blind, guns ready and

*The ducks must suffer.*

ammunition handy. Night was lifting rapidly. Through the cold dull gray of dawn, hundreds of ducks could be seen leaving the water and alighting. It grew lighter. "Mark!" A bunch of mallard came straight for the decoys. As they whirled to settle, the innocent brown grass in front of the blind became a line of fire. Black-powder smoke erupted from our four 12-bore guns, and seven of their number were left on the water.

One old drake arose seventy yards away and was killed stone-dead by Mr. Cochran with his left barrel, an extraordinarily long shot. The dogs retrieved the birds in good form. The little gate was hardly closed when the shout went up: "Mark! canvasbacks way off, coming in from the sea." We counted nine flying high. Would they swing in? They did not seem inclined to do so. Dropping my gun into its rest in front of me, I quickly seized duck after duck from the coop and threw them into the air until seven or eight were circling in front of the blind. These decoys, with our other stool ducks swimming and resting far out, caused the bunch to break their line of flight and drop down to the water. The canvasbacks saw the line of decoys, some swimming and some feeding on the corn scattered onshore. The canvasbacks settled on the water fifty yards away. After looking things over, they began to paddle our way. Meanwhile, three large flocks of mallards, bluebills, and teal had settled among the decoys, many of them within fair range.

Inside the blind there was suppressed excitement and agonizing suspense. We focused on the king of waterfowl, the canvasback. Nearer and nearer they swam, until the last one in the flock was within range. Each man singled out his bird. At the word each pressed his trigger, and five ducks lay dead and fluttering. The air then filled with ducks. One mallard was killed over-head and fell inside the blind. I saw a pair of black ducks making for the woods; as I covered one duck they crossed paths, and at the report both dropped behind the shanty, killed clean. The shooting was rapid and continuous, all wing shots, and the forest echoed with the roar of the 12-gauges. Snow fell occasionally in the cold, gray light. The wind had gone down some, but still blew hard enough to keep the birds moving. My score book shows the joint bag for that morning to have been forty-seven birds: eleven canvasbacks, and the remainder broadbills (or bluebills), mallards, black ducks, whistlers, teal, and one old squaw.

As bird after bird splashed on the water, the retrievers filled their retrieval contract admirably. One dog, Hal, pursued a wounded whistler I had dropped with my second barrel. As he approached, the dark, glossy greenhead dove underwater. Hal paused and watched. Shots from two guns behind me dropped a mallard and two broadbills almost on top of him. He paid no attention; his business was to fetch the whistler. The greenhead bobbed up twenty yards away and desperately begin to swim seaward. With great plunges, the dog came to within five yards of the bird, and then the latter dove; so did Hal, who came up with the greenhead in his mouth. The dog Colonel was also busily engaged. For an hour and a half these dogs were constantly in the water, working like beavers. But if I ran my hand through their coats close to the skin, they were warm, even though the animals had moments before left their ice-cold bath. Chesapeake retrievers have been a constant source of admiration, wonder, and study to me: They are strong in their likes and dislikes, generous friends and uncompromising foes, faithful in all things, and the best watchdogs on earth. But to be happy they must be near the water, and salt water at that.

After breakfast Mr. Cochran and I boarded the boat for an excursion around the island, half a mile away. We landed and were soon participating in good sport, shooting teal, bufflehead, and a few other varieties of marsh ducks. We had boated a dozen or so, and I was standing in the bow with gun raised to cover a bird quartering right, when Mr. Cochran said, "Hold! Don't shoot. Down quick, mark high left." I glanced up and counted thirteen geese that looked like they were ready to land.

At this instant came a loud *honk! honk! honk!* from the direction of the blind. We looked and saw three of the live geese decoys in the water, and then two more flew up from the dead grass and bushes on shore. The boys in the blind, always on the lookout, had seen the flight. At sight of the decoys, the high-flying geese wavered for an instant. Then with a long, graceful, sweeping turn, they slid down an invisible ladder and struck the water in a show of spray amid much "goose talk."

My friend and I were left out of the action. We could only look anxiously at the big birds and hope the boys in the shanty would have their hands full. I imagined Frank standing behind the blind with his 8-gauge ready: a 13-pound gun with seven drams of powder and two ounces of No. 2 shot. Whew! It was just like the old Allen pepperbox revolver Mark Twain described: "If she didn't bring what she was aimed at, she'd fetch something else."

The leader of the flock swam toward his tame friends, followed at a distance by the remainder of the bunch. He was going to inspect this fine resting place and possibly make acquaintance with the tame geese

# Duck Shooting on Delaware Bay

busily diving and feeding near shore. After carefully looking things over, he would give the signal of peace, safety, and prosperity, which is simply *honk! honk! honk!* This means, "Come on, all is well, this is a good place. Pleasant and friendly ganders live here."

When the leader was within ten or fifteen yards of the shore, he paused. The flock also halted forty yards behind him. He spun around, craned his neck, went a little nearer, and then shied off. But then he swam boldly in until he touched the sand, and, rising up, flapped his wings and gave the signal. Oh, what I would have given for a place in that blind! The flock hurried forward to join their leader. They came nearer and nearer, and were finally within range. Would the men in the blind never fire? Then erupted flashes, smoke, flutters, splashes. *Honk! honk! squawk! boom! boom! cheer! boom!* came the dull roar of the guns across the water. Four geese went down! *BOOM!* There went another down! The 8-gauge leveled the wise leader as he made a vain attempt to climb skyward.

The dogs retrieved four geese, and then a wounded bird began swimming and flapping toward our position two hundred yards from the blind. The dog Colonel started in pursuit. He gained rapidly, but the goose was soon aware of his danger. The chase eventually brought the game within reach of my friend's gun. As he steadied himself for the shot, the dog saw the movement and stopped pursuit. The next moment the big bird lay dead on the water. Colonel swam up, retrieved the goose, and at command brought it to the boat.

It must not be supposed that the duck shooter and bayman has such sport every day, or even half the days in the season. Sometimes, for days or weeks or more, there is no shooting. The principal cause of bad shooting days is mild weather. No cold, no wind, no freezing rain means no flights coming from the north. And the ducks that have already arrived are far out in the open water, rafted or packed in bunches here and there with no inclination to break up. Rough, cold, stormy weather keeps the game moving. To be successful, the duck shooter must be out when the elements are at their worst. He must endure nipping air, high winds, frozen spray, and a good soaking. But to be successful, he must also keep his health, and above all, his temper.

# Batteries on Sandusky Bay
## by "J. J. B."

For twenty years or more I shot ducks on Sandusky Bay, and am therefore qualified to compare what shooting used to be with the shooting of the present day. Before the advent of batteries or even decoys, there was no better place for ducks than the bay and its bordering marshes and tributary streams. Our boathouses were situated on the banks of Pipe Creek, about half a mile from its mouth in the cove by Big Island Point. From thence we could get down to the marsh in any weather, a thing greatly desired, for as a general rule, the stormier the day the better for ducks. Starting early in the morning, we almost invariably found good shooting all the way down the creek. The water was always black with mud hens and a goodly sprinkling of ducks. The great flock would spread open for us to pass through and then would close in behind us at a few rod's distance. The ducks, of course, took flight before the less cautious mud hens. If the wind was too strong from the eastward and the sea too heavy in the open cove after passing Big Island, we struck across the sniping ground into Pond Lilly Channel, down Black Channel, through Plum Brook, and into Graham's Pond holes.

This chain of ponds in the midst of the great marsh was the favorite feeding place of ducks, and countless thousands were constantly flying from one pond to the other. This spot afforded the best possible shooting to anyone who cared to shove his hunting skiff into the narrow strip of cane grass (locally called "flags") that separated one pond from the other. It awakens the old thrill now when I think back to the hundreds of times I had been thus hidden. I can picture the long lines of bluebills with their black necks and white breasts, skimming along about three feet above the water, until, with a sudden rush, they rise over a bunch of cane grass, then resume their previous altitude. In those days I would see them in my dreams at night after banging away at the reality all day. To those who did not care to travel to the ponds, the points and channels along the creek afforded good shooting, too. The constant fusillade, at times, sounded like the Fourth of July. In stormy weather there was good shooting for everybody and plenty of it. If a duck hunter got no ducks it was his fault, for there was game enough for every hunter's powder flask or shot bag to be empty at day's end.

# Batteries on Sandusky Bay

I well recollect the first decoys I ever saw used. Old Uncle Jim Paul, with McKinster and J. D. Bourne (the three of them in a rowboat), had shoved into the cane grass off Ned's Point. They set their decoys out in the open water so the countless flocks of ducks coming down the bay could see them. Those decoys were primitive enough, I assure you: mere chunks of white cedar, sharp at one end, a chuckle head stuck onto the blunt end, painted with lead color and black, and with a dab of white paint on each side for the wing coverts. But the way the ducks came down to them was a caution, and with those three men shooting, the number of dead ducks in the water was wonderful to see. The three men soon had imitators, and in a year or two, every man who owned a boat and a gun also had his flock of decoys. No one would think of going down for ducks without at least a few decoys to throw out in front of his hiding place or blind.

*Up Black Dog Creek in canoes after the ducks.*

In those days the whole lower cove was always full of live ducks, and if disturbed by the sand scows after dark, the roar of the flock as they took flight could be heard miles away in the city. They could not be driven away by any number of hunters, boats, guns, or other appliances then in use, and year after year we saw no diminution in their seemingly inexhaustible numbers.

Finally, in an evil hour came the batteries, and from then on the preeminence of Sandusky Bay as a shooting ground was gone. Year by year the numbers of batteries increased, and in less than five years there was no shooting for anyone outside of a sink box. What twenty-five years of shooting by men and boys from points and boats had failed to do, these batteries did in less than five years. The feed is just the same today as it was then, but the great flock is a thing of the past. You may paddle from the drawbridge down to Black Channel and not see a duck where there had once been millions of them. There is no open-water shooting around the creek except from batteries, and it is no use going down the channel to the pond holes, for no ducks are there. One would naturally suppose that, being so disturbed in the open water, the ducks would go to the channels and ponds where the batteries never come, but this is not the case, as we shall see further on.

To see how this battery business works, let us take our position on Sunken Island, from whence we can see both up the bay and down toward the mouth of Black Channel. A quarter-mile out rests a flock of perhaps a hundred ducks that to a practiced eye reveal themselves to be decoys. Apparently among them, but in reality a little to one side, is something that looks like a rail floating in the water. That is a battery, and you can just see a portion of the man's hat near one end of the innocent-looking rail. Beyond him is the tender, whose sharp "M-a-a-r-k" we hear coming across the intervening space. Down goes the man's head, and the decoys are alone upon the water. Coming down the bay is a great flock of redheads. They catch sight of their kind on the open feeding grounds, set their wings, and with a whistling rush swoop down among them. Scarcely does the advance guard slide into the water when up rises the man in their very midst. *Bang! bang! bang! bang!* go the guns, and all is tumult and confusion. The terrified flock goes up, up, up out of rifle shot, and bewildered by the onslaught that they cannot account for or understand, their only thought is to get away from there entirely, and get away they do. Crossing over Cedar Point at a safe altitude, they fly for hours before alighting again.

These open-water ambushes are why ducks no longer visit the marshes and pond holes. A duck's common sense tells him to avoid points and bunches of grass, but, even if shot at from one of these points, he will descend to open water to the first flock he sees feeding. But when, in fancied security, he goes down into a flock of hundreds of his kind out in open water with no cane grass or other cover within half a mile, and is shot at by a man getting up out of the water within ten feet of him, he is a scared duck, if not a dead one. If he escapes, he will get entirely out of the country before he stops again. Thus the great feeding flock no longer exists in open water, because there is no chance for the nucleus of such a flock to form. Each flock is terrified, in turn, as it arrives, and this prevents the ducks from becoming accustomed to the feeding ground, even though the feed is the same as of old. As I said before, there is no longer any shooting for anyone outside of a battery. My friend and old hunting chum, Houser, went down before daylight three days last fall, and each night he brought home the same two shells he put into his gun in the morning. When he can't get ducks, there's no use for anyone else to try, for a better shot never sat in a boat.

Some of the battery men say, "Oh, well, there are so many shooters and so many cussed boys pounding away at the ducks all the time, that's what's the matter." Yes, but for twenty years there have been just as many shooters, and the "cussed boys" with their three-dollar

*Paddlewheel steam launch* U. S. Grant *with a boatload of "sports" and a nice mess of ducks.*

single-barreled shotguns or old muskets have always been as omnipresent as they are now. Indeed, I think there was more shooting in the past, for back then there was the unfailing evening flight, and one could hear a perfect cannonading from sundown to dark and even after dark. Now you can't hear a gun, for there is no evening flight; that, too, is a thing of the past. With all the shooting year after year, the ducks continued to come in undiminished numbers until the advent of the batteries, but since that evil day the shooting has been ruined. Pardon me for this extended complaint, but I think it proves beyond all doubt that whenever batteries are systematically used, a diminution, if not the entire disappearance of wildfowl, is sure to take place.

## *Editor's Note*

The terms "battery" and "sink box" are often used interchangeably, but there is a distinction. When John Krider wrote of a "sunk box" (chap. 5), the device was actually a battery by description. The sink box, however, was a very low, decked-over boat with just room enough for one shooter to lie down. It had water compartments which, when filled, sank it down nearly level with the surface. The smoother the water, the lower the box was sunk. If the wind picked up and the water got rough, the gunner lightened his boat by pumping out some of the water ballast. Sink boxes were generally small enough that when the water compartments were not fully filled, the boat could easily be moved about with oars.

By comparison, the battery was a much larger outfit and had to be carried in a large skiff or aboard a sail- or powerboat. It consisted of a box to accommodate one to four gunners, built in the center of a floating deck. A one-man rig would be about twelve feet long by six feet wide, with a folding canvas wing on each side and a canvas head-wing across the bow. When the canvas wings were spread, the battery covered an area about eighteen feet long by twelve feet wide. The battery was sunk down to zero freeboard with heavy iron decoys set on the wings. The largest battery of record in the Long Island, New York, area was a four-gun rig, with a deck twenty-five feet square, upon which a man could walk. This was surrounded with three to four hundred floating decoys; another hundred were fastened to the deck at close intervals, making the battery look like a veritable island of birds.

# Coot's Revenge
## by "Kanuck"

Great Scott! Is that an earthquake or a cyclone?
Neither—it's only the alarm saying, "Five o'clock,
boys." Up we jump, wash in the creek, snatch a hasty
breakfast, and paddle down the creek to our stand.
Out go the decoys, and then we crouch in our blind in
anticipation of the morning flight. It's 6:30 A.M.—
no birds. At 8 A.M. John takes a tramp and bags
two wretched peep (drawing cheers from the blind),
then comes back exultant. He knows there are
more coming.

Hello! Look at that big black fellow coming straight
in. What is it? Never mind, bag him first, and we'll
name him afterward. He's almost over us; wait till
he's passed. Now! *Bang! bang! bang! bang!* go four
barrels, and the bird concludes to stay with us. We

rejoice, and execute a war dance around him that would do credit to a band of Pawnees. We return to camp jubilant, for we have game.

"Only three birds," I seem to hear some crackshot mutter. Well, do you suppose we want the whole earth

*Collecting old-time sporting images is frustrating when there is no description of the event or identification of the persons pictured, as is the case here. For all we know, these two could be the spectacularly unsuccessful wildfowlers who cooked their coot "from a sense of duty." Photo courtesy of Herb Peck Jr.*

# Coot's Revenge

and all the birds on it? No, my sarcastic friend, we are not that sort. We are content, and so draw the three birds for dinner. We don't know what the large one is, but we are going to eat him from a sense of duty. Anything so unsportsmanlike as killing game and leaving it to rot is something of which we are incapable, even if we are poor shots. (Take that, my crackshot friend.) But the bird's revenge comes after death, and don't he just smell after we have cleaned him. We soak him in many waters but the odor is still there. I tell John it is only the gamy flavor peculiar to denizens of marshy districts, but he doubts me and even mutters "chestnuts" under his breath. Finally we throw the bird away, for John says it is poison, and even my dog agrees with him after one sniff. Then we feel better and content ourselves with bacon and griddle cakes, which are good enough for any man.

In the afternoon we paddle down the creek and across the river to the tidal flats. We spend the afternoon reclining on the beach, smoking innumerable pipes and reveling in the salt air. We decide to have the peeps for supper, almost a mouthful apiece, and are just lighting our campfire when there comes a sudden hail from the marsh. Jim appears. "Jest slipped down to see how ye wus faring," he remarks. Down he sits on half of my blanket, fills his pipe, and after a pull or two inquires, "Wall, what luck?" We tell him about the big black bird and ask him what it was. After various queries as to its head, plumage, etc., he delivers our answer thus: "Mus' hev bin a coot. 'Twas curious ye shot him in the marsh, though. Mebbe he was kinder prospecting round. They do smell almity strong. An' so ye couldn't eat 'em, hey!" and he roars with laughter.

# When Ducks Were Plenty

The next morning we are up bright and early and try the woods for partridge, but without success, so we give up after a while and tramp home. Is the day lost because we haven't bagged all the game we can carry? You don't know us. Many a time we have unjointed our rods and left the trout still jumping because we have had enough, and we would do the same with the birds, only—well, there seems to be no danger of our ever getting a great many of them.

# A Shooting Box Named City of Saginaw

## by William B. Mershon

I wrote the following account in 1884, and I have found it among my old hunting records forty years later. I am not reproducing it because of literary merit by any means, but because it teems with the enthusiasm of youth.

Ten of us, all born-in-the-bone waterfowlers from Saginaw, Michigan, owned a rail car called City of Saginaw, which served as our traveling shooting box for many years. On Saturday, 10 October 1884, our party of four hunters and a cook boarded the private car for Dakota. We stopped Monday morning at Moorehead, Minnesota, and as I stood on the rear platform, I could see dozens of flocks of geese, hundreds of ducks, snipe, and curlew, and even flocks of "chickens" booming over the prairie. We breakfasted near Fargo just over the Dakota line, and at ten o'clock were put on a siding at Buffalo. Our local guide, Mr. Goodsell, came down to meet us, but did not give very encouraging accounts of game, as the weather had been so fine that the ducks and geese were still north.

After eating dinner aboard City of Saginaw, we loaded ourselves, traps, and dogs into wagons and set out for the ranch twelve miles distant. As we drove over the wheat stubble, great flocks of sandhill cranes would take wing just before we got near enough to shoot. Once, however, Charlie blazed away and killed a great big fellow even though he seemed out of gunshot. We were all delighted, of course, as the crane was very fat, but plans for a roast were quickly dispelled when Mr. Charles said that he was going to express it home to a taxidermist. He lugged this specimen around for two days and finally left it one night at the depot on the platform. I saw it going off under a chap's arm early in the morning, and said nothing, as it would probably do someone some good.

We arrived at the ranch about three o'clock and, after making an engagement for supper, we headed out along the sloughs. I saw at once that our shooting would be poor, for where the year before the pond holes had been black with ducks, now only a scattered flock or two were to be seen. Early next morning we tried again, and by noon we were ready for a change, having only bagged eighty-four ducks, four geese, and few snipe. We held a war counsel and determined to pull up stakes and make for a place from which we had heard great reports. We got into Buffalo just in time to hook the car to the afternoon train, and arrived the next morning on our hunting ground, some two hundred fifty miles farther west. Here we had all the shooting we wanted, as you shall see.

# A Shooting Box Named City of Saginaw

Our first concern was to secure some means of transportation to and from our shooting grounds, so Bob and I were appointed the transportation committee. We interviewed the livery man. Like a great many of his class, he sized us up for our pile, wanted $8 per day for a rig that would carry but three people, and said we must pay extra for bringing in our geese. We did not care to pay $16 or $20 per day for riding six or eight miles. We had hoped to stay several days, but Mr. Livery Man thought he had us and would not come down a cent. Thus we shopped around and soon arranged with a fellow by the name of Long, who had a good outfit that would carry our entire party at a reasonable figure. And I will say that Long proved to be a treasure. A little at a time we heard his story, though a small portion of it I am sure. He was educated at one of our eastern colleges, and for some reason or other had gone west soon after graduating. Long had spent the last winter trapping on some Indian reservation where he had no business being, and lost all his traps, pelts, outfit, and almost his life. A mule team and puppy were his only companions. At night he would spread his blankets under the wagon and sleep the sleep of the just; he called it putting up at the "Globe Hotel."

Bob was bent on duck shooting, while the rest of us hankered for geese. So we divided, Bob taking the buggy to the sloughs four miles south of the rail track. We three piled into Long's wagon and went in the opposite direction. Soon we came to a large wheat stubble covered with geese, some feeding, but most of them with necks stretched up looking right at us. We drove a few miles to the shore of a large lake and unhitched the team. Ducks and geese covered the surface, and clouds of waterfowl were flying. The roar was like thunder as flocks circled and gradually resettled on different parts of the lake.

About noon the geese began to leave the stubble, and after the first flock they flew in a steady stream, alighting far out on the lake. The din was deafening as each flock was welcomed by those already there. After hastily eating our lunch, we loaded the traps into the wagon, and back we went to the stubble where the geese had been feeding in the morning. They were sure to return toward the latter part of the day. We then began the hard work of goose shooting: digging the pits. These pits were between four and five feet deep and about thirty inches in diameter. The earth was spread out so as not to make much of a mound around the pit. We pulled stubble in bunches and replanted it around the pit so the ground would look undisturbed. After an hour's digging, three respectable pits were finished about twelve feet apart, covered with short stubble, and so well disguised that we were confident the most wary

*A morning's sport over Danz goose decoys.*

old gander would not be suspicious of danger. Then we placed our Danz metal profile decoys in the most bewitching positions.

After all our hard work we took some pulls at our water bottles and discussed our plans. The man in the center would act as captain and give the word; the others were supposed to keep down and not move. Charlie had a new 10-gauge Westley Richards hammerless, and Eben a 10-gauge Scott, which were both heavy guns. They were shooting five drams of powder and 1¼-ounce No. 2 shot. I was the odd one, being a 16-gauge crank. So there I sat in the middle pit as "goose captain"—with my W. & C. Scott & Sons "pop gun," as they called it—and I suffered no end of chaff. All I could say was, "Wait and see." But to tell the truth, I thought Charlie and Eben would clean me out, as they were both crack shots. And they certainly had the advantage with their 1¼-ounce shot, against my little ⅞-ounce loads.

Meanwhile, I had my eyes peeled in the direction of the lake. At half past three I caught sight of a long, undulating line low on the horizon. "Down, boys! Quick! Here they come!" I whispered. Then all was quiet with suppressed excitement. On they came, saw the decoys, and made straight for us, honking, necks outstretched, with lazy wings. I can't say who fired first, but we all rose and pulled when the birds were twenty yards too far. In the cold, clear air, the great fellows looked to be right on top of us, when, in fact, our first shots were at sixty to seventy yards. If we had only waited they would have come right over, but what's the use of kicking ourselves now? We would know better next time, and besides, four Canada geese lay dead on the hard ground, the result of six barrels: not so bad.

I was to take the middle birds, Eben those to the left, and Charlie the right. Two had fallen in the center, but both avowed they had fired at the old gander slightly ahead and leading the gang. So it was ever after; I could not keep one or the other from shooting at my center

birds. At any rate, I claimed them, as they had no business shooting at my geese.

Now that the ice was broken, in came flock after flock.
Oh, for another hour of such excitement! The sport lasted
but an hour, and then not a goose was to be seen. It was
grand. I heard no more from my companions to the right
and left as to the shooting qualities of my pop gun. I
killed my geese slick and clean. When the flights ceased,
we gathered up our dead, and what a pile they made!
We had four or five different kinds, including pure white
ones with black on the ends of their wings, and one
yellow-legged fellow with a blotchy black breast that the
natives called a California goose. We also had both large
and small Canada geese.

Charlie counted our pile and found it contained fifty-
eight geese. Whoopla! Talk about fun. We headed back
to the little village in the soft twilight that comes over
the great Dakota prairies after a bright October day. With
songs, laughter, and tales of how this one missed and that
one hit, we drove among the twinkling lights to our car at
the rail siding. Soon Bob came in from the slough with
reports of ducks without end, but claimed he did not shoot
well and should have had more game. We all said the same
thing, as Bob's geese and great greenhead mallards were
added to our already shamefully large pile. All hands turned
to, and the birds were soon drawn, tied in bunches, and
expressed to friends in St. Paul and elsewhere. Then came
supper, smoking the pipe of peace while arranging for the
next day's fray, and well-earned sleep.

After breakfast the next morning, Mr. Long's wagon was
brought to the door, and in we piled, bound for the slough
and mallards. After arriving at our destination, we took
possession of a small shanty once used by some hardy

pioneer as a roosting place while tilling the large fields around us. No other buildings were in sight. To the southward for two or three miles stretched Sam Devor's slough, and such a place it proved to be for birds. As we stood on the edge of the slough, something alarmed the waterfowl. When they arose they darkened the sky, and the roar reminded us of a heavy train rapidly moving over a long, resonant trestle.

It was early afternoon before Bob and I lugged our gear out to an advantageous point for the evening flight, for we were satiated with shooting and had been loafing around all day. At dusk, just as the great red glow of the gorgeous Dakota sunset was at its best in the west, the ducks came on fast and furious. I do not think I shot more than twenty minutes. My gun was hot. Frequently I had to dodge to avoid being hit by teal coming into the hole like bullets. Sometimes they came so fast and so low that they startled me, and I had to put up my arm as a shield. It seemed as if they wanted to knock me over. I only shot those that passed between me and the clear, red bit of sky, so that they would fall free in the open water.

We shot until dark and did not attempt to pick up our birds that night, as the trail back to the hard ground was long, and the water was knee deep. My shooting companion claimed a big bag, and was rubbing it in to the rest of us as usual. I said nothing, but asked him to go out with me and help gather birds in the morning. We picked up and brought in my forty-six ducks, largely teal and mallards. Bob's 10-bore had scored only forty-three. This may seem game-hoggish by present [1923] standards, but we had not yet begun to appreciate that game was disappearing. This ended our 1884 shooting trip to Dakota. Two days with the ducks and one with the geese was sufficient.

# When Ducks Were Plenty

The biggest shoot we ever had in Dakota was in the early 1880s, on the Troy farm near Tappan, the station just east of Dawson on the Northern Pacific. It was a stormy day with snow squalls. The field was a square mile of wheat stubble. Our party of five divided: Three went to one part of the field, and two to the other. We had a farm wagon with extra side boards that would carry eighty bushels of wheat. We killed 163 geese that day, and they nearly filled the wagon box. That night when we drove back to Dawson, eight miles distant, we were cold and wet. We all stuck our legs down in the geese, and the warmth of their bodies kept us comfortable.

Our group continued going to Dawson with City of Saginaw every year until 1899, when the goose hunting failed there, and after that we changed to Pleasant Lake. We frequently brought three hundred or more geese home with us, and the arrival of our hunting car in Saginaw was telegraphed ahead, so that our friends could flock to the station and share in our good fortune. Bag limits and laws against shipping out of state in those days were unknown. City of Saginaw had a large ice box, so not a bird was ever wasted, and our wheat-fed young geese were highly esteemed for the table. After the turn of the century we would sidetrack the car in town and commute by automobile to the hunting grounds. In 1914, City of Saginaw was sold.

# Never on Sunday
## by E. A. Leopold

Few ducks have visited the Schuylkill in this vicinity during the past month. They were terribly persecuted during their stay and so do not tarry long. A flock of twenty-five or thirty took up quarters along the shores of Barbadoes Island on 18 October, and, although it was Sunday, a large number of boats and shooters (I will not say sportsmen) pursued them all day. Before nightfall most of the ducks were driven westward beyond Catfish Dam, four miles from here.

I was on the river Sunday afternoon and accidentally chased two ducks within easy range of three young men in a boat. One of them raised a double muzzleloader and snapped twice, but it did not go off. They called to me, "Have you any caps?" I answered, "No, I use a breechloader, *but not on Sundays*." They explained that they had killed a duck in the forenoon and had exhausted their supply of percussion caps. They had sent a boy to a drugstore for more, but the druggist had sold out, and the gun stores were not open. Here is an illustration of the human thirst for gore. These young men were rowing a 300-pound boat around all afternoon after ducks, snapping the hammers of their gun at every opportunity, hoping by some miracle that it might go off and kill something. Such perseverance deserves a better cause.

In another boat a young man was practicing with a revolver. He would get in one shot at the ducks on the water at about twenty yards, and then give them two more on the wing. The bullets were not likely to hit the ducks, but the spectators on shore were in great danger.

On the Monday following, I went out and killed two ducks, presumably the only ones remaining within two miles of the borough. On my return to the boathouse I met a man who informed me that one of my ducks was a "crow duck" [mud hen] and said that if I would throw it away he would sell me four good ones. He further informed me that he was a great duck hunter and had killed sixteen the day before. I thanked him and said that I would risk the crow, and had enough for dinner. Such market men make me tired, and there are so many hereabouts.

ANNA HELD CIGARS

"TRY THEM"

They outclass all five cent cigars. Jos B. Moos.

# A Shameful Fashion
## by "Special"

A thing of beauty is a joy forever, but a thing of
beauty when distorted and out of place distresses
thinking people of fine sensibilities. It is customary to
compliment the fair sex under all possible conditions,
but for the present distorted fashion that trims nearly
every woman's hat with some form of a dead bird, there
are no words of praise or excuse. A bird's wing is beautiful as it cuts the air, bearing a joyous bird in freedom
among the trees. Ten million dead birds with glass or
waxen eyes, withering beaks, and shrunken skins,
perched above the noses of ten million fashionable
women, are anything but a source of joy.

Look at the displays in the millinery windows of today:
dead birds to the end of the chapter! An importer of
millinery informs me that the demand for dead birds is
enormous. A thorough system of collecting tropical birds

is in operation abroad, extending even into Africa and Australia. The killing of sea swallows and other handsomely plumaged but dull-colored birds in this country, and the sending of them to France to be dyed, is appalling. Look about you, and what do you see? Six women out of every ten have some representation of a dead bird on their hats. It is natural to start calculating. There are over 50 million people in this country alone [in 1886], and fully half of them are of the dead-bird-wearing gender. Only a few are too young or too old to wear dead birds. Allow us only ten million females wearing bird corpses in the United States. Give us ten million for England and ten million for France, and keep all the rest of the fashionable world to make our estimates good. What have we found? Thirty million lives of birds have lately been taken solely to deck out the hats of women. How long can the birds stand such a strain? Does not utter extermination stare us in the face?

# Duck Shooting on the St. Lawrence
## by "Rambler"
### (pseudonym of Melvin Oscar Stinson)

One glorious October morning in 1888, my chum, Jones, threw open my bedroom door at the St. Louis hotel and gave a loud "*Vieu hullo!*" He awakened me and also considerably startled certain worthy French Canadian guests at the same Quebec hotel. "What do you say to going somewhere at once," quoth he, to which I replied, "Where shall we go?"

The day before we had tried Chateau Richer for snipe. The result was disastrous. One Wilson's snipe and six couple of sandpipers had rewarded the persevering efforts of two grown men and a brace of superior dogs. So as soon as I had dressed and fortified my inner man with an excellent breakfast, we started to explore and

*(Picture: Col. Schmidt's J. & W. Tolley 4-bore with author's Parker 16-gauge to compare. The shells tell the story!)*

collect information.  In the course of our ramble we received free advice galore, and it was worth what we paid for it.  According to one intelligent native, ducks were so thick at a certain point as to seriously impede water traffic.

Having enjoyed the advantages of a liberal education, I knew well enough to keep exploring.  In due time we met a well-known club sportsman who strongly advised a trip to a small island some fifty miles from the city.  This island was preserved by a merchant who occasionally rented the shooting on it and the use of his 12-ton yacht.  The proprietor was interviewed, terms arranged, and the rest of the day we spent busily freighting the noble craft with stores, ammunition, guns, and dogs.

About sundown we were ready for "sea," and under a salute of two blank cartridges from Jones's gun, which was much appreciated by the solitary spectator (small boy/wharf rat), we hauled out into the stream.  Fortune seemed to smile for once, as the wind was dead aft, the weather fine, and our progress during the night most satisfactory.  The next morning by daylight we hove-to off the island preserve.  A more dreary spot for a layman could hardly be found short of Patagonia, but to the shooter, sundry teams of duck flying to and from the feeding grounds enlivened the picture surprisingly.

In response to our signals, a small skiff with a very dirty French habitant floated up to take us ashore.  How many trips were necessary I do not recollect, but I do remember most painfully that the skiff's freeboard was barely three inches when I made the passage.  I have since calculated that as Jones was nearly double my weight, the freeboard must have been negative when he submitted to the short but perilous transit. This is a somewhat surprising result, I admit, but as figures won't lie, the reader only has the choice of two alternatives, and it will save unpleasantness if he accepts my facts.

The shooting lodge measured perhaps ten feet square and had been dug out of the bank near shore. A roof covered with sod was all that showed above ground—a cunning device, built so as not to alarm the wildfowl. There would have been no difficulty in shooting black duck and teal from the door any day during our stay, had we so wished, as the birds saw nothing dangerous about the lodge. The old Frenchman in charge was assisted by his son, one, I believe, out of his family of seventeen. The lad cooked for us while the old boy acted as guide, counselor, and friend, at a certain fixed rate per diem, of course. All the sport was over decoys, and the rules about promiscuous shooting at ducks outside the preserve were very strict. A fine lot of tame duck, marked liked wild ones, were on hand to help their wooden counterparts.

Although the tide did not serve for shooting on the first morning of our arrival, the old man volunteered to show us some birds. On a small rocky island off the main one he showed us a flock of at least five hundred snow geese, and on a point a short distance beyond roosted another flock of Canadas. Dozens of ducks flew over the saltwater marsh a few hundred yards from the island.

We swallowed our dinner and then, as it was half ebb, our guide told us to get ready. We each took two guns and plenty of ammunition. Mine were both

# When Ducks Were Plenty

12-bores: a seven-pound gun by Rigby and a heavy
Parker that weighed close to nine pounds. Both were
good, but I fancied the heavy gun doubled the birds
in better form.

The shooting stands were pits blasted out of the
slate rock, and were uncovered by the tide at half ebb.
They had to be bailed out before use and evacuated
again by half flood. In front of each was a splash of
water with feeding grounds all around. Before we
reached the pits, the cautious Frenchman made us hide
while he crawled ahead. By gently elevating his hat
on a stick, he put to flight the ducks that had already
dropped in without alarming them very badly. Soon
we were both comfortably established about one hundred fifty yards apart, with decoys out, and left to our
own devices.

I had not long to wait. A small flock of bluewing
teal made a dart for the decoys. I got seven with both
barrels. Then the black ducks began to come in, two
and three at a time. The guns stayed warm. Jones was
firing away like a battery in action, but being excitable,
shot most of his birds before they had wheeled round to
alight—a great mistake. Occasionally when I had time,
I looked in his direction, and more than once saw black
ducks brought down from the clouds in fine style. Still,
he would have done better had he waited for the birds
to turn and drop to the decoys.

By the time we were driven out by the rising tide, I
had seventy-eight duck and teal, and my chum's contri-
bution made the total bag considerably over a hundred.
This was enough glory for one day, and we returned in
great spirits to the den. The next morning it was much
the same; we were blessed with a northeast wind, and

the birds were coming in from Labrador all day. Guileless and trusting were these strangers, and we took them in.

On the evening of the second day I had great luck. Friend Jones possessed a 4-bore single-choke that weighed seventeen pounds. Of this child of a cannon I stood somewhat in awe, notwithstanding it was fitted with a rubber recoil pad. The sight of hundreds of snow geese squatting on that barren rock the day before had filled me with a wicked wish to possess a specimen or two before leaving. The evening previous I had observed the line they took at sundown as they flew from the rock to their feeding grounds. They flew high, but I thought the 4-bore loaded with large mould-shot might reach them. That afternoon, therefore, about an hour before sunset, I borrowed the toy mentioned above and posted myself behind a boulder under their line of flight.

In due time they came over, calling like a pack of harriers in full cry. Raising aloft the mighty tube, I aimed for the front of the wedge and, closing my eyes, fired. For a few short seconds I gyrated like a top. On regaining my equilibrium, I saw that one beautiful white bird was lying dead as a doornail a few yards away, another nearby was just expiring, while a third lively cripple was making tracks for the nearest water. I ran after him, but weighted as I was with the young cannon, could not gain an inch, and it seemed that he would reach the water before me. Dropping the weapon, I spirited and headed him a few yards from the shore. He tried to sham dead, but it was no go. Then he turned and came after me, but I prevailed. That night I returned to camp, exhausted but happy, carrying seventeen pounds of gun and thirty of goose.

# When Ducks Were Plenty

On the last day of our stay we went for snipe and got sixteen couple.  I have hunted wildfowl all my life and do not recall a more successful outing.  We arrived safely back in historic Quebec, and for a few days were the envy of the men and the admiration (?) of the women.

# Spring Goose Shooting on Bay Chaleur
## by "C. B."

For five long dreary months winter had the earth wrapped in its frozen shroud, and there were no inducements to the wingshooter to venture forth. Bird life was limited to a few repulsive crows that pecked a precarious living on the shores, and to small flocks of snowbirds that frequented the country roads and village streets. Only occasional companies of mergansers enlivened the channels of black water between the ice flows in Bathhurst Bay. On St. Patrick's Day, however, the winter of my discontent seemed drawing to a close, for then the first flock of geese appeared from the south. I rushed hatless from the house to feast my eyes upon the half-dozen birds that were flying over the frozen waters of Bathhurst Harbor. What a majestic appearance they presented, and what an electric thrill their sonorous honking sent through me.

A small crowd stood on the wharf watching the aerial revolutions of those heralds of spring. There is a free-masonry among sportsmen the world over, and in the crowd I soon spotted a fellow shooter. He turned out to be a visiting dentist. But what mattered that? Great Scot! Had not the fowl arrived? Our mutual interest in the geese served as an introduction, and the next day we started before dawn in a "paddle boat" that we had hired and equipped. The craft merits a detailed description, as it certainly was a most effective machine for slaugh-tering ducks and geese. It was about eighteen feet long and three feet wide, with a flat bottom. The means of propulsion was two paddle wheels, worked with handles by one man who lay on his back, while his comrade, reposing forward, attended to the shooting. We hid the revolving wheels by nailing strips of white cotton in front of them, and further disguised the boat by placing a lump of ice on the bow. The bottom of the craft had runners that enabled us to push her over the floes.

As we drifted seaward along the narrow channel, I realized that there was some danger in the course we were following. Blocks of ice three feet thick frequently threat-ened to squeeze our frail boat to matchwood, and it was only by Herculean efforts and a liberal use of the boathook that they were successfully evaded. After an hour's run we passed rapidly between the two points that formed Bathhurst Bay. There we beheld an open sheet of water, ten acres or so in extent, hemmed in by densely packed ice floes. Some

# Spring Goose Shooting on Bay Chaleur

of the cakes had been piled up one on another by the wind and tide to form miniature bergs. The scene was striking.

On the other side of Bay Chaleur, the high range of mountains loomed rugged and wild. Extending north and east to the distant horizon, the sea was covered with ice floes: some level and spotless as they had lain in midwinter, others broken and piled in the wildest confusion, giving out blue and green prismatic flashes as they rocked slowly in the ground swell. The tide was setting toward the opposite ice floe, and there was some danger of our small craft being sucked under the ice. We made haste to reach and hang on to a large floe, and this safely accomplished, the boat was hauled up and our arrangements for slaughter perfected.

As a start, I constructed some goose decoys. We had brought with us several sticks cut to represent the heads and necks of Canada geese. These sticks are made by first rough-cutting them into shape, then charring them in the fire, and finally whittling out the white markings of the bird. These I stuck in the ice and added bodies of seaweed that admirably represented the backs of geese. At forty yards a man would have been deceived, let alone a goose. Then we erected a blind with cakes of ice, and disguised the upturned boat in a similar manner. It is true we might have saved ourselves some trouble by merely removing our craft to a distance, but old goose hunters make it a rule never to separate from their boat. Occasionally the ice floes are influenced by a distant gale or change of tide and break up rapidly, and many lives have been lost through neglect of this precaution.

The sight of Canada geese is extraordinarily keen, and they depend on it to detect danger. Hence it is necessary to be dressed in immaculate white, and some men even paint their gun barrels white. We simply drew a white nightshirt over our clothes and tied a handkerchief on our caps. After making this truly elegant toilet, we crawled into our white canvas bags, which contained straw, and awaited the birds. Our heads and arms were outside the bags and our guns and shells at hand, while we rested our heads on a pillow formed by the bottom boards of the boat. The weather was fine, though cold enough to freeze a brass monkey. Thus we lay side by side like babes in the woods, doubtless forming a charming picture, only there were no spectators. The contrast between the white nightshirts and our purple noses must have been exquisite.

Off to the east we saw a small flock of geese flying in their naturally listless way, evidently looking for a place to alight. Now was the time for my friend to show his skill. He began to honk in such a startlingly realistic manner that I had serious thoughts of putting a charge of shot into him, then hanging his remains in a cool place with an onion inside until tender, but I resisted. After a few melodious honks from the dentist, the geese yielded to his blandishments, and, answering vociferously, swung round and headed for our decoys. It was terribly exciting and very trying to lie still and rigid while those superb birds were sweeping rapidly nearer with each beat of their powerful wings, and the air resounding with their calls. But it had to be done; a single movement would have dashed all our hopes to the ground, and in agony and remorse of losing our prey, we should probably have flown at each other's throats and become only a memory to our best girls and creditors.

We resisted all the weaker promptings of our nature and managed to keep perfectly still while the flock circled slowly over us. Finally, seeing nothing alarming, they slowly descended to alight among the decoys. Now was our chance. Precisely at the same instant we arose to a sitting posture and blazed away at the geese, not over thirty yards from us. I was shooting an 8-bore weighing fifteen pounds and carrying seven drams of powder and two ounces of B shot. Two geese fell to my first barrel. Then, with powerful, long strokes the frightened birds hurled themselves higher into the air, and I dropped another with my left. My dentist friend had done very well by getting a bird with each barrel of his 10-bore.

The geese were all so hard hit that there were no runners, and we soon had them set up along with the other decoys. Our method of setting them up was to sharpen a small twig and insert one end under the bill and the other in the ice, while shaping the neck artistically. During the afternoon we had a chance at another flock, but killed only two birds. We had stupidly neglected to cover up some bloodstains on the ice, and the birds detected it fifty yards out. They sheared off and gave us a long shot instead of a near one. Thus our bag consisted of seven geese, but we were more than satisfied. Indeed, we never did so well again, although we had good shooting for the next three weeks.

# Selfishness Cured
## by "Kansas Chief"

At one time in the late 1880s, a wealthy young man—whom I will call George—boarded with my parents. George had quite a streak of selfishness, and I will tell how I repaid him in his own coin, and perhaps cured him.

My father sold a bunch of hogs in the fall. I was to deliver them at Iola, Kansas, twelve miles away, so George and I planned to take our guns and have a preliminary duck hunt on the beautiful Neosho River. We got everything ready the day before, loaded up the hogs in the morning, and got an early start. We both wore our Hallabird shooting suits. I had my three-barrel Baker gun, and George carried a Moore 12-gauge. We saw a bunch of ducks on the way to town, and George got four mallards with two shots before I could load my gun. We delivered the hogs,

# Selfishness Cured

put up our horses in the livery barn, ate dinner, and secured permission from Dan Horvilla to shoot in his pasture pond that afternoon. I made up my mind to teach George a lesson in selfishness if given the chance. It so happened that I had the chance and gave the lesson, although it went sadly against the grain.

The pond we went to had been dry all summer, and large sunflower weeds, sixteen to twenty feet tall, had grown around the edge between the timber and the pond. On the bottom of the pond had grown smartweed and other weeds that were rich in seeds. A recent rain filled the pond, so the weeds came up just to the top of the water. It was a quarter-mile from the river and an ideal duck resort. Ducks had just started arriving in large numbers, and many hunters were out on the river and on the three big lakes nearby. The gunners kept the ducks constantly stirred up. No one had been to Horvilla's pond as yet, so we had a fine chance to approach the game. We went cautiously in sight of the pond and could see many ducks on the water just beyond shotgun range, so we stopped to form our plans. George took the choice side as usual, and he proposed that we should not shoot until a large bunch had settled near us in good range. I knew exactly what this meant, and later my surmise proved correct.

My Baker was the better duck gun, with two 10-bore shot barrels and a .44 rifle barrel, and I had the best ammunition. The time was at hand to give George a hard rub. But I decided to wait and allow my companion to break his own plans and give me a good excuse to cut loose for myself. We separated, George taking the east side, which had a natural blind close to the water. Meanwhile, I took the west route and had poor cover.

The ducks arose without a shot from us. I could have killed two, but I wanted to give George the chance to break the plans he had made.

The wind was blowing quite hard from the south. We both understood that the ducks must, of necessity, alight while flying against the wind. As they were coming downwind from the south, they could not brace their wings to drop onto the pond until they had turned and circled back. We spoke of this and agreed not to shoot until some had alighted against the wind between us. I had to go much farther than George to get in position, and I could see him in his blind long before I got to mine. Then he did just what I expected. He shot at a pair of mallards that came downwind like an express train. He missed them both and thus broke

Baker's patented three-barreled shotgun from the 1 July 1884 L. C. Smith catalog. Prices ranged from $75 for Quality No. 1 with English stub twist barrels to $200 for Quality No. 5 with the finest Damascus or laminated steel 10- or 12-gauge shot barrels and .44-caliber rifle barrel.

his own plans and showed his selfishness. All the ducks came in downwind, as they had just been scared up from the river or lakes by other hunters. I said nothing, but shot and killed two out of four that came my way. Meanwhile, George was shooting and getting nothing. George was a splendid wing shot on chickens, but did not allow for the greater speed of ducks and held "dead on," and, of course, shot four feet or more behind them.

When I had bought my gun, all the catalogs seemed to harp on the great advantage of having the hammers below the line of sight. (The hammerless gun was yet in its swaddling clothes.) My own desire was to have a combined gun, so I bought the three-barrel Baker with hammers above the line of sight. I had much experience duck shooting and had learned how far one must hold ahead of a swift bird. Thus to fix my gun for pass shooting, I took off the hammers and filed notches in both of them to act as sights when the hammer was at full cock; then I put them on again. When the birds flew swiftly from right to left, a bead through the notch in the left hammer would throw the axis of the bore just enough ahead to center the bird. The farther away the bird, the farther ahead the true aim. And by always shooting the right barrel first, I had no trouble in killing my ducks, as the gun was an extremely close and hard hitter.

All the ducks came downwind, and George shot at them as they came in. George did not believe it was necessary to hold ahead, and the result was that I did all the killing. George did get three birds by shooting at the leader and accidentally killing one behind. The ducks came so fast that my thirty-six loads were soon exhausted, as were George's. We left a good number of birds with our host and took thirty-six to town.  I traded twenty-four for ammunition and took the rest home.

George never said anything about breaking his plans, and neither did I.  He asked me if I held on the birds, and I replied that I always took deliberate aim and distinctly saw the muzzle sight on the bird when I pulled. George could not understand his poor shooting and was just superstitious enough to think that it was all bad luck caused by breaking his own plans.

DAY'S HUNT of WILD GEESE near WILLOWS, CALIF.
Kittinger, Artist

# Duck Shooting in Southern California Years Ago

## by Robert E. Ross

The sport of duck shooting in southern California has seen many changes since 1887, when I first began hunting. In that year and for some time after, there were no laws of any kind protecting the birds, no bag limits, and, with one exception, no duck clubs. In the immediate vicinity of Los Angeles there was then a good bit of marshland and a number of ponds and lakes on which wildfowl of all descriptions were plentiful. At that time Los Angeles was a small town; now [1920] it is a city of almost 700,000 souls. Many of the marshes and lakes have been drained, the open season is three and a half months, the bag limit is twenty-five, and practically the only shooting to be had near the city is on the preserves of the many ducking clubs.

# When Ducks Were Plenty

I have kept an almost unbroken record of my shooting for the past thirty-two years, and, in looking over my old journals, I am impressed that shooting opportunities have remained here. The birds apparently still visit, though their feeding and resting grounds have been so much restricted of late that fewer birds stop here throughout the winter season than formerly. To give eastern sportsmen an idea of southern California duck shooting as it was in the good old days of the 1890s, I will select from my journal a day typical of the sport back then.

In November of 1893, I was shooting at a club's preserve in Orange County, about sixty miles south of Los Angeles. The marsh was located on the banks of the Santa Ana River, about three miles inland from the coast. The preserve, controlled by the Greenhead Club, was only a few hundred acres in extent, but the adjoining marsh spread out for thousands of acres: tule land, threaded with sloughs and dotted with ponds and "holes" in the tules. At the foot of a bluff the growth of tule was so thick and the fallen tules so matted that a natural dam was formed. The river, meeting this obstruction, backed up its waters into a shallow lake covering three or four hundred acres. It was from stands in the tules on the border of this lake that our shooting was done.

A heavy wind began to blow that day, a wind that we call here a "Santa Ana." It should be called the "Cajon," for it roars down the pass of that name, and generally blows for three days with high velocity. The birds had been driven out of the marsh by the morning shooting and had gone to raft at sea. The bulk of them would ordinarily have remained offshore until evening, riding in immense bands, acres in extent, about a mile beyond the line of breakers. But when the Santa Ana started to blow, flocks of ducks began pitching into the marsh and whirling down the lake in battalions.

About an hour before sunset we loaded every decoy we could find into a light skiff, or "tule splitter." Wading along the edge of the lake, we pushed the skiff near the head of the backed-up river where it divides into several shallow channels. Here we used dead cockleburs to construct an inconspicuous circular blind, and left two wooden shell boxes for seats. We set a hundred or more decoys in two stools, hourglass fashion, with the smaller stool heading upwind from the blind. Then we went back to the cabin, had supper and a nightcap or two, and retired to our bunks. The wind was howling like a band of demons loosed from the pit, and the cabin rocked and groaned.

It seemed that I had just gone to sleep when Sarnow, our Alsatian keeper, was shaking me by the shoulder and calling "four o'clock!" We reached the blind shortly before dawn, and, seating ourselves on wooden boxes, we opened the shell cases to have our ammunition supply within easy reach. Kenneth was shooting an L. C. Smith, and I had my Parker—both 12-bores.

The east was flushed with an angry crimson from the dust raised by the Santa Ana. Great banks of tules stood black against the east and were whipped almost level by the screaming wind. We were cold, even in our heavy sweaters and jackets. Bands of birds constantly flashed over us, blown like down before the wind; or else, with laboring pinions, and making poor headway, they bravely tried to breast it.

Kenneth, rubbing his hands to keep warm, leaned over and howled in my ear, "Let's take only bull widgeon!"

# When Ducks Were Plenty

I nodded. "All right!" It was light enough to distinguish the colors of the different species, so it was time to shoot. Heading upwind toward us and moving slowly was a band of about fifty widgeon, necks outstretched, pinions beating rhythmically, the white splotches on the wings of the drakes plainly discernible in the dawning light. Kenneth and I half rose. There were two sharp cracks — the bark of three and a half drams of Schultze — followed by two more cracks and four birds crumpled. They were then caught by the wind, and landed in the marsh grass twenty yards back of the spot where they had met the charge of shot.

The four reports caused great bands of widgeon and other fowl to rise from the marsh downwind, and these birds began flying into the wind and passing over us in a steady stream, not more than thirty yards high. For a while the shooting was as fast as we could load and fire, and with a proper allowance for the drift of the shot, it was the easiest and prettiest sport we had ever enjoyed. The birds were not all widgeon. There were many swirling flocks of teal, strings of mallard and pintail, and the ever-present shoveller. But we passed them all up for the widgeon, and of these we shot only drakes — "bulls" as we called them.

Steadily the wind hummed and roared over the marsh, and just as steadily the layers of shells in our cases grew lower. Still the wonderful flight continued; the birds were unwilling to beat to sea, as it was then too rough to raft. We kept careful count of our fallen birds. A little before nine o'clock Kenneth called to me, "I have fifty-six down, let's stop!" I had counted fifty-one to my gun. We withdrew our charges, left our guns in the blind, and went out to gather the birds.

# Duck Shooting in Southern California Years Ago

Half an hour later, after we had scoured the marsh grass in a wide circle about the blind, we piled up our morning's bag and started to string them on straps. There were 104 widgeon, and all were bulls save three! Sarnow had been watching our shooting through the glasses from the shelter of an old shed on the bluff, and, seeing us gathering in the birds, came out to the blind and slung one heavy strap across his shoulders. The other strap Kenneth and I slung on a willow sapling, and the three of us trudged back to the cabin, turning our heads to breathe, for the gale drove the breath back in our teeth when we faced it.

After we rested a bit and had loaded the birds in the wagon for the drive back home, we walked to the edge of the bluff and swept the lake and marshes with field glasses. There were apparently more birds than ever. Great banks of fowl formed dark splotches on the lee of every wall of tule and sheltering bank, while in the air, level with us as we stood on the bluff, great flocks were still battling the wind we call "Santa Ana."

# No Ducks on Currituck Sound

## by Alex Hunter

My shooting diary for Tuesday, 3 March 1891, has the following entry: "Bitter cold—got up at three A.M.— a heavy norther blowing." Now here was a day that should present Currituck at its best. Wilson, my guide, declared that there would be royal sport and urged me to carry an extra supply of ammunition. Alexander, Valk, and I sat silent and inert in Wilson's boat as we traveled to the hunting grounds at one mile an hour. Our marrow nearly froze in our bones, in spite of heavy clothing. But we stood it without a murmur, eagerly anticipating abundant wildfowl and good shooting.

# No Ducks on Currituck Sound

On reaching the sound, Alexander chose the point, while Valk and I decided to occupy the sink box that was situated about two hundred yards from land. These boxes are a favorite with the Currituck clubmen and are by far the most comfortable places to watch and wait for waterfowl. Sink boxes are about five feet square, made of cypress plank about two inches thick, and are carefully caulked and pitched. They are sunk in the feeding grounds, with about four or five inches left above the surface of the water.

It was a disagreeable and chilly task to set out the decoys, and it took us over an hour to arrange them properly. Then, with numbed hands and stiffened bodies, we crawled into the box. It protected us from the icy wind so that we were almost comfortable. We told Wilson to go to the swamp but remain in sight so we could signal when we wanted him.

We had some shooting for about half an hour after daylight and knocked over exactly twelve ducks between us. Then came a lull that lengthened into a long interlude, with not so much as a feather moving in our vicinity. We crouched down in the box for several hours, getting colder and colder, until at last we could stand it no longer. Slipping a few shells in our pockets, we waded to shore and found Wilson asleep in a bed of rushes where the long swamp vegetation afforded shelter from the careering blast.

We got out our lunch and started a fire, and such a fire it was! There was no driftwood or bushes in the swamp, only stalks of the slender cat-o'-nine-tails. Wilson went to work on these stalks with his knife and succeeded in keeping up a spasmodic flame that served to warm our hands if nothing else. Every now and then an eddy would find its way through and blow dense aromatic smoke in our eyes, causing them to smart like fire. Wilson got tired, so we took reliefs. Valk and I managed by careful nursing to keep the flame alive for a couple of hours. We then returned to our sink box, feeling smoky, blinded, and miserable. We were there until dark, but didn't fire half a dozen shots between us.

It was after 9:00 P.M. when we returned to the club-house and found that Alexander had left for home at noon. His sole spoils were one goose and one duck. We had noticed that all the blinds, as far as we could see, were manned by anxious gunners—mostly keepers, natives, and guides—but few did any shooting. Indeed, one blind was set with goose decoys alone, and its occupant did not fire once. Whoever that man was, he certainly possessed as much patience as an Indian brave and enough hope to stock a colony.

On Wednesday the wind had lessened. Valk was so tired and disgusted that he refused to heed the guide who entered our room with his lamp to announce, "Time to get up." I therefore started out alone and spent the entire day at a new point a couple of miles higher up the sound, where not a gun had been fired throughout the season. A broad

*We got 11 out of 12 this time.*

creek emptied into the sound, and Wilson said it was as good a stand as could be found in the section. He told me of having killed one hundred fifty canvasback and black duck with a muzzleloader five years ago in this very spot. But my all-day vigil was rewarded with only two geese and five ducks, all strays, and we did not see a respectable flock all this time.

Ten to twelve days passed with every variety of wind and weather. We gave the place a fair and impartial trial, but our conviction was that the wildfowl are not in Currituck Sound. We got the news of all the other clubs from the sportsmen's rendezvous at the post office at Knotts Island. It was the same dreary tale. Our club of nearly thirty members was not largely represented, as only a fourth had put in an appearance, and most of them left after a day's experience. Our party of two was the only one that remained.

The splendid club of Swan Island had but one solitary clubman who had been alone for a couple of weeks. Currituck Club with its valuable territory was entirely tenantless, not a single member having appeared on the scene. The fine establishment of Monkey Island was practically closed. I stopped for a short while at the Martin Point Club, which had as much territory and profitable franchises as any club in the sound, and found the keeper leading a more lonely life than Robinson Crusoe, for that charming castaway had his man Friday and a tame goat, while the keeper had only his dog.

The famous Palmer Island Club, the richest and most exclusive one in Currituck Sound, was as empty as a church on weekdays. The explanation for the absence of the clubmen was that they were in direct communication with their keepers by the wires of the lifesaving stations. The keepers occupied the boxes, blinds, and batteries on likely days. Had they killed fine bags and telegraphed that fact, in a couple of days there would have been a rush of clubmen from every quarter of the union to Currituck. But the wires flashed back to all inquirers: "No weather and no ducks; no use to come."

The few clubmen who wanted an outing and had been at these places when the season opened had nearly all gone back home. Great as their disappointment had been, it was tenfold more bitter to the keepers and guides. A bad season for them is what a short session of Congress is to the average Washington boardinghouse keeper: a crusher of hopes and a house of sorrow. Yet I have no sympathy for the guides and keepers, for it is as much their fault as any other that the ducks are gone. Every local mother's son will shoot ducks in the night if they can make half a dollar by doing so. "If I don't, the others will," they argue. "What's the use of stopping?" As it is, many of them are reduced to as near ruin as one can get in Currituck. But it is their own fault. Not content with their legitimate gains, they want every dollar possible, break all the laws, and kill every waterfowl they can, in and out of season.

The natives say, "It's the weather; a hard winter will bring the ducks." But I think the open winters are not answerable for the absence of ducks; the causes I have enumerated must bear the blame. I believe in calling a spade a spade. Under the existing state of things, the place is dead for duck shooting, and the costly shooting privileges are not worth the stock of a bankrupt railroad.

# A Day's Hunt at Lily Lake

## by Alex Friend

No doubt most readers, after looking at the accompanying plate, will picture Lily Lake as a remote haunt far from civilization, one of those inaccessible and lonely hunting grounds that our imaginations hold dear. But they will be mistaken. A two-hour run by conveniently timed trains links Chicago to this paradise for businessmen with hunting instincts and limited time. Lily Lake is almost a suburb of the Windy City.

# When Ducks Were Plenty

One day last fall, a friend gave me the tip that jack snipes had begun coming in from the north. With praiseworthy promptitude, I pulled my 12-gauge out of the office vault, rubbed the dust out of its shining barrels, laid in a supply of sixes and eights, and added a box of threes for a chance shot at ducks. Then I telephoned George Reitz, an avid gunning companion who's always ready for a hunt at the drop of a hat. George said he could have his gun, paraphernalia, and dog at my office by three o'clock, so I rearranged some business affairs to make room for my intended trip. A little before three o'clock, Reitz came in with boots and dog and a happy look on his face. An hour later we were steaming out of Grand Central Station on the Mapleleaf train for our fifty-mile run to Lily Lake.

Suppertime found us making swift tracks for the comfortable abode of my old friends, Mr. and Mrs. James, half a mile from the Lily Lake Station. We were soon settling comfortably around a hardy meal of honest country cooking. Long experience has made Mrs. James the perfect entertainer of that particular species of mankind, the hunter. She has studied his peculiar habits and tastes and understands him through and through. After supper we went out for an evening stroll about the "corners." As we walked down to the town's single store, the frequent *honk! honk!* of passing flocks of geese convinced us that the next day's sport would prove interesting. We bedded down early, and my night's sleep was one continuous vision of flying ducks, geese, and jacks.

The next morning we were up before light and, having packed our coat pockets with the ample lunches left out for us, made haste for the lake. After putting out our decoys, we sat listening to the sounds of ducks flying by in

# A Day's Hunt at Lily Lake

the dark. We longed for dawn. Hardly had the sun's first rays glinted the promise of a glorious October day when a pair of mallards wheeled and would have settled in our decoys, had not a loud report and several ounces of our lead caused them to drop in the water some thirty yards from the blind. Reitz and I had agreed that the first man to miss a bird was to pay all the expenses of our outing.

"Well, George," I said, "why didn't you shoot? This cost you the trip!"

"Me shoot!" exclaimed Reitz in his usual positive way. "Why, you dunderhead, I killed those ducks. I don't even believe you were loaded!"

Investigation, however, proved we both had shot simultaneously, and all bets were declared off. The ducks now came in swiftly and kept us busy until the heat of the sun began to make our blind uncomfortable. George then suggested we try the marsh for jacks.

Shooting Prairie Chickens.

*Back in the bad old days before Schultze wood smokeless powder, double barrels were no guarantee of a second shot.*

# When Ducks Were Plenty

We were just stowing our game away when a whirr caused me to raise my eyes and gun. A covey of prairie chicken, flying like the wind, went over us in perfect duck style. "*Bang! bang! bang! bang!*" went our four barrels, and then three chickens kept the ducks company in the tails of our coats.

The marsh proved full of jacks. At three o'clock we had killed seventy-five, and were so well satisfied that when a heavy rain caught us on our return trip to the James's house, our soaked clothing could not dampen our high spirits. We topped off a great day's hunt with a great supper and declared by our actions and words that it was much appreciated. Then we took the late train back to the city, feeling full and contented, and carrying an usually heavy game bag for city suburban shooting.

# Black Duck Thanksgiving

### by "R" of Lowell, Massachusetts

I had the pleasure of visiting a friend in Hancock, New Hampshire, last season and enjoyed two days of sport with the gun. On Thanksgiving morning of 1896, we learned there were some ducks on Rye Pond, a small muddy place on the road to Stoddard, about four or five miles from the village.

We put our guns into the buggy and drove to the woods on the east side of the pond. The wind was north-westerly and blowing quite hard. We thought that with careful work we might get a shot at the ducks by crawling toward them from the edge of the meadow to some large stones near the water. We stopped at the foot of the pond near the road and took a survey through field glasses. The wildfowl were at the upper end of the pond in shoal water among the lily pads—five, all black ducks.

# When Ducks Were Plenty

We could see them as they tipped up and worked along the bottom, feeding. The black duck, or black mallard as it is sometimes called, is the finest of all ducks found in this section.

The horse was driven a short distance down an old road and hitched to a sapling. Our plan was to approach the birds from downwind so they could not wind us and or hear us. All was well until we came to the edge of the meadow, where we had to leave the woods and crawl about seventy-five yards in the open. It was necessary to crawl low and keep the rocks between ourselves and the birds to block their view, for had they seen a motion or heard a sound they would have jumped instantly.

We found that there were one to two inches of water in the meadow under the dead and seemingly dry grass. But the genuine sportsman is seldom thwarted by trifles when there is game in sight, so back we went to where we had seen several boards on a little bridge over the brook. We selected two of the best and returned to the meadow, where we launched the boards carefully and noiselessly, side by side, on the wet ground. Then we pushed one ahead of the other and crawled along, drawing the first one up and then pushing it ahead, and so on, until we had gone the whole distance, not in solid comfort, but after a fashion. When we peered over the top of the rocks we saw that the ducks were still there. Their demeanor while feeding revealed their utter lack of suspicion.

We waited a few minutes, hoping they would bunch more tightly. Then we trained our guns on them and agreed to fire at the word, each selecting a duck. The birds were at about forty yards and moving away from us. The signal was given, and the birds jumped—that is, the two that were able to did. So did we. As soon as we were on our feet, we pulled on the other two as they were climbing fast, and between us got one down. Three had stopped at our first fire—two dead and the other one hard hit—but it took two more charges at sixty or seventy yards to put him on his back.

The birds were all in sight, but how were we to retrieve them? They were so near and yet so far. We had a hundred-foot line that would not reach even if we could throw a forked stick over them. But my friend had not come all this way to lose the ducks after shooting them. He scavenged a few rails from a nearby fence and retrieved the two bridge boards we had left at the rocks. With a few green withes cut from the osiers at the edge of the meadow, in half an hour he had tied together a raft on which he was poling out among the lily pads and merrily singing, "A life on the ocean wave, a home on the rolling deep." His navigation may not have been of the highest order, and the time was not the quickest ever made for the distance sailed, but with raft, pole, and hip boots, he managed to recover all four of our ducks and return to the landing without being shipwrecked. They were a pretty bunch, with bodies plump in hand, and feathers dark and glossy in contrast to their orange legs. We felt well paid for our hard work.

We hid the birds under the buggy seat and went home, assuming a "fisherman's luck" aspect as we drove into the yard. We gracefully submitted to considerable chafing from the "boys" for half an hour or so. We allowed them to have all the fun they could, and we played our parts well, for we enjoyed it as much as they did. One old gentleman said he was sorry that apples had been so plentiful this year; barrels were scarce and high, so we could not barrel up our game to send to market. Then they all laughed heartily at what was considered a good joke. As soon as the old man could recover his speech, he added that there was plenty of ice in the cellar, and he would furnish cold storage for us until barrels were cheaper and obtainable. After another round of laughter we pulled our four plump black ducks out from under the wagon seat, and the mirth suddenly ceased. We put them on the scale, and they weighed eleven pounds even. Thus the good-natured joshing turned to gratitude as we were asked to accept a vote of thanks for furnishing Thanksgiving dinner.

# My Three Blackbreasts

## by Wilmot Townsend

Weeks ago I cut the cedars that serve as my blind. I selected them from a grove some two hundred miles from their eventual destination of the marshlands on the coast. As I sent the hatchet thwacking into their soft stems, I thought of how they had stood watch in company with the forest patriarchs for years. Could they but speak, what tales they might tell of huge owls that make the woods echo at night with uncanny laughter, of browsing deer and flocks of turkeys. But they were mute, and I toiled among them until a goodly number were piled in my boat, to be stowed later on board the yacht.

# When Ducks Were Plenty

It is possible to construct a blind from materials found at the marsh, but for the spring flight I prefer the young cedar so plentiful on the upper farms in Virginia. The color blends with the tender green of the marsh at this season, and one or two good armfuls may easily be carried in a small boat to a shooting place. I select young trees from four to five feet in height and trim the butt to a point for easy thrusting into the soft sand or mud. Thus prepared, a cedar blind may be constructed in a few moments.

I usually build in the shape of a small square and interlace the twigs after I am seated therein. Of course, the smaller the structure the better. A dozen well-covered young cedars will suffice, and I prefer to let the breeze circulate freely, as it keeps the bugs away. One cannot be careless of his motions in such a loose structure, but I would rather be careful than suffer the misery of a close-built blind with its hoard of bloodthirsty gnats.

One recent morning I went to the margin of a shallow pool, perhaps half an acre in extent. Just where this pool is situated I am too selfish to tell, as this spot is known to but few of the native gunners. I discovered it accidentally by watching the flight of birds above the marsh when they were returning from the bars and flats as the tide rose. With the glass I had seen bunch after bunch pitch into the marsh about this spot, and this led to my investigation of it.

After taking ranges, I started into the marsh with all my paraphernalia in the small boat. Following the windings of a broad stream branch that seemed to head in the right direction, I pulled for a long time along its tortuous course. Finally, weary of investigating blind leads, I ran the boat on the mud and scrambled ashore

# My Three Blackbreasts

to look about. The same unbroken level marsh was everywhere. I could not even discern the glint of a pond hole. As I was about to retrace my watery way to the yacht, I chanced to glance seaward and saw a thin wisp of plover head in over the meadow from the beach half a mile away. They flew straight as an arrow until almost out of sight. Then I saw them pitch. In five minutes I was lugging a backload of cedars, decoys, gun, and shells over the marsh.

Before leaving the boat, I took the precaution to fasten the painter to an oar thrust deep in the meadow bank. I tied my handkerchief aflutter from its end to guide my return, well knowing that the tenderfoot can lose all sense of direction in the monotonous level of these marshlands. It was a hard tramp of some two miles, but worth it, for when at last the glistening water of the little pond caught my eyes, I found it alive with birds. Some were basking on little sedge islets that dotted its surface, while hundreds were grouped about the sand on its margin. Advancing steadily, I drove them all up and resisted the temptation to dust the more tardy flocks that waited for the last moment before leaving.

In half an hour I had rigged out, and there you would have found me that bright morning. How still it was! There was no wind that I could detect, so I was forced to guess at the best location for the blind. I selected a spot where the meadow jutted well into the water and planted my cedars just where the tender green of the springing sedge ended. Then I scattered my decoys well about, some twenty yards in front, with an odd space here and there. My seat, built after the fashion of a ship caulker's stool, was set firmly in the turf within the blind. I opened my cartridge box at my feet. Then I bent and interlaced

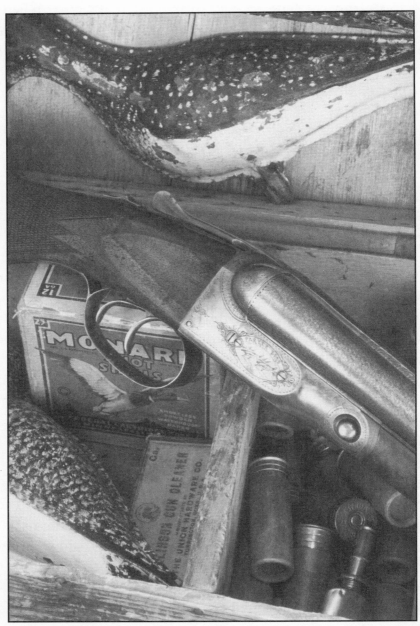

*Parker Brothers GH grade 20-gauge with fine Damascus steel barrels. "Tinnies" are Strater and Sohier 1874 patent shorebirds. Gun courtesy of Pete Wall.*

the cedar twigs in front and on the sides until they were nearly level with my eyes when sitting upright, and I left many untouched so that the blind would not appear too artificial. This done, I stepped out to survey the structure from a bird's eye view and, after a touch here and there, found it to my liking. I lit my pipe. There is no time that a pipe tastes so good as under these circumstances.

Quietly smoking, I awaited the return of the birds, removing my pipe now and then to call. A turkey buzzard dropped to the meadow on one side and stalked about slowly, peering under every patch of drifted sedge and into each tussock that came in his way as he searched for eggs. Vagrant crows dotted the marsh, busily engaged on the same quest.

I had just given a plover call, when, to my surprise, it was almost immediately answered from behind. An instant later three superb blackbreasts hissed right over in rapid flight. How I pleaded with them to return. In silence they sped on, until, at the far side of the pond, they seemed to think better of it and turned. They headed back for the decoys darting on curved wings. I got a lap on two and actually saw them both twist over the sight as I pressed the trigger. I tried to swing on number three, but he doubled back and came right in before I could cover him. I rose and turned and cut him down directly behind the blind out on the meadow. They had been so sudden, so unexpected! It was all over before I had time to think of what I was doing. Then the immensity of my success began to dawn on me. The very suddenness of their onset no doubt contributed to the result. I shot instinctively and well.

Was I elated? I am not one of those human gunning machines who shoot every bird that passes his blind.

# When Ducks Were Plenty

Although not adverse to achieving precision in shooting, somehow it never seems to happen. But those three dead plover, two in front and one in the rear of my blind, gave me a sensation that I shall never forget. I picked them up and put them gently to one side, smoothing the ruffled plumes and feeling good all over.

While admiring my blackbreasts, I chanced to look, and there over my decoys were several dowitchers. To raise the gun and fire was the work of a second. But to my utter astonishment they whirled away untouched, and even my second barrel yielded the same results as the first: nothing. Evidently the giddiness of success had for the time-being unnerved me, though I soon came round. For three hours I had grand sport. Then, as the tide fell, the flight slackened and soon no birds were in sight, save the buzzards and crows.

I made two trips to my boat that afternoon, one with my rig and another with an elegant lot of birds. But of all I carried, my three blackbreasts were my finest cargo.

# Close to Home in Minnesota
## by "J. W. G. D."

This is not a story of big bags and fine shooting, but rather a plain, unvarnished tale of moderate bags and many misses, of outings of immeasurable pleasure, all within an hour's ride from St. Paul, Minnesota. We hunted in places where one could go out Saturday night after work and return early enough on Monday morning to get brushed up and open the office at nine o'clock. Birds were fairly plentiful last year, and the weather on Sundays was all one could wish for. Minnesota weather is quite different from that in the east, where two, three, or more days of every week one stays home and listens to the drip, drip of the rain off the roof, and spends his time between a book and watching the weathercock on the barn, praying for it to turn westward.

# When Ducks Were Plenty

My first spring hunt last season was on 27 March 1899, a little over two weeks before the ice had left the river and ducks were reported on their way north. My friend Sam and I had gone out at daylight, waited patiently until nearly noon, and killed but two ducks. It then started to rain and sleet and, as there was not a feather moving, we gave it up as a bad job. The following Thursday morning, I called Sam and asked him to go down again that night for a shoot on Good Friday, but he said that he'd had all the spring duck shooting he wanted. I was compelled to travel alone to my friend's farm.

That afternoon I was lucky enough to get through my work and change my clothes in time to take the five o'clock train. A ride of three-quarters of an hour brought me to a little way station where I met Olie, and we were soon covering the three miles to his farm. The country was just beginning to look spring-like; the buds were swelling, and in some places the farmers were breaking ground in preparation for their spring sowing. Olie said that no ducks had been about since the previous week's storm, although the sloughs had been free of ice for a week or more, and the weather had been mild and clear.

When we reached the farm, I put on my long boots and got out the boat. One of Olie's brothers wheeled it down to the slough, a quarter-mile below the house. My boat is a Mullins metal duck boat, and in spite of being called a tin pan by some of my friends, it is a nice little thing for two medium-weight men to shoot out of. I have used it three falls and three springs and shipped it nine times by freight, and it is as dry and light as the day I bought it. I had an axle and pair of wheels made for it, and it can also be strapped to the top of a wagon. A couple of fellows could take it any-where on land, and it has saved us many a sore shoulder.

# Close to Home in Minnesota

When we reached the slough, not a feather was moving, so I cut a boatload of rushes and willow brush and then sat down to look for birds. A pair and a small bunch passed by heading north. Then it grew dark, so I turned the boat over and returned to the farmhouse for supper.

We got away early the next morning when it was still as black as midnight, and a lantern was necessary to find the path to the slough. Two men from town were at the head of the slough where they had built their blind the morning before, so I went down a quarter of a mile to my boat, launched her, and rowed across to the opposite shore. I found the muskrat house that Sam and I had used the Sunday of the storm and soon had my dozen decoys blown up and anchored, just as it was beginning to get light. The muskrats had thoughtfully built a large house in the best position for a blind. I dug out the rear side to form a little fort that reached nearly to my waist when standing up. By using the reeds and brush I had brought with me, I soon had an ideal blind.

As I sat looking toward the decoys strung out in front of me, I faced north. The opposite shore, distant a couple of hundred yards, was high and under cultivation, while back about three hundred yards were the woods, separated from me by reeds and low marsh. This slough lies in a bend of the Mississippi River and is about half a mile long. By looking behind me, I could see over the trees to the bluffs on the opposite side of the river.

It was getting light enough to shoot, despite the low clouds. I began to wonder if the day was to be a bust, when two ducks swung into the decoys. Both dropped dead when I fired right and left. Three more birds came in; I let the first two alight and killed the third as it hovered for an instant. Then I did the same to the others as they jumped. I began to think it was dangerous for a duck to come my way, and could see myself carrying a nice bunch of birds back to town that evening.

Soon birds were moving steadily up the river. They came up over the woods at the east end of the slough, dipped down, flew straight up the middle, and, seeing my decoys, made a big swing and headed into the wind that now was blowing a gale from the east. It seemed they wanted to settle down and have a rest. A pair of bluebills flew up and decided to stop when I gave them a couple of shots. Then a lone bird came straight across the water. I pressed the trigger and expected to stop the incomer, only this incomer kept on going.

Next came three mallards, high up. They flew to the slough with their leader, an old drake, letting out a regular *quack! quack! quack!* I squawked back in my best mallard style and could see the old fellow turn his head and look down at the decoys. When they reached the end of the slough they turned back and circled three times. On their fourth trip, just as they were over the decoys, they set their wings and dropped until they were about ten feet over the water. They

*Flight shooting.*

caught themselves and hung for an instant, with red legs dangling. This is what I had been waiting for. Selecting the drake and his partner next in line, I gave it to them right and left. But instead of dropping like two wet rags, all three climbed at least twenty feet in one jump and away they went, with me watching them until they disappeared in the west.

This was too much to stand, so I got in my boat and took a little row to steady my nerves and perhaps change my luck. I picked up my four birds. The first two were bluewings, but to my disgust the second pair were mud hens. I then changed my decoys, setting them farther downwind and above the blind, as I found I was getting too many shots away to my right. I do better work when the birds pass from right to left. As soon as I got back in my blind, a bunch of bluebills came in low, but instead of dropping three or four, I only wing-tipped one. I stood up and gave it the right barrel as it swam clear of the decoys. The shot splashed the water three feet to the left of the bird, and the second barrel gave the same result. It suddenly dawned on me that the east wind was blowing a gale straight across the decoys from my right and had affected my shooting. Birds fly slowly when coming upwind to the decoys, and I had not allowed for the drift of the shot. My third shot at the cripple did the work, and the bird drifted down with its white breast uppermost and its legs waving a last farewell.

I profited by my discovery. As the flight kept up well, by eleven o'clock I had an even dozen birds in the blind, after having lost three or four cripples. Of course I missed a good many birds, but they dropped often enough to make it interesting. My luncheon had long since been exhausted, so I paddled back to the landing and returned to the farmhouse for dinner. I found the other men had quit in disgust and started for home. I was not much surprised, for one of them was stout, wore a black hat, and seemed to dislike sitting down and keeping out of sight. It was a wonder to me that they ever got a shot. He loomed up as big as haystack, and a nearly blind duck could easily have seen him a mile away.

Olie was waiting with the team when I returned to the farm. After retrieving my decoys and piling my hunting gear in my boat, we started for the station. Thus an enjoyable trip was ended. My bag consisted of two bluewing teal, five baldpates, and the rest bluebills. They made quite a nice little bunch when tied together, and we found them excellent eating the following week.

On the drive back to the station we had a fine view of the river, and it made me think of my initiation into Minnesota duck shooting two springs before. But now it looks as if our spring shooting is a thing of the past, as the legislature, at the behest of the sportsmen's clubs, has closed spring shooting for an indefinite time. While it is nice to get out into the country after four months of close confinement in an office, I will gladly give up spring shooting in hopes of being amply repaid with improved shooting in the fall.

# A Comparison: 1844 to 1900

### by "Adirondack"
### (pseudonym of L. E. Crittenden)

Before me lies a copy of an old New York Central time-table printed in 1844. The contrast between transportation then and that of today provides a striking object lesson in the progress of the United States over the last fifty-six years.

In 1844 it took Frank Forester 30½ hours to travel from Albany to Buffalo by mail train. In 1900, by the Empire State Express, it now takes 5 hours and 37 minutes. In 1844 the Albany to Buffalo fare was $11.50. In 1900 the fare is $6.15. In 1844 the route from Albany to Niagara Falls was by rail to Syracuse, then via Oswego Canal and Lake Erie, a distance of 333 miles, with a $10 fare, and 32 hours travel time. In 1900 the distance by New York Central is 305 miles, the fare is $6.15, and the travel time is 6 hours and 14 minutes.

In 1844 the cars were lighted with candles. There were no sleeping cars, and meals were obtained at primitive taverns.  The physical conditions of the roadway made long and tiresome delays necessary and a journey an irksome undertaking.   In 1900 the cars are lighted by both gas and electricity; they consist of luxurious sleeping cars for night travel, and magnificently equipped parlor cars and coaches for day trains.  Dining cars furnish meals equal to that of the best hotels.  There are luxuriously furnished smoking and library cars, and magnificent observation cars where a person may sit and study the ever-changing scenery and the constant succession of cities and towns that make the New York Central famous.

## *Editor's Note*

The current *Rand McNally Road Atlas* shows Albany to Buffalo via the New York State thruway as 301 miles. Until recently the speed limit was 55 miles per hour, and the trip would have taken 5 hours 45 minutes by car, without any allowance for toll booths and pit stops for fuel, food, and drink.  According to "Adirondack," the same trip would have taken eight minutes less by rail in 1900.  The IRS allowed 31.5 cents per mile for business use of an automobile in 1997, which for the Buffalo trip comes to $95 for auto mileage plus tolls.  Therefore, the $6.15, turn-of-the-century transport to good hunting grounds was faster, more luxurious, considerably more productive, and a lot cheaper (inflation notwithstanding) than it is today.  Perhaps by now many readers share my conclusion that when it comes to wildfowling, we were all born a hundred years too late.

In 1848, Henry William Herbert wrote of transportation in the "Introductory Observations" for *Frank Forester's Field Sports of the United States and British Provinces of North America*.  In it he lamented that "the country is

# A Comparison: 1844 to 1900

*A prairie shooting wagon.*

everywhere intersected by railroads that enable the city
pot hunter to move about with his dogs and to transmit
the subject of his butchery to the market cheaply and
speedily. . . . [His plunder is] easily disposed of by the aid
of conductors and other employees on the railroads who
share the spoils with the killers." Frank Forester's observations on expeditious rail travel were in the context of a
circa 1844 mail train taking 30½ hours to travel 305 miles
from Albany to Buffalo at an average speed of 10 miles
per hour.  By 1900 the train was in its glory days, with
193,000 miles of interconnecting track crisscrossing the
United States, and a train on the Albany to Buffalo run
could average 50 miles per hour.  Although the railroads
would remain a popular mode of travel for another fifty
years, the advent of the motor car in the late 1890s made
hunters even more mobile, and the haunts of wild game
and wildfowl became increasingly accessible.

Frank and Charles Duryea built the first American
"horseless carriage" in Springfield, Massachusetts, and
manufactured thirteen of these gas-powered inventions

# When Ducks Were Plenty

*The Stevens-Duryea automobile.*

in 1896. There were 8,000 motor cars on the American roads by 1900, but these first automobiles were extremely expensive—costing from $1,200 to $5,000—and country "roads" were then little more than wagon wheel ruts that turned to mud when it rained. Henry Ford founded the Ford Motor Company in 1903, and five years later introduced the relatively inexpensive Model T. By 1915, approximately 2.3 million autos were registered in the United States—about half being Ford's Model T—and the price dropped from $850 in 1908, to $440 in 1915, then to $275 in the 1920s. Suffice it to say that improved transportation and modern firearms had a doubly deleterious impact on wildfowl numbers.

# Slaughter of Wildfowl at Hog Island Light Station

## by Dr. R. W. Shufeldt

A remarkable flight of ducks, brant, and geese converged on Hog Island Light, off the coast of Virginia, for three nights on 22 February 1900. The keepers of the light were aroused from their slumbers by the honking of brant. The man in charge of the lighthouse had to call for assistance, as the wildfowl were breaking window panes from the top to the bottom of the tower. Some geese would even go through the wire mesh that protects the revolving beacon. When the keeper's assistant arrived with guns, they shot for an hour and a half as rapidly as they could load. The guns soon began to get hot and the men's shoulders sore, but the wildfowl kept coming. Finally, the cry for ammunition was heard, but none could be had. The keepers had shot 225 times and bagged 228 wildfowl while defending their lighthouse, and when they ran out of ammunition they had "enough geese for a mess." The birds were in fine condition and were boxed up and shipped as presents to friends of the keeper.

On the following evening this wonderful flight commenced again, made up principally of brant and geese. There being no ammunition on hand, the lighthouse party took to capturing the fowls alive, and this sport did not cease until one hundred fifty of the birds had been taken, including several geese. The enormous rush of the flight eventually drove the men from their positions, causing them to take cover, while at the same time all the lamps were extinguished in the watch room and the panes completely knocked out of three windows. The revolving light had attracted thousands of ducks, brant, and geese, a circumstance supporting the conclusion that waterfowl are not yet extinct on the coast of Virginia.

# Brant Shooting on Great South Bay

### by C. R. Purdy

Brant shooting on the Great South Bay is confined entirely to the spring months. Although a few flocks pass through in their southern migration in the fall, they never stop in the bay in any numbers. In the spring, however, they select these waters as a resting place on their return to the northern breeding grounds. A few scattered flocks drop in about mid-March, and the flight improves each day until at its height about the first week of April, when the brant are in the bay in great numbers.

If we could have as many brant in the fall as we have in the spring, they would furnish magnificent shooting. But when they arrive in the spring after being shot at all winter in southern waters, they are all too familiar with the devices used by man for their capture, and it takes hard work under extremely favorable circumstances to make a fair bag. My average, as I find by looking over the score book, is thirty to thirty-five birds a week, and my best day in fifteen years yielded forty-seven brant.

Brant prefer to feed on shoals near a beach. They cannot dive for their food, so they wait until low tide when they can reach the young marine grasses by dipping. It is in such shallow places that the gunner rigs out his shooting outfit, which usually consists of a single battery with about seventy-five brant decoys, or a double battery with up to one hundred decoys.

Old eel grass on the shoals will often collect until it forms a small island, with the top just below the surface of the water. These seaweed bunks vary in size: Some are only large enough to protect the battery and make a lee for it, while others are up to sixty feet wide. When a bunk forms on a good brant shoal, the gunner who rigs out under it may remain in his battery even in a heavy blow, while the same battery could not stay afloat on open water. In heavy wind the brant do not fly high as they do in light weather, but hug the water and decoy readily. The following is an account of brant shooting from a battery behind a seaweed bunk on the Great South Bay:

"It's no use talking," said the captain, "These old birds are getting too well educated for us." He was remarking on a group of five or six hundred brant that we had discovered living at Flat Beach. Although bunch after bunch had headed for our decoys, we were able to kill only seven. They had a bad habit of rising in the air when about two gunshots from the rig, apparently to see whether there was anything dangerous beyond our nice-looking decoys.

"If there had been more young birds, I think we would have done better," the captain continued. "I don't know what we should do next. I suppose we might as well go east as far as Old House Flat and look around."

So we raised sail on the sloop and stood east. We had been working the brant since the twentieth of March, and it was now the third of April, but as yet the big flight had not arrived. Some days we picked up three and others seven or eight, but the season's score looked as if it would be slim. However, we had a comfortable thirty-foot sloop with a large cabin and plenty of good things to eat, so we could afford to wait and see. It was almost dark when we sailed into the cove near Old House Flat and anchored close under the beach.

"I don't like the looks of the weather," remarked the captain, as we were tying up the sails. "I'm afraid we are in for a nor'easter." After supper I went on deck to take a last look at the weather, and things did not look promising for the next few days. The wind had pulled in to the northeast, and a heavy scud was driving across the moon. So, paying out more chain, we turned in, to be lulled to sleep by rattling blocks and the dull boom of the surf on the beach.

The alarm clock got us out at four o'clock next morning, and after a quick breakfast we went on deck to look about. It was dark, and the wind still blew hard from the northeast, almost at a gale. This meant too much sea on the flats for a battery. I resigned myself to a day in my bunk reading. But by seven o'clock the tide began to ebb, and the captain announced his intention to go ashore and collect driftwood for the stove. He had been gone about half an hour, and I was dozing over my book, when I heard the scraping of the sharpie alongside, followed a minute later by the captain's head thrusting in the cabin door.

# When Ducks Were Plenty

"The quicker we get a move on the better," he said. "There's a good seaweed bunk in shore to the east of us, and brant are going to the beach."

That was enough for me. I was out of the bunk in a minute and on deck with the glasses. I could make out a hundred or more brant on the flat, about a quarter-mile to the east, and several bunches were swimming around to the windward of the sloop, heading toward shore. We wasted no time. The stops were thrown off the head fender of the battery, and the sloop's stern shoved around until she lay broadside to the sea. Then the centerboard was dropped to hold her there. This made a lee for the battery, which was launched over the side. But the seas were so rough that the battery could not carry the iron duck decoys when clear of the boat, so seven of them—each weighing twenty-five pounds—were lowered into the stool boat. My 8- and 10-gauge guns in rubber covers and two rubber bags containing shells followed next; then I threw in an old gunning coat for a pillow and a rubber blanket for the bottom of the box. We towed the battery with the stool boat, using the anchor rope of the head fender for a tow line, and reached the seaweed bunk after twenty minutes of hard work.

Our seaweed bunk was a good thirty or forty feet wide and formed a splendid shelter for the battery. It was the work of only a few minutes to throw the head fender anchor under the lee of the bunk, straighten the battery downwind, and drop the tail stone. Guns and traps were put in the box and the decoys deployed. We were using eighty brant decoys with our single battery. Leaving me in the box, the captain started back to the sloop to exchange the stool boat for the sharpie. He would have to tend the battery from shore, as the shallow water and direction of the wind prevented use of the sloop. After getting the sharpie, he rowed over to tell me that he was going to send up the brant that we saw feeding on the eastern shoals.

Then I was alone, with only the wooden decoys bobbing and moving around me. I dropped down the side fender and walked around to wet down the deck. The old gunning coat was doubled up on the headboard and the rubber blanket spread on the bottom of the box. I took the covers from my guns, loaded the 8-gauge with No. 2 and BB shot, and the 10-gauge with No. 4s and 2s. With the 10-gauge on my right and the 8-gauge on my left, muzzles sticking over the foot of the box, and shell bags between my feet, I lay down to wait for something to happen.

I wondered if the captain had started the birds and rolled partly over to look back. No, he had not gone far enough, so I dropped back down in my box and watched a three-masted schooner outside the beach going west under lower sails. Suddenly the air behind me was filled with a sound like tearing muslin. I grabbed the 10-gauge and twisted around to take a part in the disturbance. A bunch of shell duck had dropped to the decoys, but were gone before I could get on them. The next minute I was pleased that I had not shot, for the captain started the brant, and they were coming down the shore. They seemed to be a large squad; too bad they would not come in smaller bunches at different times! I hugged the bottom of the box and began to calculate. Should I try the 8- or 10-gauge first? Should I let them alight, or would it be better to shoot them in a bunch in the air? I was considering these things, when, to my horror, I saw the whole flock going to leeward and not noticing the decoys at all. This would not do, so off came my old black hat; flirting it with a quick motion along the edge of the box, I called brant talk as loud as I could. How quickly they noticed! The leaders of the bunch lifted in the air and caught sight of the stool.

In an instant everything changed. The head birds turned for the decoys; the rear birds mounted the air and fell in behind. They were all talking at once and hugged the water where the heavy wind was least felt. "They will come in like chickens," I thought, "and if I work those two guns all right, the brant are going in the pot tonight." Along they came, a regiment of them, beating slowly against the wind. How big they looked! Soon the half-dozen birds in advance reached the decoys and dropped in, but something alarmed them. It was useless to stay down out of sight any longer. I seized the 8-gauge and aimed at a thick bunch of birds to the left. How they tumbled out! Those No. 2s did great work, and nine birds dropped out of the sky.

The captain came rowing down like a steamboat to gather the birds. He shot over the cripples, and we owned nine brant. I stood up in the box to receive the captain's congratulations and was staggered by his question: "What's the matter; weren't they near enough?"

"Near enough! Of course. Didn't you pick up nine?"

"Well, then, you must have had buck fever. Two guns in the battery and you only fired one shot at a crowd like that!"

But no matter, I had no time to indulge in regrets and felt that we must take advantage of the ebb and get what birds we could. The captain had just gotten nicely out of the way when seven brant came in from offshore and four dropped in around the decoys. Picking up my 10-gauge, I scored a clean miss on the three flying birds with the first barrel, but managed to kill two with the second, and, catching up the 8-gauge, I stopped two others as they started out of the decoys.

After looking around and seeing nothing on the wing, I sat on the edge of the box for a while, when a low *k-r-r-r-k* from the decoys drew my attention. A single brant was swimming through the rig. It is strange how sometimes they will come up and alight when you are sitting up, while at other times you cannot get them near the decoys no matter how well you are hidden. I made sure of our solitary friend, for I wanted to get out of the thirteen hole.

Soon another flock came in sight offshore, and I got down in the box to watch them. I hoped they would not get around behind me, for this turning one's self into a corkscrew to peek backward in a battery is not agreeable. They didn't show up on the other side of the box for some time, but at last I saw them well up to windward. They had dropped in and were swimming toward the beach. There was nothing to do but lie close. Five minutes passed, and an old black duck came over the box, looking down in my face. I detected a leer in his cunning old eyes, as if he knew I would not shoot at him with all those brant around. It seemed as if by this time the brant must have drifted down before the heavy wind, so I rolled over a little and saw one swimming just outside the decoys. The rest were almost at the head fender.

When the brant were close enough, I swung around with the 8-gauge and took careful aim at the waterline of the nearest three birds. They jumped as I pulled. My first barrel scored a blank, and the second barrel stopped but one bird. Now for the single one! He headed down-wind and was a long shot off. I sent both barrels of the 10-gauge after him. The first hit him hard, but it looked as if he might get away. He set his wings and scaled in toward the sharpie, where a puff of smoke rose, and a moment later he was tossed rudely onto the stern seat. Then the captain shoved slowly toward the battery, picking up the dead, and came within talking distance.

"We will have rain soon; it's getting thick off there to the east," was his first remark. "You didn't do much with that last bunch," was his second. But just then a boat going to the beach west of us sent up a big cloud of brant, so the captain started back for shore. I stood on the deck to look around while he was rowing away, and offshore to the east and west I could see the white tails of brant, bobbing up and down on the waves. The wind was doing big work, and the birds were stopping in the bay, tired from facing its force.

More brant were coming now, flock after flock, and the shooting was brisk. I made some rank misses that I could explain to myself, but not to the captain, who was watching me from the sharpie with a powerful pair of field glasses.

Forty-seven brant lay in the bottom of the boat when the rain began to come down in torrents. I tried to stand it long enough to bring the score to fifty, but the shower bath on my upturned face was too much. I reluctantly called it quits, and the captain brought me back to the sloop. Those forty-seven noble birds were stowed away, the rig picked up, and rubber boots and wet clothing taken off. Then with dry clothes, feet in old comfortable slippers, and a stiff hot scotch to take the chill out of the bones, we loaded our pipes and proceeded to talk it all over.

"Well, what do you think of today, Cap?"

"I would like to have made fifty," he replied, "but if we do half as well tomorrow I will be satisfied."

We came near it, but that is another piece of history. The day behind the bunk has always remained my big day at brant, and, with the great increase of batteries and the brant

# Brant Shooting on Great South Bay

growing wilder each year, I know only too well I will never duplicate that day's bag, at least in the Great South Bay.

## Editor's Note

The preceding passage was taken from *American Duck Shooting,* written by George Bird Grinnell in 1901. In the book Grinnell credits "Mr. C. R. Purdy, whose long experience as a brant shooter entitles him to speak with all authority, and who has kindly contributed his notes on brant shooting in the Great South Bay." Grinnell's book was a bestseller at the turn of the century, and remains a popular and relatively easy

Brant or "Brent" geese.

acquisition for today's gunroom library. According to Riling's bibliography, George Bird Grinnell was the author or editor of at least nine other books about hunting big game, small game, upland birds, and wildfowl from 1883 to 1926. *American Duck Shooting* is perhaps his best known title as an author, even though he collaborated on several books with Theodore Roosevelt.

Grinnell's *American Duck Shooting* is a seminal work on wildfowling, and the section titled "The Decrease of Wildfowl" defined wildfowling (fact and fiction) as it was at the turn of the century. William Randolph Hearst's "yellow press" was then engaged in various crusades against such outdoor sports as live-bird trapshooting and fishing with live bait. The editorial mentality was, "My mind is made up; don't confuse me with facts." For example, the *Chicago Times-Herald* condemned a National Fly-Casting Association tournament held in Chicago's Garfield Park in 1897, because one event specified "half-ounce rubber frogs." According to the yellow press:

> "Use him as if you loved him," said Izaak Walton, when advising the neophyte how to best adjust his frog on the hook. Surely these Chicago votaries of old Walton must have forgotten this advice when they jerked the poor frogling through the air, not for the purpose of ultimately catching a fish, but simply to acquire the art of casting. Would not some substitute of proper weight have sufficed them? There was no more necessity for them to use live frogs than there is for holiday soldiers to use bullets when fighting a sham battle. It was cruel—unnecessarily cruel—and ought not to be repeated.

Hearst and his cohorts railed against almost anything, without regard to the actual merits or demerits of the situation, just to sell more newspapers. Other Hearst articles condemned the shooting of "Peoria blackbirds" (manufactured by Fred Kimble) as being unnecessarily cruel to clay pigeons. It was all but impossible for non-shooting sportsmen to get a grip on reality. And although the constant decrease in wildfowl numbers in the 1890s added genuine fuel to the editorial fires set by the yellow press, it was hard to separate fact from fiction. Perhaps the most colossal sham scandal was contrived by the National Game, Fish and Bird Protective Association, in collusion with Hearst's Chicago newspaper. According to Grinnell:

# Brant Shooting on Great South Bay

One of the most grotesquely fantastic explanations of the scarcity of wildfowl was put forth several years ago in the newspapers, and was soon afterward attributed to a society bearing the impressive name "National Game, Fish and Bird Protective Association." This story told of the enormous destruction of wildfowl eggs in the northwest for commercial purposes; millions, shiploads and trainloads of such eggs, it was gravely related, were gathered annually in Alaska and British America, and shipped thence to points in the east. There they were manufactured into egg albumen cake. The story was taken up by the newspapers, and those who had fathered it were eager to be interviewed and tell all they knew.

In 1895, *Forest and Stream* set out to investigate what truth there was in the story; the basis, if any, for the alarming statistics quoted; and whether an abuse that required checking actually existed. It was obvious that if anything approaching the quantity of eggs mentioned were shipped each season from railroad points on the north Pacific coast, someone would know about it. Yet a careful inquiry among the persons who professed to know most about this subject, and who were most eager to be quoted on it, elicited no information whatever. Then *Forest and Stream*'s investigation turned to the transportation lines, custom houses, and those persons concerned with the manufacture of commercial albumen, where these carloads and shiploads of millions of eggs were supposed to be consumed.

It was found that the transcontinental railway lines, which by necessity would have taken the wildfowl eggs to the east, had never transported any. Inquiry at the different custom ports showed that wildfowl eggs had never been imported through any of the custom houses along our northern or northwestern border. Finally, the largest manufacturers of albumen in this country stated that practically all their product was obtained in Russia, Germany, and France, where hens' eggs are very cheap.

This, then, was the conclusion to the matter: Those who professed to have information on the subject were unable to substantiate the stories they told; the transportation companies carried no such eggs; none were ever received at ports of entry; the albumen trade knows nothing whatever about them; and, in view of the total lack of evidence, the story proved to be pure invention.

A century later we get our information from radio, television, newspapers, magazines, and the Internet, and presume (perhaps in error) that each medium audits the veracity of the other. One would think that there is little present risk of being led down the primrose path of disinformation by yellow journalists, special interest groups, and political jive jobbers. Yet, consider the current media debate about tobacco in the context of a supposed national consensus against smoking: More people smoke than voted in the last presidential election! Visualize the "information superhighway" as a narrow one-lane road of tabloid "yellow" newspapers, and you have some idea of the late-nineteenth-century media blitz that prompted state-by-state regulation of hunting and fishing.

# Market Shooting on Chincoteague Bay

## by Howland Gasper

The number of wildfowl in Chincoteague Bay, Virginia, recently has been augmented by the arrival of large flocks from the south—chiefly redheads and broadbills, though there are at least a dozen other kinds. A few days ago I accepted the invitation of a local market hunter to accompany him on a shoot, and we had an excellent day's sport. But what I most desired was to become acquainted with the methods of the pot hunter, which contribute more to the extermination of wildfowl than the ordinary shooting practices of sportsmen.

After sailing to the edge of a flat about two miles from shore, we drove some bushes into the sand to make a small pen about three feet across and ten feet long.

# When Ducks Were Plenty

The hunting boat was drawn into this by the man who had carried us to the spot. He then withdrew to stir up the ducks. About one hundred and fifty decoys were scattered to windward, the avowed purpose of this arrangement to secure a closer approach of ducks.

Our arrival at the blind at ten o'clock in the morning was not very propitious, as during the noon hours the wildfowl rarely fly. A few singles and pairs approached and were shot down with such skill by my companion that I could not refrain from an expression of admiration. In the late afternoon, when the great flocks began to seek resting grounds, he was afforded an even greater opportunity to exhibit his ability as a marksman.

The vanguard of the afternoon flight consisted of small bunches of birds. Shooting into those, he averaged three and four at a shot and, on one occasion, killed four on the water with the discharge of one barrel. About half an

*A big day's luck at Black Dog Lake.*

hour after the first scatter of ducks had arrived, the larger bunches began to move. One flight of about fifty ducks detected our decoys, changed direction, and approached the stools. They soon arrived and spread their wings, preparing to alight. I raised my gun to my shoulder and was about to shoot when my companion said, "Don't shoot yet." As I lowered my weapon, the flock detected my movement and flew away. When I realized that the chance of obtaining another shot at the same flock

# Market Shooting on Chincoteague Bay

was past, I inquired of my companion his reason for refraining to shoot, as the birds were in range. "Why," he replied, "I never shoot into a bunch of that size unless there's a good chance to kill more than a dozen. Them birds was so scattered that a fella couldn't kill more than a couple with each barrel."

The wisdom of his policy was well exemplified, when, a little later, a flock of about thirty redheads flew down and turned toward the decoys. Throughout their maneuvers my companion's power of mimicry was allowed full scope. Under his seductive influence the whole bunch drew together, braced their wings, and prepared to alight.

Then my companion, realizing an opportunity to earn a week's income in a trice, raised his gun and discharged both barrels almost simultaneously. The loud report of the gun was followed by several dull thuds, and when the smoke had cleared away, the surface of the water was covered with dead and wounded ducks. I snap shot a cripple that was preparing to dive, while nearly all the others which had been simply wing-tipped were allowed to escape, with no effort to secure them by "wasting" ammunition. I paddled out from the blind and retrieved fourteen birds, mostly redheads.

Other flocks continued to visit our decoys until dark. Then we loaded up, and our little bateau was almost submerged by the weight of decoys and ducks. Scarcely had we removed the last decoy before our sailboat came within sight, and in a few minutes we were homeward bound. Our spoils for the day totaled eighty-five ducks; about sixty were redheads, the remainder being broadbills, whistlers, and black ducks.

My companion, while acknowledging that the day's kill had been a fair one, stated with pride that he had frequently shot more than one hundred ducks in a day. The eighty-five ducks of that day were almost exclusively killed by the market hunter, I having been content with occasionally dropping a duck that held aloof from the main flock.

The methods of the above marksman may be regarded as representing the methods of all market hunters in this area. The appalling decrease in numbers of game must be attributed, in a large degree, to this sort of whole-sale destruction. These men, despite the rigors of cold and force of winds, pursue the wildfowl day in and day out as their main source of income.

Sportsmen, to whom the love of the art is above the greed of possession, should make an effort to secure legislation and its rigid enforcement to protect and perpetuate wildfowl shooting, so that not only ourselves but posterity may regale in pursuit of this sport of kings.

## Editor's Note

Howland Gasper's 1893 book, *The Complete Sportsman*, is of the old school: an instructional treatise along the lines of Dr. Lewis's *The American Sportsman* (1855) and John Bumstead's *On The Wing* (1869). Gasper's book is rather dry reading, in marked contrast to his turn-of-the-century column, "Long Island Game Notes." The column, from which this chapter was extracted, was published regularly during hunting season in *Shooting and Fishing*. Gasper used his access to the sporting media to forward his opinions on the then-contentious issue of government regulation of wildfowling. The next chapter describes regulation as it existed on the cusp of the twentieth century.

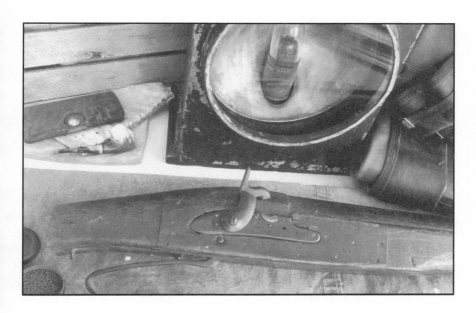

# Lacey Interstate Bird Law of 1900
## by Ed Muderlak

Let us go back for a moment to the early 1870s, when Wilbur F. Parker used his *American Sportsman* newspaper to promote local and state sportsmen's clubs affiliated with national associations. He stated in a February 1875 address to the Massachusetts Sportsmen's Association that:

> [T]he whole question of preserving game is a new thing with the many. We have no power yet of passing a central national law on the subject, because we would arouse prejudices and get into conflict with state jurisdictions. . . . [But a] national association . . . constitutes a central point from which action can be directed on Congress . . . [and] . . . would give harmonious and one-minded support to the efforts of gentlemen who were acting not for a particular locality, but for the whole nation.

*(Picture: Destry's 1⅛-inch-bore Illinois River punt gun and light for night shooting.)*

# When Ducks Were Plenty

At the dawn of the twentieth century, state and local sportsmen's clubs had become a real factor in the promulgation of shooting regulations, closed seasons, and licensing. A civil enforcement action had also evolved, whereby the sportsmen's clubs, on their own initiative, could have an accused violator summoned to court to answer charges brought in the name of the club. As an aside, this power was wielded both ways, as sportsmen's clubs found themselves defending civil enforcement actions brought by humane societies to curb their use of live pigeons for trapshooting. Suffice it to say that enforcement of game laws through the 1890s was confusing and contentious at best, and had few positive results.

Starting about 1895, the editorial positions of the various pulp weekly sportsmen's newspapers—*The American Field*, *Forest and Stream*, *Shooting and Fishing*—strengthened against game hogs and market hunters. Feather hunters were particularly frowned upon, and "foreign" (immigrant) songbird hunters were considered beneath contempt. "Self-restraint" was the after-dinner buzzword of sportsmen at every game-protection association banquet. The diners at these banquets feasted on canvasback duck and terrapin stew, and were, in the words of Wilbur Parker, "without inquiry as to the month or the day of the month."

Jacob Pentz, whose sketch in chapter 11 showed his sensitivity to the passing of the passenger pigeon, had a long career as an outdoor writer and sportsman. As a contributor and editor of *Shooting and Fishing*, he promoted the conservation of game and wildfowl. Note the tone of his editorial, "Babylon Has Fallen," taken from the 26 December 1895 issue of *Shooting and Fishing*:

# Lacey Interstate Bird Law of 1900

We recently printed a communication describing a prodigious bag of ducks made at Great South Bay by a Babylon gunner. Accompanying the article was a photograph, as if to substantiate the almost incredible tale of the killing of 264 ducks in a single day's shooting by a single gunner. Nothing has appeared in print for a long time that so completely aroused the indignation and disgust of sportsmen as this immoderate and selfish bag. Not even the skill of the gunner, nor the statement that no birds were wasted, can lessen the disgust that every true-minded sportsman will feel in reading of this wholesale slaughter by a Babylon gunner. We do not regret publishing the article and illustration, for it has created such a widespread indignation as to probably cause legislative action to restrain insatiable game hogs.

Most sportsmen today intuitively refrain from killing more birds than are sufficient. The man who exceeds moderation is no longer regarded as a sportsman, but is classed as a game hog or a market hunter; he cannot be regarded as a conservator of game, as conservation is recognized as a cardinal principle of sport hunting today. Congratulations by the game hog's friends intensifies the outrage of true sportsmen, who see the waste and say, "Babylon has fallen!"

Never mind the strong editorial position of *Shooting and Fishing* against game hogs and hunting for the market; the sportsmen's consensus had not yet shifted focus from state-by-state regulation to federal government regulation. The following editorial, "Protect the Migratory Game Birds," was taken from the 14 January 1897 issue of *Shooting and Fishing*:

Letters to the editor have advocated national legislation for the protection of migratory waterfowl. This is a subject that few well-informed sportsmen care to discuss. Good reasons are numerous against such fancy relief. The deliberations of Congress are not famous for haste, and when sportsmen see their favorite game being exterminated, they will never ask relief from the legislative body which, if it ever gives it, will certainly not do so until too late for practical use.

National legislation would be exceedingly unpopular. It would not be possible to adjust laws suitable for each state, and so voluminous would a set of national game laws become, that in a short time an extra Congress would be needed to revise and adjust them. Cooperative legislation between the states is the only answer, and every year it becomes more important that sportsmen and lawmakers realize this growing need.

We need only reflect on the extermination of the bison. Men became hide hunters because they knew it was only a matter of months or weeks until the great animals would be gone forever. They argued that as long as other men were rapidly thinning out the herds, they should, in self interest, get their share of the plunder. So widely was this policy followed that men were almost falling over each other in their haste to do what they in their hearts deplored.

And so it is today with our migratory birds. There must be cooperation among sportsmen before cooperative laws can be made. If southern sportsmen follow shady methods, missionary work should be done whenever possible, but sportsmen of the northern states must never go beyond moderation in their shooting, and, as an excuse, say that if they permit waterfowl to escape their guns, the birds will surely be slaughtered in another state.

By the late 1890s, Jacob Pentz's serendipitous call for cooperative state laws had become more shrill at the

# Lacey Interstate Bird Law of 1900

same time cooperation became less likely. Nevertheless, sportsmen pressed for more and more government action, even though it then would have taken a Talmudic scholar to make head or tail of the conflicting game laws already passed by states, counties, and local jurisdictions.

Meanwhile, letters from readers to editors of the various sportsmen's newspapers had gravitated away from discussions of big versus small-bore guns and black versus smokeless powder, to criticism of virtually every method of wildfowling save the one practiced by the writer. If one waterfowl hunter wrote of using live decoys, retorts condemning the practice would appear in the next issue. This condemnation had a chilling effect on reports of large bags and successful hunts as sportsmen feared being called game hogs. Thus many of the stories in this book were written under pen names, or as retrospectives with the implication that "It was thus and so in the good old days, but we don't do it this way anymore."

Sportsmen's clubs and game protective associations were well established at the turn of the century, but the prevailing opinion—almost dogma—was that everyone was a game hog "except me and thee, and I'm not too sure about thee." Meanwhile, the passenger pigeon was all but extinct, bison seemed to be next, and, believe it or not, deer were virtually nonexistent in Illinois and Connecticut and points between. A blurb in an 1897 issue of *Shooting and Fishing* stated:

> The presence of wild deer in the state of Connecticut has been doubted by many, but the 1897 annual report of the Fish and Game Commission says there are at least a dozen wild deer within the borders of the state at the present time. The commissioners

are making earnest efforts to preserve these few
remaining deer.  A fine of one hundred dollars is
imposed on anyone killing a deer within the state.

The dearth of deer had little direct connection to the
extinction of the passenger pigeon, the near-extinction
of the American bison, and the alarming reduction in
migratory wildfowl, but the evidence overall led to the
obvious conclusion that hunting had to be regulated.
Small birds were always considered "fair game" by the
turn-of-the-century flood of immigrants from the south
of Europe; some of the first effective state game laws protected songbirds from the depredations of mostly Italian
and Greek immigrants.  The following is an editorial titled
"Greece and Italy" taken from a turn-of-the-century issue
of *Forest and Stream*:

> Our Boston correspondent records another
> personal encounter between a game warden and a
> foreign shooter.  A warden came upon two Greeks
> killing songbirds, and when he undertook to arrest
> them, received into his body a charge of bird shot.
> He was removed to the hospital.  These Greek and
> Italian and other foreign-born shooters have become
> an unmitigated nuisance, a peril to life, and a con-
> siderable factor in the destruction of song and
> insectivorous game birds.  The Italian immigration
> is bringing to us hoards of people who dream that
> America is a free country.  But in this particular
> respect, they think it means a country where every
> mother's son of them is free to carry a gun anywhere
> and at any time, and to shoot anything that flies,
> without let or hindrance.
>
> It would be a great mistake to imagine that
> these foreign-born shooters and bird snarers are

confined to the neighborhoods of large towns. On the contrary, they are scattered over the country, and their destructive work is not confined to any one climatic zone. New England is full of them, New York has an army of them, and on Long Island the roads and fields and woodlands are full of Italian bird shooters, both weekdays and Sundays. New Jersey has its quota. In Pennsylvania they have given so much trouble that the legislature has sought to check the evil by requiring the unnaturalized gunner to take out a $10 gun license.

We have in this office information on the deliberate shooting of five citizens during the past fall by these people. One gentleman living near the city limits of Pittsburgh saw three Italians shooting song and insectivorous birds in his orchard and ordered them off his land. One of the foreigners said, "This is a free country. We don't have to go." To this the owner replied, "Yes, you do," and thereupon received two loads of shot in his stomach and legs. Fortunately he wasn't killed, although he was compelled to stay in the hospital for many weeks.

How shall we control this pernicious element in its relation to the life of the sportsman in the field? Manifestly the remedy may be found in abridging the privileges of the man with the gun. In short, we are reaching a point where shooting and carrying guns must be classed as privileges accorded under restriction, and not as rights exercised without leave asked of anyone.

By 1900 all states had enacted nonresident licensing laws and at least two states prohibited nonresident hunting altogether. Meanwhile, most states had laws against shooting during spring and summer, and against the possession of wild game out of season. However, some states—New York in particular—allowed wild game to be possessed during New York's closed season, as long as shipping documents showed that the game was procured at least 300 miles beyond state borders. In other words, New York legislators didn't care if the canvasback ducks consumed at their political fund-raising banquets were taken in or out of season, as long as they were procured from out of state.

Apparently the editorial suggestion by *Shooting and Fishing* that states should cooperate in the reciprocal enforcement of game laws was another fine theory that would never become practice, at least not voluntarily. Thus the stage was set for the first federal game law: the Lacey Act of 25 May 1900, which prohibited interstate transportation of game taken in violation of state laws. According to an editorial titled "The Interstate Bird Law" in the 7 June 1900 issue of *Shooting and Fishing*:

> The Lacey Game Bill passed Congress, President McKinley has signed it, and it is now a national law. Briefly described, this law will prohibit interstate traffic in animals or birds killed in violation of the laws of a state. It also prohibits traffic in foreign animals, game, and song birds, and the carcasses or parts thereof. The shipper, the carrier, and the consignee will each be subject to a $200 fine on conviction.
>
> The importance of this new law is great, even though it comes several years too late to save countless animals and birds from extermination that should be alive now. It is not likely that persons who are accustomed to laughing at state laws will laugh at the national law, now that the federal government is to aid each state or territory in punishing violations of its laws by persons living in other states and territories.

# Lacey Interstate Bird Law of 1900

The loophole (and fatal deficiency) of the Lacey Act was that traffic in market game had to be in violation of a state's law for the federal law to kick in. Neither buyers nor sellers were complaining about market game violations, and it was all but impossible for a third-party enforcer to trace the origin of game that was by its very nature best consumed sooner rather than later. In retrospect, it's all too easy to condemn turn-of-the-century hunting and eating practices, while our own grocery shopping and restaurant dining experiences are sometimes suspect. Have you ever questioned the legal origins of that walleyed pike *almondine* or duck *à l'orange* on a restaurant menu? Was the walleye caught commercially in season by a properly licensed fisherman? Did the duck originate from an egg hatched on a properly licensed game farm? Who knows? Who cares? Let's eat!

Not surprisingly, the Lacey Act was (and is) almost universally ignored. Although on the books a century later, the Lacey Act is seldom enforced, except when the federal government helps states with sting operations involving illegally taken game moving across state lines. *The American Field* published this editorial four years after the Lacey Act:

> It is reported that over 50,000 wild ducks have been killed in Barton County, Kansas, this fall [1904], and the larger part of them have been marketed. Most of these ducks were killed on the Cheyenne Bottom, and one dealer is said to have purchased from hunters 2,000 birds a day for several successive days. A good many birds have also been killed on the salt marsh south of Ellinwood, and on Walnut and Cow Creeks and the Arkansas River. It is said that one hunter on Cheyenne Bottom killed 133 ducks in six shots with a magazine shotgun, and that with these guns other men have

killed over 100 birds in six shots; also that one
man has a record of over 500 ducks in a single
day. These reports are enough to make a true
sportsman's blood boil with rage, for it is well known
that such slaughter would not be made if it were
not for the money the birds bring in the market.
So great has been the slaughter of ducks this fall
in different parts of the country that sportsmen are
seriously discussing the question of having laws
enacted prohibiting the sale of game at all seasons,
contending that in no other way can the game be
protected and preserved for future generations.

The fact that over 50,000 ducks were killed in Barton
County, Kansas, and the larger part of them marketed,
was not illegal under federal law in 1904, as long as the
game had been taken legally in Kansas. Further, even if
the 50,000 wild ducks had been killed in violation of
Kansas law, the Lacey Act would not have been violated
if all the ducks were marketed and consumed in Kansas.
There was little incentive for the Kansas legislature to
restrict the shooting; increased numbers of ducks would
only migrate south, to be killed by market and sport hunters
in Arkansas, Louisiana, and Missouri—and these states
prohibited Kansas residents from hunting within their
boundaries. Nevertheless, pressure from sportsmen's
clubs was incessant, and one by one the states began
passing laws to curb market hunting, spring and
summer shooting, and hunting practices that seemed to
violate sportsmanlike conduct in the field. Still,
regulating restraint in one's own state was difficult in
the face of a demonstrated lack of restraint elsewhere.

The "Age of Progress" presented its own special
stresses on wildlife. Firepower improvements, from the

# Lacey Interstate Bird Law of 1900

Punt guns in America were always considered by gentlemen sportsmen to be a tool of market hunters. The British, however, considered "punting" great sport, with Sir Ralph Payne-Gallwey the leading proponent. Sir Ralph's Holland & Holland double-barreled punt gun had 1½-inch bores, weighed 200 pounds, and was 9 feet, 6 inches long. From Lord Walsingham's and Sir Ralph Payne-Gallwey's 1886 book, Shooting: Moor and Marsh.

1860s muzzleloader to the 1870s breechloader to the repeating shotgun of the 1890s, combined with improved rail travel to accelerate the decrease in wildfowl. The draining of marshland, clear-cutting of forests and conversion of wildlife habitat to agricultural and urban uses further depleted wildfowl populations. The advent of the automobile in the late 1890s so improved mobility and access for the masses that it seemed only a matter of time before ducks, geese, cranes, shorebirds, and all other wildfowl would be as scarce as passenger pigeons.

Meanwhile, the various states perfected systems of licensing resident and nonresident hunters. Licensing revenue provided for the establishment of departments of fish and game, and for the hiring of wardens to enforce the proliferating state game laws. These laws protected mostly indigenous nonmigratory game such as deer, turkey, and grouse. But migratory wildfowl continued to be a special problem, as there was little incentive for the states to protect birds that yesterday had not yet arrived, tomorrow would be in another state, and in a week a thousand miles away.

The tug of war between the states to divvy up myriad migrating wildfowl would ultimately be resolved by federal legislation. However, the complex constitutional and political issues implicit in such a remedy would take another twenty years to resolve, and only then with the cooperation with the British Commonwealth and Canada, and several appeals to the U.S. Supreme Court.

# Section III
## 1900 to 1920

By the first years of the twentieth century, most states and territories had laws restricting the "depredations" of nonresident and market gunners, but the federal government had not yet stepped in to protect migratory wildfowl from residents and nonresidents alike. Meanwhile, market hunting and sport shooting continued on an all but year-round "season," and waterfowl were still relatively abundant if one had a place to get at them. This inaccessibility generally necessitated membership in a private duck-shooting club, and travel by yacht, rail, or the newfangled horseless carriage.

The flood of immigrants from Europe, coupled with the dividends paid by the industrial revolution, shortened the work week and increased the demand for recreation. Proletarian shooters with inexpensive repeating shotguns took a toll on wildfowl numbers, and the resulting crowded shooting venues and smaller bags were a rub to the influential clubmen who paid big money for their sport. By the late 1890s, sportsmen no longer exercised gentlemanly self-restraint toward market hunters and game hogs, but called loudly for government action to decrease the slaughter. Thus from 1900 to about 1920, state and federal governments intervened to control and protect migratory birds. The laws passed during the first two decades of the twentieth century spawned the waterfowl hunting regulations as they now exist at the beginning of the twenty-first century.

# The Shadow of a Gun
### by H. Clay Merritt

When we consider water birds—and mallard ducks
in particular—we would naturally expect them to exist in
large numbers. Water covers a large part of the globe, but
most of it is unfit for the home or haunts of wildfowl. The

ice pack covers the north part of the continent for eight months of the year, and drives the birds to warmer climes when winter is on. The great oceans produce no bush, no vegetation, no plot of land upon which the weary traveler from arctic seas can rest. The shores of the ocean are silent, and there are fewer and fewer duck sanctuaries where the bottom is easily reached for food.

As the cities enlarge and spread, and white sails dot seaside resorts, the ducks must go to sea or take their chances in freshwater rivers and lakes. American genius and enterprise are scouring the back bays for new railroads and new lines of travel into the wilderness. Cities are planned, new ships come to port, rivers are locked and dredged, and their treasures transported away.

Many years ago the ducks nested in large numbers on every marsh in which wild flags and course water grass appeared. The Annawan [Illinois] swamps, in common with many others in the country, produced mallards and teal in profusion. Then came a dry spell of several years' duration. Farmers, who had seen a chance to enlarge their realties, made a deal with the holders of these flooded lands. With a system of ditches, the farmers reclaimed so much marshland that the ducks eventually avoided it, and they never cared to come back.

For a while these same ducks bred and thrived on the waters of Wisconsin and Minnesota. Inside the timber belt of northern Minnesota lies an immense prairie country full of rice ponds and laughing lakes that encouraged the ducks to tarry. Here the ducks filled in as they left Illinois in the spring. But the waters were troubled. The ring of the carbine in those wilds was heretofore almost unknown, but then the markets opened for ducks. The ducks could not rest, and they moved again. This time they passed northward, so far that the blast of steam whistles could not reach them. How far northward the ducks have emigrated is unknown, but it is believed many are very near or within the Arctic Circle.

About 1885 we had our last flood of ducks. The waters of the Mississippi were congested with mallards. The same phenomenon occurred along the Chariton in Missouri, and doubtless many other points. The birds were not hard to reach. It was winter, and the slaughter kept up until nearly spring. As one flock was destroyed, new ones came in. Whole carloads were killed and sent to market at ridiculously low prices. Where freezers could be had, hundreds of barrels were carried over into the next year. The market hunter, though, did not consider these mallards as desirable as many other species.

*Clay Merritt from the frontispiece of his 1904 book,* The Shadow of a Gun.

# The Shadow of a Gun

The mallard is a native of no state or territory exclusively. He is known in the waters of Long Island Sound, and also on the Croton River that supplies the aqueduct of New York. He is an inhabitant of the entire west and south, besides his active visits to the extreme north. His lines of travel in the spring and fall carry him along the important rivers. He turns off whenever he can see an open pond to feed and rest. He is always on the lookout. No other duck sends so many scouts ahead to spy out the land. He knows every defense that hunters make to lure him within reach. He knows that the safety of other ducks he sees in the water will grant him like safety. Where redheads and canvasbacks alight, he is all patience and fearlessness. He is less likely to alight by teal and small ducks, which use shallow water near cover, and he has been surprised so many times that at every motion he is fearful an undiscovered enemy will spring up. He is partial to the flags where they fringe deep water and he can sit unnoticed. He is a bird of many associates and is not coy or critical about his companions. He will sport in the air with a flock of teal or even scaup ducks, and on the arrival of a new flock of any kind he is liable to light down among them.

Where hunting is good, many persons seem to desire mallard shooting above all other. But I did not spend much time with them, and what little I did was generally unprofitable. Size considered, they are the cheapest ducks in the market. They are heavy to carry where you have not the convenience of a boat, and the best shooting is often where a boat cannot travel. Besides teal, especially the greenwings, mallards are the most liable of all wild ducks to spoil in a sudden change of warm weather. To draw them reduces their best appearance and value. I am not certain after handling many thousands of mallards that I derived any profit from them. In a few instances they sold remarkably well, perhaps for a first time and under new circumstances, but I never sold any higher than $1.25 a pair, and then only in the winter season just after the Civil War. A dollar per pair had always been the objective, which was rarely reached.

There are wonderful stories about immense numbers of mallards killed by fortunate hunters, but I am not one so fortunate. I never killed but fifty birds in one day, and that only once in the course of three or four hours' shooting. This was in a cornfield adjoining Coal Creek, a mile and a half north of Annawan, and the circumstances were all favorable. Large numbers of mallards had sat in the creek all day, and in the late afternoon they came out over the field, attracted by a thin strip of buckwheat which cut in twain twenty or thirty acres of corn. I had only to step inside the shadow of the corn to hide. A new breechloader had just come out, and I had one of them. It was a pinfire, and already the defect of this kind of gun was apparent. The smoke constantly worked out around the pin. The strain of firing the gun gradually separated the stock and barrel, and it appeared no great prophecy that the breech bolt would soon shoot loose.

I threw down a handful of shells on a corn hill and began to blaze away. The shot seemed to have unusual effect, as perhaps the birds were closer than I imagined. I seldom fired in vain. Small detachments of birds came up steadily from the creek and, viewing the ground, prepared to light down. They returned with one or two less each time. My dog sat by me and picked up all the wounded birds. He knew when a shot was effective, and no matter if the bird fell at twenty or forty yards, he bounded away and brought it in, not once missing a bird. I never shot so fast before, as all my experience had been with muzzleloaders. The loads were strong, and the gun was light. I constantly felt at every recoil that the fastening was gone or giving way, and even doubted whether my head remained. I examined the smoked barrels, saw they held nearly in place, and drove in two more cartridges. In the course of a few hours I secured the fifty mallards above stated and never lost one bird.

With my last cartridge I broke a drake's wing. The bird settled over the top of a hill, and the dog tarried too long, so I went after him. On the way I ran into another hunter who was anxious to know how many men were shooting. I told him there was no one but myself, and explained the action of my new breechloader—the first he had ever seen. He said, "Sounded like all hell was broken loose," and declared that he was going to have a breechloader as soon as possible.

## Editor's Note

Clay Merritt was born in Carmel, New York, in December 1831, and he wrote in the preface to his 1904 book, *The Shadow of a Gun*, that "I was born with a gun . . . [and] I think there was a taint of wildness in my ancestors." But Merritt characterized his parents as backwoodsmen who "carved their way with the ax, and passed their lives with modest comfort, thrift and industry. A gun to them was like a bird of ill omen, and those that followed it were denominated lazy." Nevertheless, the family did have an old flintlock fowling piece—more heirloom than weapon—and Merritt started shooting at an early age. His father had powder but not shot, so he loaded the gun with small white beans and stalked predatory birds to keep them out of his mother's chicken coop. As to first blood: "One day a big owl alighted . . . and I snapped the old king's arm some minutes before it would go off, but at last a spark fell, and the owl was no more." Thus Clay Merritt took up the gun as a child and matured to be one of the most successful market hunters in northwestern Illinois and southwestern Wisconsin.

Clay Merritt was an accomplished market hunter by age thirteen, and plied his trade in New York to subsidize his education. When he graduated from college in 1855, game was getting scarce in New York, and one of his customers said, "You are such a good hunter, I should think you would go west to Illinois where there is plenty of game." Three days later (14 June 1855) Merritt was on the Illinois River at Peru, and began a market hunting career in the west that spanned more than forty years. His contemporaries along the Illinois and tributary rivers were Joe Long, Fred Kimble, Adam H. Bogardus, and a youthful Charles Askins. Merritt was one of the first market hunters to adopt the newfangled breechloading shotgun (albeit pinfire), and he perceived that loss of habitat was a prime cause of declining wildfowl numbers. His occupation was outlawed in 1900 as a result of the Lacey Law and concomitant regulations. Thus he became a writer, and his book is the definitive text on late-nineteenth-century market shooting on the Illinois prairie and western rivers.

# *Breechloading Shotguns*
## *by Ed Muderlak*

America was a rifle- and pistol-oriented country before the Civil War. After General Lee surrendered his Confederate army at Appomattox on 9 April 1865, peace-time production of arms took off in a different direction with the first generation of American-made, breechloading, double-barreled shotguns. Charles Parker of Meriden, Connecticut, built the first "tipping" breechloader for use with a self-contained, 12-gauge brass cartridge in 1866. About 1868 Ethan Allen & Co. introduced a lid-opening 10- and 12-gauge shotgun that used Allen's patented steel cartridge; Whitney was selling 10- and 12-bore breechloaders by mid-1869; and Sylvester Roper manufactured a small number of four-shot, auxiliary-chambered revolving shotguns in the late 1860s. Parker's "tipping" breechloader proved the success, however, and defined side-by-side shotgun and metallic shotshell development through the mid-1870s in the United States.

# When Ducks Were Plenty

Wilbur F. Parker was in charge of the Parker Brothers gun works from the late 1860s through his untimely death in 1876. But Parker Brothers was more than a gunmaker in the decade just after the Civil War. The manufactory fabricated everything from steam engines to drop forges to rotary printing presses, and was the publisher of a weekly newspaper, *The American Sportsman*, from 1871 until 1875. Wilbur Parker was sometimes listed as "Editor and Proprietor" of the paper, which featured articles by leading sportsmen and conservationists of the day. John Bumstead of Boston was a contributor, and in 1869 wrote *On the Wing—A Book for Sportsmen*. This book served as a primer for the then emerging class of sport hunters who adopted breechloading fowling pieces in the late 1860s and early 1870s. Ethan Allen's lid-opening "new-patent" breechloader is pictured in the book, but Bumstead failed to even mention the more popular Parker

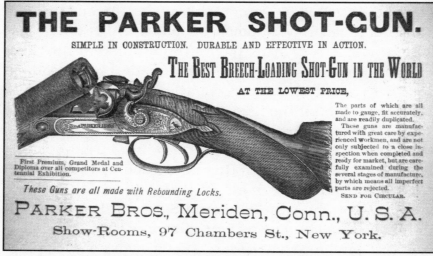

*This circa 1876 Parker hammer gun reflects the state of the art when one-piece extruded brass shotshells had just become available, and "black" was the only powder. From Joe Long's 1879 second edition of* American Wild-Fowl Shooting.

# Breechloading Shotguns

breechloading shotgun. The irony is that by the time Bumstead's book rolled off the press, Allen's new patent proved to be a gunmaking dead end, while Parker's tipping breechloader was the definitive side-by-side double-barreled shotgun of the 1870s and thereafter.

Joe Long was another Boston sportsman who traveled the country in pursuit of game and then wrote about his shooting experiences. Long's book, *American Wild-Fowl Shooting* (1874), told of duck hunting with Fred Kimble of Peoria, Illinois, using muzzleloaders on the Illinois River in the winter of 1870–71. After the season they entered into a friendly competition to have closer-shooting, better guns made for their next outing. Long chose his hometown gunmaker, Tonks of Boston, while Kimble had a muzzleloader built by Secor of Peoria. As the story goes, Tonks refused to build a muzzleloader for Long, telling him that if he wasn't satisfied with the breechloader he proposed, he would give him the gun for free. Long was more than satisfied with his new Tonks gun, and wrote about it at length in his 1879 revised edition of *American Wild-Fowl Shooting*. Meanwhile, breechloaders and the associated paper and brass self-contained ammunition had swamped the market, and Kimble gained fame as "Master Duck Shot of the World," first with his Tonks 9-gauge, next with a 6-bore of his own making, and later with a Parker.

All through the 1870s and 1880s, side-by-side breechloading shotguns were state of the art. Duck shooting usually involved at least two and sometimes three heavy 10-gauge guns in the boat, blind, or sink box. The approved shooting method continued to be that espoused by Bumstead in *On the Wing*: "If a number of ducks are on the pond, wait until they come together so that you can secure as many as possible, and endeavor to shoot them when their sides and tails are toward you. After having discharged both barrels at the ducks on the water, [etc.]." Apparently *On the Wing* was just a book title and not yet the sportsmanlike way to take water-fowl. Meanwhile, upland bird hunters came to favor wingshooting with lighter 12-bores so as to mitigate the rigors of a ten-mile tramp through the boondocks. Also, at the urging of Parker's A. W. du Bray and others, elite waterfowlers and clubmen soon adopted small bores as a means to—believe it or not—conserve game.

Christopher M. Spencer, of Civil War-era Spencer carbine fame, upped the ante in the mid-1880s with the first successful American-made slide or "pump"-action repeating shotgun. Winchester then introduced their Model 1887 lever-action shotgun, and next the Model 1893 slide-action repeater. The first generation of repeating shotguns had five- and six-shot magazines, but weight, balance, and mechanical problems often negated the firepower advantage over contemporary double-barreled guns.

The Winchester Model 1897 "pump" literally blew away the competition. Winchester built and sold roughly 1,025,000 of this most popular five-shot repeater. The new gun was an instant success and became the bestselling slide-action shotgun until the Model 12 was introduced fifteen years later. But it was an article of faith in 1897, among the side-by-side *cognoscenti*, that no repeater could ever balance and shoot like a Parker, Lefever, or L. C. Smith. Repeating shotguns, however, were the future. The new "pumps," especially the Model '97, and the 1900 Browning-patented semiautomatic shotgun, made the double-barreled fowling piece a collector's item by 1905.

One man was responsible for the new wave of shot-guns. John M. Browning designed the Winchester Models

# Breechloading Shotguns

1887, 1893, and 1897, and sold his patents outright to the Winchester Repeating Arms Company. Browning patented a gas-operated semiautomatic repeating shotgun in 1900, and, knowing he had a winner, tried to cut a deal with Winchester for a royalty contract based on guns built. Winchester, to their everlasting regret, balked at such an arrangement. Browning took his patent to Belgium and had his new gun manufactured by Fabrique Nationale (Browning Auto-5), and he licensed his patent to Remington for American manufacture in 1911 (Remington Model 11).

The combined firepower of the Winchester '97, Browning Auto-5, and Remington Model 11 took a toll on wildfowl, and the clash was on between market and sport hunters. California tried unsuccessfully to outlaw repeaters, but the Supreme Court held that a restriction on the design of a shotgun (repeater versus multi-barreled) was a violation of "equal protection." Meanwhile, market hunters were

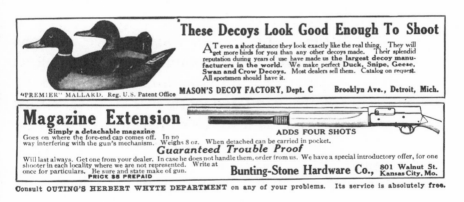

*Mason decoys and a magazine extension for the Remington Model 11 semiautomatic shotgun meant double trouble for waterfowl. Some repeater magazines could be extended to allow as many as twelve shots. Not surprisingly, today's federal regulations limit waterfowlers to three shots, and magazines are plugged rather than extended. From the November 1914 issue of* Outing *magazine.*

extending the magazines on their repeaters to as many as eleven shots without reloading. The inventive genius of American gunmakers had so increased the firepower of shotguns that it seemed only a matter of time before all wildfowl would be eliminated by sport and market hunters, notwithstanding the Lacey Interstate Bird Law of 1900.

The Lacey Act of 1900 was the first federal intrusion into police powers that had previously been considered reserved to the states by the Tenth Amendment. The constitutional issue of states' rights was avoided simply by making it a federal offense to move "illegally taken" game across state lines ("interstate commerce"), but only if the game was taken in violation of state law—an all-but-fatal defect in the Lacey Act. The next chapter, "Shooting the Chesapeake Duck," can be read in the context of the state of Maryland protecting resident market hunters and their shooting concessions with restrictive licensing, thus relegating the migratory wildfowl to the status of "fuel" necessary to run the state's "economic engine." Suffice it to say that little in the way of constructive wildfowl protection and control was accomplished by the federal or state governments prior to 1920. But in that year (1920) the Supreme Court validated both the Migratory Bird Treaty of 1916 with Canada and the Migratory Bird Treaty Act of 1918, which implemented the provisions of the treaty. Meanwhile, it was mostly business as usual in the sink boxes, sneak boats, goose pits, batteries, and blinds, except that ducks were no longer plenty.

# Shooting the Chesapeake Duck
## by David Bruce Fitzgerald

On the Chesapeake things are not as they once were. Old men who have lived half a century or more in the vicinity of the bay tell of a time when the upper waters of the bay and tributary rivers—Gunpowder, Bush, Sassafras, and Elk—were literally black with wildfowl. They say it was then sometimes necessary to place a man in the bow of a boat to sweep the ducks out of the way with a pole in order to make a passage through the great huddled flocks. There were then no ducking laws, no closed days, and no restrictions. Sport shooting was just getting started, but there was an immense, wholesale slaughter for the market in which the old-fashioned bored-out musket and the swivel gun played important parts. If stories told on the ducking shores may be believed—and there seems to be no reason to doubt their truthfulness—there was a long series of seasons when one had only to throw a few bushes together for a blind, seat himself behind this screen, and blaze away as rapidly as he could load. There were millions of ducks in sight, and they had not yet learned the caution that is now apparently instinctive. The size of a gunner's daily bag was limited only by his supply of powder and shot, the toughness of his shoulder, and the coming of darkness.

The swivel gun was simply an enormous shotgun that rotated on a pivot in the bow of a boat, thus taking up the recoil. It was used at night when the sleeping birds were huddled closely together on the surface of the water, and, as this "son of a cannon" carried a full pound of shot, each discharge cut a distinctive lane through the mass of ducks. Almost from the first, however, the swivel gun was held in disfavor. Long before its use was outlawed, no man would admit to the ownership of one of these weapons, but scores of them were hidden away about the Susquehanna flats and along the shores of Bush River.

As might have been anticipated, this enormous slaughter rapidly thinned the flocks that year after year sought the headwaters of the Chesapeake. Finally, when

*The long gun. This circa 1884 etching courtesy of Dan and Jane Behr.*

# Shooting the Chesapeake Duck

diminished numbers of birds suggested total extermination in the near future, the legislature of Maryland stepped in and placed a score of restrictions on the duck gunner. One must now approach the ducking shore only after elaborate preliminaries. The first step is to secure a license, and this costs twenty dollars to shoot from a sneak boat or fifty dollars for use of a sink box. Also, when this document is read, it is found that it confers the privilege of shooting only on Mondays, Wednesdays, and Fridays, and it is absolutely prohibited to use a gun larger than 10-bore. When the sportsman reaches the scene of actual operations he soon discovers that the restrictions legally placed on his work are not mere formalities, but are very practically enforced by police boats that regularly patrol the entire ducking territory.

The one obvious defect of the Maryland ducking law is that by subtle interpretation of the statutes, a license is

*"The surface-boat, coffin-boat, battery, sink, or box." From Dr. Lewis's 1857 book,* The American Sportsman.

understood as granted to a boat rather than an individual. If the owner of a sloop has an official shooting permit nailed to the cabin wall, he feels at liberty to set out more than one sink box, and the police will not molest him. This legislative oversight, judicial leniency, tacit understanding, or whatever it may be enables the sportsman who has no equipment of his own to shoot under the license of a regular ducker or market gunner whose entire outfit he hires by the day. This arrangement does not augment the number of gunners to any alarming extent, however, as any sportsman financially able to engage a ducking outfit could certainly, if necessary, supply himself with an individual license.

The sportsman of moderate means may shoot the Chesapeake duck, but would better select some locality other than the flats at the mouth of the Susquehanna. There at the head of the bay, on the best shooting ground in the world, the price of sport runs very high, with one hundred dollars a day usually asked for rental of a sloop, sink box, and the services of the owner. However, except at the height of the season during the first half of November, when the hotels in Havre de Grace are crowded with gunners from the north, it is possible to reason with ducking outfitters; a sportsman who is acquainted with the situation and has a little time to bargain can often secure a reasonable discount. The marking down of prices is as much a feature in duck shooting as in the dry goods trade, but it is useless to expect cheap and good sport at any time in the vicinity of Havre de Grace.

To all intents and purposes, duck shooting on the Susquehanna flats is restricted to wealthy men and market gunners. With the one class it is a sport; with the other an industry, and a profitable one. Canvasbacks killed on the flats or in the immediate vicinity are worth ten, sometimes twelve dollars a pair, and the price of redheads is only a shade lower. If shot lower down the bay, the same ducks would bring only a dollar a pair. This extraordinary difference owes entirely to local conditions. The Susquehanna flats are alluvial deposits, widening in fan shape from the mouth of the river, thinly covered with water, and extending three or four miles into the head of the bay. A peculiar water plant, the valisneria, or wild celery, grows abundantly in this soft, alluvial mud. This plant at once furnishes to the wild duck a food of which it is very fond, and in the course of a few days transforms it from a bird of fishy flavor into the most delicate gastronomic tidbit with which the epicure is acquainted.

The headwaters of the Chesapeake produce the celery-fed duck. Therefore, if the sportsman merely wishes shooting, let him go somewhere else — to Deal's Island, Hog Island, or the environs of Synepuxent Bay. Let him select the Susquehanna flats only if he desires to bring down birds of the finest and most elusive flavor, and is able to pay from five to fifteen dollars each for the privilege of shooting them. This is the minimum price, and no one knows exactly what the maximum is. It is said in Havre de Grace that each duck killed by the wealthy clubmen, who have houses on the Bush and Middle Rivers and in other nearby localities, is brought down at an outlay of seventy-five dollars. This outlay is determined by the equipment used, which ranges from the yacht maintained at an expense of five hundred dollars a day, downward through all classes of small craft to the tiny sloop or scow of the market gunner who only desires a clear profit. The entire value of a market gunner's equipment, including boat, sink box, and gun, is probably not more than two hundred dollars, and to him the first cost of the birds brought down is comparatively nothing.

Save for enthusiasm, the work of the average market gunner leaves nothing to be desired. His shooting is marvelous. Indeed, he hardly considers himself professionally qualified unless he can kill eight birds out of a flock with four discharges of two double guns. There is a local explanation for this phenomenal skill that I will quote: "When a market gunner has a canvasback within range, he sees five dollars at the end of his gun, and he never lets the money get away."

The average sportsman, much less the novice, must not expect to rival the performance of the man who shoots to sell his birds. Familiarity with conditions is essential to success, and one's first day in a sink box is almost certain to prove a tremendous disappointment. That a particular "nimrod" can kill quail and snipe on the wing does not mean he can hit a wild duck, even when the bird is well within range, as "ducking" is quite a different art from field shooting. In a sink box the position is painfully cramped and awkward, the eyes are blurred from staring at the sky, the expedient of handling two guns is confusing, and a dozen unfamiliar conditions combine to make the novice nervous and his shooting unreliable.

About two o'clock in the morning of an "open" day, the scores of ducking sloops and scows in the harbor of Havre de Grace get underway and drop down past the lighthouse. At this point the vessels scatter, each captain steering for a locality that experience or intuition suggests as favorable. As the flats are wide, there is room for all, though, for obvious reasons, the sink boxes must not be placed within gun range of one another.

# Shooting the Chesapeake Duck

Imagine yourself a passenger on one of the ducking sloops. As a paying customer, you may well remain asleep in the stuffy cabin; but if this is your first day out, the anticipation of unfamiliar sport will inevitably bring you on deck to see what is happening. After discovering that the man at the tiller is decidedly uncommunicative and will not even hazard a conjecture concerning the quality of the sport to be expected, you meditate in the darkness and mentally estimate the size of your probable kill. Though it makes you shiver, you welcome the stiff breeze from the north, for rough weather is an almost unfailing precursor of good sport. Wild ducks will not dip to motionless decoys. All the better if there is suggestion of rain in the air. You are after a winter bird, a bird of cold and wind and white-capped waves. No small part of the excitement of this sport lies in braving the elements.

By the time you have finished a couple of pipes, the lights of Havre de Grace are far behind you, and there is a faint, gray streak in the eastern sky. Suddenly the captain growls out an order, and his helper, who has been catching a catnap in the bow, springs to his feet and replies, "Aye, aye, sir!" in true nautical fashion. With great flapping of canvas, the sloop comes into the wind, the anchor falls with a splash, and the sail is lowered on deck. The time has arrived for the second stage of preliminary operations, which includes setting out the sink box, arranging the decoys, and placing yourself in position to shoot. The resemblance of the sink box to a coffin is peculiarly impressive, and the inexperienced are often haunted by apprehension. This long, narrow box made to contain (but not accommodate) the body of a man lying at full length is let into a floating platform

twelve feet long by six feet wide.  The craft will show
nothing above the water except a deck flush with the
surface, and this deck is painted a dull gray to make it
less noticeable.  As far as the ducks are concerned, the
deception is perfect.  They will alight in the vicinity of a
sink box without the least hesitation, apparently unaware
of its existence.

After the box is safely launched, the captain and his
assistant embark in a small boat and tow it to a selected
location, where it is anchored.  The wooden decoys are
then grouped artistically and irregularly within close gunshot range to leeward, and a few are reserved to represent
stragglers, disposed at varying distances from the main
body.  Each decoy is anchored to the bottom by a cord to
which a weight is attached, and, generally speaking, the
more numerous the decoys the better, as a larger flock is
more likely to attract the attention of passing birds.

Five minutes later you are lying flat on your back in
the sink box with two guns and a box of shells.  The
waves are lapping close to your ears, and you are gazing
straight up at the sky.  The rattle of cordage followed by
the flapping of canvas informs you that your companions
have sailed away and left you to your luck.  You find it
necessary to assure yourself repeatedly that your guns
are cocked.  There is a mist before your eyes that you
feel will spoil your aim when the moment arrives.  These
symptoms of nervousness may be expected to disappear
after the first fire.

Your results will depend largely on experience.  If
you have learned this lesson, your disappointment at
seeing no dead ducks floating among the decoys on the
first try will not be so keen.  A duck is rarely killed or
even crippled by the first fire of an inexperienced

sportsman. This applies with equal force to subsequent fire, as no man makes a large kill on his first day, and beginners often return in the evening without a single trophy. It requires a certain degree of self-restraint to shoot ineffectively, time after time, and then sit and watch the speedy withdrawal of successive flocks, without wasting expletives as well as powder. But the eventually successful man is invariably he who regards failure merely as something to be redeemed at the earliest opportunity. If it is a fairly good day, you will not have long to wait for a chance to redeem your first failure, and if your fire is followed by a splash of a canvasback or redhead floating breast-upward on the water, you may consider the day's sport well opened.

If the birds fly freely and decoy readily, the excitement will make the morning hours pass with astonishing rapidity, and by ten o'clock the work of the day is practically over. In the absence of rain or storm, afternoon shooting is generally unsatisfactory. About three-fourths of all ducks killed are brought down between dawn and nine in the morning, and the inexperienced gunner will find that five hours in a sink box is an amply sufficient time in which to acquire chills, cramps, rheumatism, and an acute attack of shotgun headache. By noon the novice will be ready to hale the sloop and seek a haven of rest.

The result of a day's outing on the Susquehanna flats will vary with the season, weather, and skill of the gunner. In the old days of indiscriminate and unreflective slaughter, when marksmanship counted for little and the size of the charge in the gun for much, the gunner stopped when he had as many birds as he could carry home. Later, after the ducks had learned to avoid the shore and it became necessary to go out on the open water after them, a good shot often brought down one hundred fifty birds a day, and this number was occasionally doubled. At present, it is impossible even to approximate this record except during the first week of the season. Beginning with the second week, the daily kill falls off

*"To all intents and purposes, duck shooting on the Susquehanna flats is restricted to wealthy men and market gunners."—David Bruce Fitzgerald. My guess is that the "dude" on this photographic postcard is not a market gunner.*

# Shooting the Chesapeake Duck

rapidly. During the remainder of the season, a show of thirty to forty ducks in the evening is considered very good. Of these, about one-fourth will be canvasbacks, and the others redheads and blackheads.

The small proportion of canvasbacks in the kill will be a disappointment only to the sportsman who, while aware of the fame this bird has acquired, is not familiar with the fine qualities possessed by the other varieties. The only points of superiority in the canvasback over the redhead are its slightly larger size and probably greater fatness. On the table, and judged by flavor, only the gastronomic expert can distinguish between them, and even he is often at fault. The characteristic plumpness of the canvasback is due to its indolent habits. In the struggle for existence, it relates to the other varieties of ducks much as the bald eagle does to the fishhawk; that is, after the other birds, with much exertion, bring the celery to the surface of the water, the canvasback dashes in and appropriates the food. This method of obtaining a living gives the canvasback many leisurely intervals for the accumulation of fat. The more active redhead, though thinner, makes a close epicurean second, and the blackhead a fair third. Indeed, any duck that has fed on the valisneria for ten or twelve days has the characteristic "celery" flavor.

There are a number of important "don'ts" that apply to the preparation of wild ducks for the table. Don't bleed, draw, or pluck the bird until the last moment; don't save it over a week to let it get "high," or subject the meat to refrigeration to make it tender; don't stuff it with bread crumbs, potatoes, oysters, or chestnuts; don't lay it on its back to roast; and don't, above all, overcook it. Affirmatively, pluck and draw the bird, wipe it off with a wet cloth, place it breast downward in a covered pan, put it in a very hot oven, and allow it to remain there for not less than twenty and not more than twenty-five minutes. If a wild duck is cooked too long and blood does not follow the cut of the knife when it is carved, it will not have the true celery flavor. My opinion is that a bird in the air is worth two on the platter if the cook bungles his art.

# *Securing a Point*
### *by Howland Gasper*

The Bellport section of the Great South Bay is considered the best shooting ground hereabouts.  A small
army of local guides there know every nook and corner
where a wild duck can roost.  The city sportsman is sure
of a good day's sport and some ducks if he joins one of
these guides.  In order to get the early start needed, the
city hunter must go into the country the night before.
The local guides have their own sailboats and are always
stocked with provisions to feed hungry guests during the

trip. There is one thing certain about a duck-hunting trip on the Great South Bay: If the gunner does not return with a bag of ducks, he always comes back with a well-satisfied appetite. The guide is usually a good cook, and roast duck, fresh from the water, is one of the gastronomic features of a South Bay ducking trip.

Bog and point shooting is allowed throughout the bay beginning the first of October. However, "securing a point" without being on the ground more than twenty-four hours beforehand is often a problem. This securing a point is no joke. A start at three o'clock in the morning for any particular place is likely to be hours too late; the hunter will accomplish nothing more than to ascertain that another gunner is already at the site with boats, men, and decoys out, holding the fort.

The Great South Bay and its tributary waters are now witnessing the largest flight of wildfowl realized on Long Island in a score of years, and, notwithstanding the absence of favorable weather conditions, some gratifying bags have been secured. The knowledge of this grand flight has extended to all portions of the state, and hundreds of visiting sportsmen, many from Manhattan and the adjacent boroughs, are competing with one another for the best stands. So great is the demand for sites that some of the more enthusiastic hunters are occupying points night and day, sleeping in the blinds, and having their meals carried to them by companions. These points, however, afford only mediocre sport, for too often other hunting boats are stationed along the shore only a few rods distant. Several of the stands are so close to one another as to necessitate the shooting of ducks from one blind over another man's decoys.

# Securing a Point

When "holding a point," it is an inflexible rule that a man must be present at the site with a boat and decoys. Hugh C. Smith, one of the best gunners ever known on Long Island (now dead), was some years ago out with a sportsman on Little Ridge, opposite Bellport. At the end of the day's shooting, the sportsman suggested that they sail across to Bellport with the catboat, leaving the decoys out, and get a good dinner at a hotel, sailing back later in the evening. That part of the proposed program went through all right, but on their return to Little Ridge later in the evening, their decoys were gone. "They didn't hold that point" was how one gunner put it. Smith found his decoys some days later, hidden in the bushes on the beach.

# Days with the Wildfowl
## by Sandy Griswold

"I would rather kill one of those birds," remarked Gerald, as he stepped over the gunwale and took his seat on the bow of the boat, "than any bird that flies." He glanced up to the long line of cranes flying overhead, now almost white against the background of a floating cloud, now bluish-gray where they sailed away from the fleecy pile, now dark where their course lay against the blue sky.

"Did you ever kill one, pop?" Gerald asked me.

"Yes, indeed," I said, "many and many a one, and long before I came to Nebraska, too. In the early '70s, I did a good deal of shooting in the spring and fall at Beaver Lake, Indiana, some twenty miles north of Kentland. Dr. Boerstler and I used to run out there from Cincinnati. In those days the flight of crane almost equaled that of geese, and when I first came to Omaha, they were very abundant in this state."

# Days with the Wildfowl

"Where did you go for them?" inquired Gerald, as we slowly pushed our way through the devious channel toward open water.

"Well, they were especially plentiful out north of Rogers. And in the late fall, huge flocks covered the plains and slopes along the Platte."

"Listen!" and Gerald chopped my remarks in half as, with uplifted hand and tilted head, he seemed to concentrate all of his faculties into that of hearing.

Shoving the push-pole deep in the mud, I stood still as death myself, and, notwithstanding that our sandhills had dwindled into specks in the distance, a weird, guttural *grrrrrrroooooo!* floated in quavering cadences through the sunlit air back to us. It sounded like a spirit voice in the heavens.

"It must have been a grand sight in the early days to have seen those birds like you did," resumed the boy. He dipped his paddle, and we started on again.

"Yes, indeed it was. The fall I was out north of Rogers with John Hardin back in 1887, I saw the birds in greater abundance than ever before. Far and wide, when the sunlight in the early morning played a thousand shades of green and yellow on the rising knolls they stood, blue or almost white, according to the light. They were always vigilant, always alert, watching for danger. At night when we lay in our tent, their rolling notes fell from the starry heavens in unearthly vibrations. By day, with broad wings and long necks outstretched, they floated across the sky with such easy grace and so high above the ducks and geese and all other birds that they seemed to belong to the celestial regions rather than to this terrestrial sphere."

"When did you kill your last sandhill?"

# When Ducks Were Plenty

"Well, the last one I only helped to kill. Tom Foley
and I both shot at a passing flock of three, and only one
fell. Of course we both claimed we shot at the hapless
bird, and probably did. Anyway, I know I did, and as
Foley is the most veracious of sportsmen, I have no reason
to doubt that he did too. It was in the autumn of 1898,
up on the Lake Creek marshes."

"Where were you?"

"We were in a blind, way out in the middle of the marsh,
and these three birds passed us flying not fifteen yards
above the tules. The bird we knocked down was not killed
outright, however, and after he had been hit, he continued
on with his mates for some few yards before falling. It was
a touching scene Tom and I were treated to."

"How was that?"

"Why, when our bird—the middle one of the
three—began to lag behind his companions, settling lower
and lower with slower strokes of his wings, the other two
cranes came back to the side of the stricken one, seemingly trying to cheer and sustain him on his hopeless way.
Yet the bird's wings beat slower and slower, and more and
more he dropped toward the top of the tules, with the
other birds clinging tenaciously to the last hope of saving
him. Suddenly there was an alarming lurch, a spasmodic
flap of one wing, and the long neck folded; the wounded
bird let go all at once and fell dead into one of the shadowy
crypts below. With a melancholy *pur-r-r-rut* or two, his
friends shot up into the sky and left him to his fate.

"When we saw him go down, Tom and I were wildly
enthusiastic, for it had been the ambition of every man in
camp to kill a crane, and each had made scores of futile
efforts. When we realized that we had accomplished the
coveted feat, our joy was boundless. We both tore out of

our blind and through the dense tules like a couple of wild men, each eager to outstrip the other and first lay hands upon our prize. But the satisfaction was left for another. In our excitement of watching the uncertain flight of the wounded crane and his two companions, Tom and I had both failed to properly mark the spot where he finally fell, perhaps feeling there was no special care necessary; we thought it would be no difficult task to locate a big fat crane carcass on that broad and unbroken expanse of brown vegetation. But search as closely and diligently as we might, we could not find him. We did pick up a stray crimson-stained feather or two that had undoubtedly fallen from his fluffy and wounded side, but the bird itself we could not discover. We searched for over an hour, in fact, until it was almost dark, beating down several acres of dead tules and withered flags, but to no avail. While we were looking for him the ducks flew overhead, but so intent were we in searching for the sandhill that neither one of us took a shot, until finally, in deep disgust and mortification, we were compelled to give it up."

"And you never got him?"

"Oh, yes, we did. Charlie Rogers and Scrib were shooting from the same blinds the next morning, and Scribner ran across our crane, lying in plain sight in a little open glade in the tules. He was stone dead, with his long neck doubled back over his shaded back, and his long, lavender wings fully outstretched. Scrib said that Tom had trampled the tules by the bird within a dozen yards of where it lay, but as he found it and Rogers carried it into Camp Merganser, they had the gall to claim a hand in our triumph."

"Well, as long as you finally got the bird, you didn't care, did you?"

# When Ducks Were Plenty

"No, not particularly. Anyway, that night we gathered round old Abner's table and feasted ourselves to almost bursting on roast sandhill crane. I can taste it yet."

"Good?"

"Good? That's no name for it. It was a young bird, fat as butter, and Abner had him dished up in a style that would have made the Waldorf Astoria's chef turn green with envy. Young turkey with chestnut and oyster dressing didn't hold a candle to our crane, and with the wild sage and onion stuffing Abner served, I thought Charlie Metz and Billie Marsh would never quit eating. But here we are. Let's string the decoys a little farther around the point to where birds coming from the west can see them quicker. From the way they are moving up the lake, I think we are going to have some great fun this evening. There, reach that decoy with your paddle and pull it along until we get 'round the point; I'll gather these in front of us."

"Before we get ready, Dad, I want to ask you if you don't think the sandhill is the greatest game bird we have ever had in this section of the country?" Gerald pawed at the nearest decoy with the flat end of his paddle.

*"Plenty of ducks in camp." From a series of stereoscopic sporting and game photographs by T. W. Ingersoll, St. Paul, Minnesota, circa 1890s to 1905.*

# Days with the Wildfowl

"No, I do not. I even think—look out there! You'll throw me into the slough if you lean over the boat in that manner—I even think he is not up to the wild goose, and so far as comparing him with the whooping crane, he is as far beneath that bird as he is superior to the sawbill."

"The whooping crane? I don't believe I know the bird you mean. Are there any of them round here now?"

"Yes, sometimes, but they are almost as thoroughly extinct in Nebraska as the buffalo and wild pigeon, although Bob Lowe came within an ace of getting a shot at one last fall near Clark's Lake, south of Omaha."

"Then they were once plentiful here, too, like the sandhill?"

"Just as plentiful. In fact, when I came to Nebraska, they were almost as numerous as the sandhills. They are larger by at least ten inches in wing span and eight inches or more in length, and have always been considered a rarer and more valuable bird. They are as white as a swan, excepting the several inches of velvet black that tips the wing. When floating in the bright sunlight of Nebraska's clear air, whooping cranes are the most beautiful of all big American game birds."

"And you say they were quite numerous when you first came here?"

"Yes, very, and as late as March 1894, Bill Simeral and I killed two out north of Goose Lake in Deuel County—the spring we made that big kill of canvasback."

"Canvasback. I haven't heard you speak of that hunt. How many did you kill?"

"Well, canvasback and redhead, but principally canvas— we brought back to Omaha exactly 604 birds after a ten-day shoot, and this number included the two whooping cranes and seven swan. No two hunters in the history

of Nebraska duplicated that bag. But I'll tell you about
that later. Just now I want to tell you about the crane—
the whoopers. They were abundant in the sandhill
country, but I never heard of many being killed here.
Hunters were always content with geese and ducks,
probably because the whooping crane is about the hardest bird to approach in the world. He is as keen-sighted
as the Andes condor, and has the most acute hearing of
any animal I ever hunted. They are great fliers, and
circle much of the time so far in the zenith that they
seem but bits of down. The whoop they send through
miles of air is as wild and strange as the ringing blast
of a silver bugle. It is almost a hopeless task to try to
get a shot at one. They—well, isn't that gall for you?
I'll kill the drake on the water, and you take the hen
when she rises."

A pair of redheads gliding like noiseless, disem-
bodied spirits had dropped right into the midst of the
decoys behind us, apparently not alarmed by my voice
and perhaps unaware of our proximity. Calling
Gerald's attention to them, I cracked away, and the
old cock dropped his bright chestnut head and fell over
on the water, kicking spasmodically. With an affrighted
squeak the hen leaped into the air and sought to get
away by whirling over our heads. She miscalculated.
Gerald's first barrel cut a handful of feathers out of her
ashen tail, and the second sent her plunging dead on a
long slant into the glistening tules.

"Well done!" I cried.

"Nothin' t'all surprisin'," he answered. "I had one of
those long-killing shells of yours."

Even before we had a chance to retrieve the pair of
redheads or push our boat back into the covert of tules,

another pair of ducks, baldpates this time, came skimming down the channel just over water. Gerald and I both saw them at the same time and crouched low down on the hay in the boat, waiting for them. The boy was in the bow and nearest the channel, so I whispered to him to take the leader, and I would attend to the one in the rear. They were soon opposite us, and the reports of our Parkers followed each other in quick succession—so quickly, in fact, that they seemed to blend into one, and two white-crested members of the wildfowl family lay struggling hopelessly upon the water.

"Oh, aren't we shooting a little bit this afternoon!" exclaimed the young sportsman as he opened his gun and slipped in another brace of shells. "Two doubles on

*"Gee whiz! What a chance!"*

single birds in less than three minutes: Looks as if things are coming our way, eh?"

"Yes, indeed it does," I replied. "All signs point toward a good flight this evening—but, heavens and earth! Look at that line of mallards coming down over the hills! Push! Gerald, push! Let's get into the tules. They're coming straight for us!"

Tugging and pushing and pulling like a couple of Trojans, we soon had our boat tucked well back in a labyrinth of tules. Stooping low, I gave a loud *quack!* on my caller, thrice in rapid succession, then waited.

As far off as they were, I saw that I had attracted their attention. In those low sandhill valleys, a caller can be readily heard for a mile. The bulk of the approaching flock flew over the lake and down toward me with a rush. I then uttered the chattering notes of an old hen, and the fragment of the flock that had deviated a trifle to the north turned and followed the main bunch. When about two hundred yards away, they all swerved a little, the way of newcomers when approaching an unfamiliar line of rushes. I called when they swung off, and I chattered as they turned again. Then down they came in a line like a charge of dragoons, with long green necks stretched to their utmost tension, and heads gleaming like flashing gems in the slanting sunlight.

They cupped their wings and dropped their brightly colored legs. Three birds some yards in advance of the main line, like generals leading their troops, alighted among our decoys before the others had bunched sufficiently to give us a good rake at them. Gerald was unnerved by the advancing line of glorious birds, and he let drive among them half a minute too soon. Then there was a whirl and a wild scramble in the air, which seemed filled with thumping wings sheering upward and outward amid a weird chorus of affrighted cries. At the crack of the kid's first barrel, a whirl of green and gray and black struck the weedy waters: Two birds had fallen in together. At the report of his second barrel, another white-collared neck drooped, and another pair of wings folded. I was a bit slow, but in the aerial riot I caught two with my right as they crossed, and got another with my left as the last stragglers rapidly approached the danger line.

Breaking my gun, I stood watching the scattered flock gathering together far up the lake. They at last united in a big bunch and went with the wind off over the hills toward Hackberry, where some of our party probably awaited them. I could not refrain from comment, nettled a little, you see, at having such a grand opportunity spoiled by the impetuosity of the boy.

"A trifle premature, Gerald," I said. "If you had only waited a—"

"Oh, get out! What do you want, the earth? Didn't we knock down five? Could reasonable men ask more?" he shot back.

"No, indeed," I said, "but that isn't the point. There is a proper time for shooting at a flock of incoming mallards, just as there is a proper time for everything else. We killed enough of them, to be sure, but I wanted you to see those birds when they poised stationary in the air before dropping into the water. They would have all stood on their tails until satisfied that the three birds already on the water had not made a mistake. And with a tremendous flock like that—"

"There must have been a hundred of them!"

"Fully. And I say, with such a flock, you would have remembered the spectacle to the end of your days. I saw just such a sight back on the old Kankakee over twenty-five years ago, and I can close my eyes now and see it again, as vividly as I did that glorious March morning long ago. But look out there! Knock that bird down! Don't let her get away!"

As I spoke, a big old hen mallard rounded the south point of the rushes and was about to settle among the decoys. She caught sight of us, and, turning swiftly, was putting as much space between her and our blind as her terror-stricken wings would permit. The lad swung on her and fired, and down she tumbled among the smartweed with a broken wing.

"Well, you got her," I told him, "but she is only wounded, and I don't think we'll be able to retrieve her. But what do you say, let's try. There seems to be a lull just now, and as a number of our dead birds have drifted out of sight, I think we'll profit by running out and gathering them before the final roundup this evening. Aren't you handing it to them; think I'll have to match you against Parker's man Fred Gilbert when we get home, and if we could only spring ducks from the trap, I'd back you for the money. Now, Gerald, you pick up the dead, and I'll push over there among the smartweed. We'll try for that old hen first."

I slowly pulled the bow over to the line of weeds that formed a thin brown wilderness along the side of the channel. Gun ready, Gerald got on his knees and carefully scanned the line of dead growth as we slowly floated along the selvedge. Failing to discover her, I said, "She's here somewhere. Let's both look sharp while I hold the boat still. These old hen mallards are about the cutest birds of the whole family, and a wounded one is tough to find. She's probably immersed her body and is lying still. But you can depend on it that her greenish bill is above the water concealed by some clump of pepper grass, and she's keeping her yellow eyes on us all the time. Hold on—still now—I think she is right under that little bunch over there." I pointed with the pole to a small cluster of leaves that were blacker than the rest, possibly from having been lately soaked in the water when the old hen immersed herself. "You see how light the surrounding leaves are; their color has not been changed by a sudden bath in the water. I'll push right up close, then you take a whack at the dark bunch with the flat side of your paddle. If she's there, we'll soon find out."

Gerald deposited his Parker in the hay and seized the paddle. When within striking distance he brought it down on the clump of smartweed with a loud whack, crushing the weeds into the water and sending circlets of waves radiating away in all directions. Immediately there was a violent commotion within the aqueous tangle, and the next instant the rufous back and snake-like yellow head of the old hen showed above the surface. A second quick blow from the paddle stretched her two brown wings out on the surface, and her short tail feathers, sticking almost straight up, twitched and trembled in a way that plainly told that she was good as a dead duck.

Another little push on the pole and the kid reached over, grabbed the mallard by the neck, shook the water from her plumage, and cast her back at my feet on the hay. Then, picking up the paddle, we started back to where our dead were floating, and so it goes. . . .

# When Ducks Were Plenty

## Editor's Note

Sandy Griswold's upbeat article, "Days with the Wildfowl," was taken from the 8 October 1904 issue of *Forest and Stream*. But a decade later, an article in *The American Field* had Griswold lamenting that "Snipe Must Change Their Migratory Route" due to rampant conversion of marshland to farmland.

> The old snipe grounds up this side of Calhoun [Nebraska], between Horseshoe Lake and the old Poncho Road, are no more. I made the trip with my old shooting friend, Billie Townsend, and was surprised and vexed to find my favorite marsh absolutely ruined. For years and years this marshy lowland has been the favorite resort of Omaha jacksnipe shooters, but now the whole vast area is dry as a bone. Huge drains and ditches crisscross the old grounds in all directions, and, while there are a few straggling pools yet remaining, they, too, will soon disappear. The progress and thrift of the agriculturist is something that the jacksnipe cannot interfere with. The system of drainage is perfect, and next year the entire expanse will be under cultivation. As Bill and I strode across the dried-up marsh, the devastation filled our hearts with sadness, regret, and disappointment.

The same year Griswold and his son Gerald enthused about abundant wildfowl near Omaha, Nebraska, another retired market hunter, Clay Merritt (chap. 45), published his book *The Shadow of a Gun* (1904). In it he complained that agricultural progress had driven the birds from northwestern Illinois. The same dredges and tiling machines that drained L. B. Crooker's (chap. 19) "disgustingly wet and muddy spot known as the Winnebago Swamp" in the mid-1870s, and Merritt's Annawan Swamps in the 1880s, moved slowly westward through Iowa to the Horseshoe Lake area of Nebraska. The "Age of Progress," measured by conversion of wetland to farmland, drove the wildfowl out of northern Illinois in the 1890s, and it was only a matter of time before Griswold would lose his snipe grounds near Omaha.

The frontier was subdued from east to west commencing in the 1700s, and the deleterious effects of industry, commerce, and agriculture on the wilderness were common conversational topics by mid-nineteenth century sportsmen. John Krieder (chap. 5), in his book *Krieder's Sporting Anecdotes* (1853), observed that "formerly ducks were very abundant on the western shore between Port Deposit and Havre de Grace . . . [but] the dredging of the Tidewater Canal drove the ducks off the flats and marshes." The dredging of a canal near Havre de Grace in the 1840s merely drove the diver ducks from one favorable place to another at the mouth of the Susquehanna. However, the dredging, channeling, and draining of Griswold's marsh near Omaha in 1913 meant that snipe had to change their migratory route—but to where? They certainly couldn't settle on the drained Annawan and Winnebago Swamps then under cultivation in northern Illinois!

Henry William Herbert, in his "Introductory Observations" to *Frank Forester's Field Sports* (1848), predicted a secondary repercussion of westward expansion. He had observed civilization's encroachment on wildlife habitat through the 1840s, and foresaw that improved rail transportation would facilitate and thereby increase market hunting. Forester stated that big game had been all but exterminated in the eastern states, and, as a consequence, the rifle there had fallen into disuse. He expressed short-term hope for shooting sports, but his long-term prognosis was not optimistic:

> So long as wildfowl and smaller game exist, the shotgun will continue to replace the rifle in the west as it has in the east, and the practice of firearms will not be totally lost. But destroy the small game, too, and the fowling piece will also fall into disuse. I do not myself believe that one century will pass in the United States, before its population, now the readiest on earth with the gun, will cast aside shooting sports altogether, and the use of firearms will be rare except in the hands of trained regulars.

As I write this in October 1998, a century and a half after Forester's prophecy, huntable numbers of small game and wildfowl persist, and the utility and honor of the shotgun has been preserved. Let us hope that reports of the impending *death* of sport hunting in general, and wildfowling in particular, are in the words of Samuel Clemens—"greatly exaggerated."

# A Flyer in Geese
## by Julian Burroughs

"Yes, I guess I'll go duck hunting today. I'm within striking distance of the end of my fall work, and if I don't take a day off now and then, I'll—"

*Honk! honk! honk!* came the wild clamor of three hundred geese rudely breaking in on my ruminations. I paused, looking up, and saw a mighty flock of wild geese bearing straight toward me, boring through the morning mist with express train speed.

"There's a flock of geese acoming," I yelled. "Come, quick!"

In a moment my whole family was out on the door stones, just in time to see the flock go over, scarcely a gunshot high. The geese's great wings drove them forward with swift, tireless beats, and their voices stirred

# When Ducks Were Plenty

our blood.  Before I could throw my things together, my father came in.  "Those geese have turned back and lit right outside here.  They're lost in the fog!" he exclaimed.

In a moment I was running recklessly to the shore, my lunch and field glasses bumping my back as I bounded down the steep path.  Quickly noting the tide and wind, and picking some weeds for a battery, I shoved my canvas duck boat into the water.  Heading into the fog, I drove the boat along with every ounce of strength I had.

Off Gordon's Point I suddenly saw the flock: a long, unbroken line of geese, dimly visible in the mist.  With trembling eagerness I rowed back toward shore until I felt that their sharp eyes could not see me.  Then the oars came in, sculling paddle went out, and, lying flat on my back, I began to creep toward the half-acre of solid geese, rapidly at first and then more slowly as I drew near.  Oh, what a sight for the gods they were!  Hundreds of geese, most of them dazzlingly white, held their reddish heads proudly alert as they swam slowly among each other.  When I approached within seventy yards, they grew uneasy and began to call.  Then, with a deafening roar of wings and water, they tore themselves from the river and climbed the air, a host in full flight.

Twice the old gun burst forth, bringing four of them tumbling down.  They were snow geese—a boatload of them!  From Grinnell or Baffin Bay or northern Greenland in the Arctic Ocean they had come, traveling two, three, or even four thousand miles to bring me that wonderful Arctic whiteness in their plumage: a whiteness born of the frozen seas and low sun; a whiteness so pure that it seemed a sacrilege to touch it.  Their heads were russet, their wing tips gray-black, their bills and feet a strange purple-pink—a jewel-like color just touched by the aurora

# A Flyer in Geese

borealis.  They had a wing spread almost as great as the spread of a man's arms.  And they were mine.

The night boats from New York, delayed by the fog, were just stealing by, stirring the silence of the Hudson Valley with their sirens, as I slowly climbed the hill.  My arms ached with the load I bore.  And I wondered if I would have set aside my fall work to pursue geese, had they not come to me first.

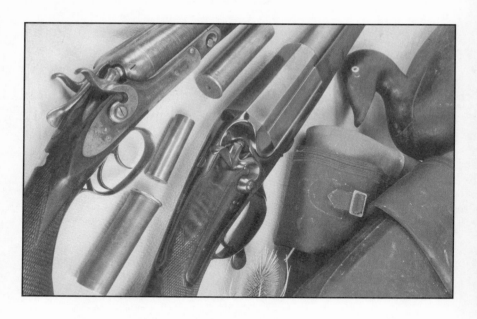

# "Ducking" with Perkins
## by Ernest Pettitt

"Perkins just rang up to say that he wants to go duck-ing on Friday, and to know whether you are game," Charlie said to me the other afternoon.

"Oh, I'm game enough," I replied. "Tell him to arrange for Sam to meet us, and for rooms at the Crown."

Now, Perkins is a bit of an oddity. One never knows where he is going to break out next. He has a nice little income, no business worries, and a natural aptitude for try-ing his hand at all and sundry occupations. As such, he enters into everything, possessed with a will that often leads to ridiculous situations. And what a boy he is for being up-to-date! He indulges in no sport—and he tries his hand at most—unless he has the latest in equipment, and everything is just "the thing." Nothing old-fashioned

*(Picture: Parker 16-gauge and J. & W. Tolley 4-bore. The shells tell the difference.)*

# "Ducking" with Perkins

will do for Perkins.  If he goes for a day's fishing, the
rods, nets, and tackle of every description that make
up his outfit as the "complete angler" require the services
of a light porter.

Friday afternoon, after having picked up Perkins at
the club, the three of us spun down the road in the
direction of our shooting grounds.  Perkins' impedimenta
was, as usual, of copious dimensions, so we—that is,
Charlie and I—allowed him to have the back seat of our
little four-seater to himself, along with his baggage and
our retrieving spaniel.  Really, we could do no other, for
he and his traps together filled the car nicely.  A couple
hours of easy running and we pulled up in the yard of
the Crown Hotel, where mine host and Sam made their
appearance simultaneously.

Sam is a good fellow as a keeper.  Rumor has it that
in the dark ages of a generation ago, Sam was a confirmed
poacher, until a certain designing person of the opposite
sex (the daughter of the head keeper on a nearby estate)
caused him to abandon the thorny path of wrongdoing.
Another rumor says that he reformed because the local
arm of the law determined to put down his nocturnal
expeditions at all costs.  Whatever his past, Sam is a
very good keeper; that is to say, he always finds us a
day's sport when we come down.

Our traps unpacked, a cold lunch demolished, and
a drop of something warm stored in our pockets for later
to keep out the cold and damp, we started along the path.
Six hundred acres of woods, field, and swamp constitute
our small though varied holding.  On it we have observed
most kinds of game and wildfowl, with the exception of
grouse.  To be sure, we have bagged an occasional mallard or teal, but to wait for the flighting of duck alone

was to be a new experience. About a hundred acres of our shoot consists of low-lying grassland and swamp that are the haunt of snipe, plover, and other wildfowl innumerable. In the middle of the swamp is a reedy pond of twenty acres, and on its verge stands a number of old pollard willows. We purchased an old boat, had it conveyed here in a farmer's wagon, and anchored it in a reedy corner of the pond, which had a convenient outlook for passing wildfowl. On the other side of the pond, Sam had driven in four posts just offshore, and on these he laid an old door, which he securely nailed to the posts. The high reeds around the new stand made a most effective screen for two hunters. Our setup had been the result of considerable deliberation, and now our hopes were high.

A solitary duck, winging across the cloud-flecked sky—a mere speck in the heavens—spurred us into readiness. Perkins and I had arranged to occupy the stand, so Sam drew on a pair of heavy thigh boots and carried us one after the other, pick-a-back, across the intervening bit of swamp to our screened position. Then Sam returned to the boat, and, with Charlie, made himself comfortable for a bit of a wait.

I must relate that Perkins had arrayed himself in a fearful rig of waterproof clothing, and was so smothered by fittings of various kinds that I wondered how he would wield his gun. His armory consisted of two guns, a 16- and an 8-bore. The latter weapon was an extraordinarily heavy double carrying a big load, and was expected to completely decimate a flock of ducks anywhere within one hundred yards.

Knowing that the duck had a long flight from the nearest breeding place, we were not afraid of our sport being spoiled by the firing of a few shots, so a solitary curlew, sweeping low across the water, fell victim to Charlie's gun, and was cleverly retrieved by the cocker. A wisp of snipe flashing over our stand met with a warm reception; Perkins got off both barrels at the lead bird, dropping it cleanly with the left, while my right accounted for another bird. Immediately the sharp, rifle-like crack of Perkins's 16-bore again broke the silence, and a green plover came down in a lovely spiral, dropping within a yard of the platform. Perkins thereupon insisted on wading after the three dead birds, which he secured after a struggle with some submerged briars. Hardly had he regained the stand when *swish-ish-ish*, a sound well known to wildfowlers, told us that ducks were on the wing. I hurriedly changed my small shot cartridges for No. 4s, and Perkins, snatching up his 8-bore, shoved in a pair of cartridges. We need not have hurried though, for the birds simply swept round at an impossible height and vanished the way they had come. They were but the scouts of an army, however. A few minutes later a solitary mallard drake swooped down from the sky, checking himself beautifully as he almost touched the water, then rose again, sweeping close by Charlie: a nice, easy shot. Charlie took full advantage.

No more ducks appeared for a few minutes, but then a nice little squad came sweeping along, out of range. At the same time an odd bird (which afterward I found to be a widgeon) took my attention by crossing in front of me, and my left barrel stopped his career at a good sixty yards. Almost simultaneously with the report of my gun came a *boom!* as of a young cannon, and a confused quacking and splashing revealed that the charge from Perkins's 8-bore had disturbed a squad of ducks near the shore. I could see one bird floating dead on the water, while another, evidently badly hit, was splashing along the surface toward a bed of reeds. Sam dispatched the dog after the wounded bird, which he recovered after a bit of splashing. On his way back, the clever dog came across the dead bird and managed, after a bit of a tussle, to carry both birds at the same time.

Only a few more ducks came within shooting distance, and all escaped. Later, when the evening shadows began to fall on the water, the fowl arrived with more confidence. An occasional *plop*, as a shot bird struck the water, showed that our expenditure of ammunition was not

*The gun on the left has Parker's trademark recessed hinge pin; close examination shows it to be Trojan grade. No more useful or cost-effective double has ever been made for upland game and wildfowl since the Trojan's introduction in 1913. More than 30,000 of this popular knockabout were made before production ceased in 1938. Thus it's not surprising that most Parker aficionados cut their teeth on Trojan grade.*

# "Ducking" with Perkins

quite in vain. The deepening silence was broken only by the whistle of duck wings, an occasional *quack!* from some impatient drake, or the mournful cry of a curlew or redshank. Meanwhile, the boom of Perkins's 8-bore put my nerves on edge. It was impossible to see the birds except at very short range, so I wished in vain that he would exchange the heavier weapon for the handier 16-bore, which would have been appropriate for the range at which we were shooting.

Suddenly out of the gathering darkness a couple of ducks flashed up directly in front of Perkins, traveling at a tremendous rate. Up went his cannon, and, with the birds only twenty yards from the muzzle he fired: "*Bang-ang!*" I thought a thunderbolt had struck the stand. Perkins, in his excitement, had pulled both triggers of his 8-bore simultaneously. As he staggered back with the force of the recoil, and before he could recover his equilibrium, a shot duck speeding forward caught Perkins fairly in the chest. With a crash of breaking branches, he vanished through the brush screen, falling with a tremendous splash into the water.

Sam came floundering across, thinking by the noise that we both must have gone to kingdom come. Before he arrived, Perkins emerged sputtering, "What the —? Where the —? Who pushed me off the platform?" It was some time before I could convince him that the dead duck lying on the edge of the platform was the cause of his mishap. Somehow he had never released his hold on the gun, having clung to it like grim death. Thinking he would be wet through, we urged him to hurry off to the hotel, but to our surprise, after a few more violent expletives, he burst out laughing. He declared he was as dry as a bone, his new wading suit having protected him admirably externally, but admitted that he was a good deal wetter on the inside with all the water he had swallowed.

Of course there was no more duck shooting that day. By the time our outburst of laughter had subsided—for it was impossible not to laugh at the ridiculous figure that Perkins presented—we could hardly see the way back to our hotel. Sam conveyed Charlie and me to land in the same manner he had brought us out. Perkins, however, insisted on further testing the efficiency of his waders by remaining to splash about with Sam in a blind-fold search for the dead birds. Eventually they brought to the bank a dozen ducks of various kinds, piling them onto the smaller birds we had collected before the ducks appeared. The other birds could not be found in the darkness, so Sam gathered these with his spaniel the next morning before breakfast.

Perkins had recovered his good humor by the time we reached the hotel, and we did justice to the repast our attentive host set before us. And for hours afterward, an occasional chuckle from one or the other of us indicated that the incident would not soon be forgotten. Perkins has since sworn off using an 8-bore for duck shooting.

# Mallard Shooting in the Alberta Wheatfields

### by Paul E. Page

I was born near the Horicon Marsh in Wisconsin. My boyhood was spent there, and many a day I pushed a canoe through the rice and studied that then great expanse of aquatic life. Nature was my teacher, for there were few books on hunting at the time. I trapped with the Indians, too, and saw them gradually melt away to the west. I have shot ducks and geese all through the Northwest since the early seventies. But this story is of a recent modern [1919] duck hunt, a story of birds living off the fat of the Canadian grain fields.

On a beautiful day last October, I stepped off a train at an Alberta siding, carrying a letter of introduction to a farmer who supposedly knew every duck and goose in Canada by its first name. But I found that Mr. Farmer had just left town for an unknown length of time, and, having only the balance of the day and all of the next in

This "Dapper Dan" went to a lot of trouble to have himself photographed in a studio with his hammer gun. Too bad he didn't write his name and some details on the back of the photograph.

which to shoot, I was up against it, as I knew absolutely nothing of the country. Fortunately a young fellow had been listening to my efforts to get shooting information, and he told me that if I wanted ducks, to come to his place, as there were millions there. I tried to pin him down as to how many flocks came into his wheatfield in a day, but he could not grasp the flock question. I was to find out why later.

He told me that he was on a rented farm about two miles from town, so I took a chance and went with him. When we drove his wagon by the field in which he said there were millions, not a duck was to be seen. About half a mile away, however, I saw a number of ducks flying over a clump of brush and asked what was over there. He told me there were three lakes and that a few ducks were flying from lake to lake. I told him to drive over for a look.

When we got closer I saw one lake of about forty acres and another of about twenty, with a little rise of ground covered with brush and heavy slough grass between them. I got out of the wagon and unpacked my gun and shells, and the boy started home with the understanding that he was to return for me at dark. I walked out between the lakes and had twelve greenheads in the grass before he got the team turned around. But then I spent an hour looking for them and did not find one, as I had no dog. I told myself that would not do, and looked around for a better location. Beyond the farthest lake, ducks were flying into a wheatfield that came down close to shore. As I waded across the lake to the field, I dropped six mallards in the water and secured them all. I found a likely place in the field, built a blind out of grain shocks, and set my dead ducks on other shocks as decoys.

In a moment the flight started. Although I have seen ducks in Wisconsin, Dakota, and Iowa as far back as 1876, when they were as thick as I ever supposed they could be, I must confess that I had never really known what ducks in numbers were. They came into that field in flocks a half-mile long and a quarter-mile wide, from hundreds of lakes near and far. These birds—thousands and millions of them, and every one an overgrown, grain-fed mallard—had never been shot at and had never seen a man. I did not see a duck of any other kind in two days of shooting. My only regret was that I did not have my .22 automatic, as the 16-gauge was too tame.

To give you an idea what it was like, I'll say that I believe I have the record for shooting ducks with a 16-gauge pump: nine mallards with the six shots. I got six ducks another time. With the nine ducks, the flock all came in about ten feet above the stubble, wings set and legs dangling. One glance at my dead decoys brought them pell-mell on top of me, to their doom. I could have put in several more shots if I had had another gun. The only time during the day when there was any rushing or jumping was when four or more ducks tried to alight in the same place at the same time. I think I shot as many birds while I was out of the blind gathering up the dead as I did when I was under cover. They could not see anything but those dead ducks on the shocks and the prospect for some good eats. Shooting ended sharply at 4:30 P.M. and from then until dark not a bird was in sight.

Next day I went to the lake and made a blind in a muskrat house. The first shot put my gun on the blink, and I had to shoot it as a single shot until noon. I went up to the house for lunch, took the gun apart, and found two screws, one bolt, and three springs broken. These I patched up with a match, some wire, and a small nail, and I got it working fine in the house. But back at the

# Mallard Shooting in the Alberta Wheatfields

lake, the first shot had the wire going one way, the match another, and the nail may be going yet for all I know. So I shot a single for the rest of the day, and in addition had to hold up the carriage with the fingers of my left hand to get it to work at all. However, I waited for every opportunity to get doubles and triples with one shot.

On the second day, while shooting from the rat house, I noticed a fringe of brush about a quarter of a mile from me. At no time during the day when I looked in that direction did I fail to see a long string of ducks flying over the brush. These strings of ducks were from a quarter- to a half-mile long, thousands of them in each string. I do not know what was on the other side of the brush, but presume it must have been another wheatfield. There were so many birds coming into the lake where I was that I did not take the trouble to go over and discover the attraction.

I have hunted ducks since 1876, and truly believe that I saw more mallards in the two days of shooting than I have seen in all the years since I shot my first bird. And I learned why the farm boy could not tell me how many flocks came to his place a day. When they got to his wheatfield there was no flock, just ducks everywhere in all directions, and then some more. Is it any wonder I am today a little homesick for the smell of that Alberta wheatfield marsh?

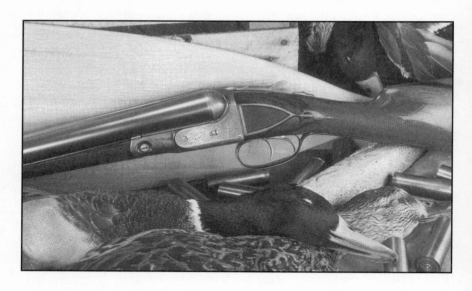

# Timber Mallards on the Illinois River
## by William C. Hazelton

Within the cobwebbed loft he sits
'Mid spars and caufs and wrecks of things,
Who, couched in sedgy marshes heard
Wheel to his lure swift vibrant wings.
—The Old Decoy Duck

Do not a few old battered decoys lead to reminiscence? Could they but speak, what tales they would tell of bygone days! I can well remember the first decoys I ever saw. They had been abandoned, left to freeze in a rush-covered pond by hunters not from our country. Who they had belonged to we could only surmise. They bore shades of Elliston, the master decoy-builder, and were wonderfully lifelike.

Many autumns have now vanished since I first shot ducks in the flooded timber on the Illinois River. Dead trees will stand upright in the water for years before succumbing, so practically all of the flooded timber is dead or dying, and, depending on the level of water, there sometimes is considerable buck brush. On the part of the river where I then lived, timber shooting was to be had mostly in the spring, and only rarely in the fall. Farther down the river at Senachwine, one could shoot in the flooded trees for weeks at a time, especially in the spring. I have shot so close to the old town of Hennepin that I could plainly hear the bells calling the children to school.

Timber shooting is the best of sports, and the Illinois River is one of the best-known locales on the continent for this form of ducking. There you see the royal mallard at his best. All the varieties of shoal-water ducks can be found in the flooded bottoms, and mallards are numerous there. However, deep-water and diving ducks such as redheads, canvasbacks, and bluebills do not frequent the timber.

Mallards love the river when it overflows, as they are never open-water birds from choice. They find both food and shelter in the flooded timber, and prefer to roost there too. Mallards feed

*Duck shooting in the timber.*

on smartweed, nut grass, and other aquatic plants and vegetable matter, and if you rout them out of a favorite feeding place, they will soon return singly and in small flocks instead of settling in somewhere else for the day, especially should the weather be blustery and chilly. Nowhere will ducks answer a call more readily than along the river, as without any large areas of open water, they are prone to be guided by the call of their kind—a fact of which the hunter takes full advantage.

Last November [1920] I enjoyed several days of shooting in the overflow timber on the Illinois River. Each experience was different, adding fascination and allure to my wildfowling experience. I will endeavor to describe but one day's sport.

After watching the flight for a time, I picked out a spot on the flooded edge of some dead trees; the mallards seemed to favor an open pond there. The water was from two to three feet deep, and the height of the trees from twenty to forty feet. Although I had decoys with me, I decided to try and get some shots without their use, while sitting in my boat.

My first two shots were at a small flock of five mallards. I killed one with each barrel. An old drake came in, his head moving from side to side looking for his kind or possible danger. I let him pass without firing. Then a flock of gray ducks (gadwalls) headed directly for me. I fired two shots when they were nearly overhead, but only scored one hit. Fortunately none of the birds went down winged, but all were dead, so I let them lie where they had fallen.

Next a pair of ducks headed my way, unsuspecting of danger. When they were nearly overhead, I fired, and one started to fall. I quickly got in the second barrel and was surprised to get my second bird also. When I pushed

# Timber Mallards on the Illinois River

out to gather them, I was astonished to find two hens: one a mallard and the other a pintail. Were they widows, divorcees, or a couple of vamps? One is confronted with a legion of surprises in duck shooting.

I did not care to build a blind, but some of the ducks would see my boat, so I decided to leave it farther back in the woods. I then waded out to an old log that was sheltered by an overhanging tree trunk. This log was blind enough and a firm seat. I had just settled in when a duck came right at me not over thirty yards high, and I gave her a shot. She fell, and I saw that she was a black duck, or black mallard, as they are called on the river. I noted the glossy feathers and darker speculums. The black duck is not a freak of nature like an albino, but is a separate and distinct species. Being in lesser numbers in the west, they often travel with mallards. They are to the east what the mallard is to the west.

As the thin ice that had formed overnight in the timber melted from the sun's rays, the ducks returned with the utmost confidence, seeming to say, "We know this place; it's safe here." But two streams of fire poured from tubes held by a figure seated on a log, and the ducks rolled away on the wind to seek a safer refuge. Long-necked pintails drifted overhead. Little flocks of greenwing teal scurried among the trees. Baldpates flitted into a large open pond just beyond, giving their musical whistling call. And I could see the white spot on the wings of gray ducks as they volplaned in the distance. After studying the gray ducks considerably, I have discovered that they are not excessively wary on the water, but on the wing they are as cautious and quick to note a suspicious object as any mallard. The gray duck is a fine sporting bird and splendid on the table.

There was a little touch of winter now, with feathery snowflakes drifting down and a stiff northwest wind. High up four large flocks of bluebills passed over, heading down the valley. They were plainly travelers from the north. Who can imagine the daily wanderings of a flock of migrating ducks?

Four years ago in southwestern Iowa, I saw tens of thousands of noble mallards flying down the Missouri River during three days of bitter weather. They would not face the cutting wind at all. They were bound for the south and knew where they were going; every flock flew its course as though following a compass. In the old days I saw wild pigeons all following the same flyway, although each flock was out of sight of the preceding one. "As the crow flies" may be a tradition, but "as the duck flies" is a revelation in directness. Their migrations are a mystery and a marvel.

*A very young and dapper William Chester Hazelton (1868–1951) shows his shooting form in this original photograph. Courtesy of Carol Barnes at Gunnerman Books.*

Sometimes one learns much by watching birds at rest and play. It was pleasant to sit in the timber, unobserved, and watch the journeying waterfowl as well as those nearer at hand. As I sat on my log, a flock of Canada geese honked down the valley with their far-carrying cries. Numberless bands of cormorants, erroneously called loons on the river, filed by in formations resembling geese, although the similarity ends there. The true loon is the great northern diver and cannot be mistaken.

I heard goldeneyes coming down the valley. Nothing stirs me more than the noise of an approaching flock of these wary birds: the first distant trilling whir as they near, the louder whistling rush as they pass, and the final distant and gradual dying away of the musical sound of their wings. Many lonely far northern marshes and lakes had they visited—Peace River, the Athabasca—and doubtless their yellow-gold eyes had swept the borders of Arctic seas. Goldeneyes are one of the keenest-sighted and alert of all waterfowl, as I discovered while studying them on the lower Kankakee River as a boy. But enough reflection—I must have a few more ducks—it's time to go into action again.

After a few hours and a succession of hits and misses, I had my legal limit of mallards and gray ducks only. It was about two o'clock, so I called it a day. On my way back to camp, I rounded a bend in the river where a fringe of ancient oak trees broke the force of the northwest wind. I passed several cabin boats moored to the bank; bunches of ducks were suspended from various places on the boats. Leaning over the rail of one boat was "Sandy," a typical riverman. With his weather-beaten visage and skin like leather, he might have been Kipling's "gentle yellow pirate," had the Illinois been the habitat of pirates. Sandy noted the generous bunch of ducks in the end of my boat and observed, "Guess ye had a purty good day, didn't ye?" Being well satisfied with myself and the world just then, I nodded and smiled and journeyed on. . . .

> To follow the way a wild duck takes,
> To the twilight of the grassy lakes,
> To the glory of the Yukon hills.

# No Spring Shooting
# on Barnegat Bay

## by Martin Hill Ittner

    For several years past, it has been my practice to
devote about four days during the season to duck shooting
at Barnegat Bay.  My shooting days are spread out, and
I do not take two in succession.  I drive down in an auto
from my farm the night before, over forty miles, and back
again the next night after the day's shooting is over.  This
is not a joy ride, especially if it is raining or cold and
windy, but a duck shooter must not mind these things.
I have gone for miles in my boat over the rough waters of
the bay long before daylight, when the top of every near
whitecap on the windward side sent spray clear over my
canvas breakwater, some of it freezing to ice before it
could all run off the sloping deck.  If fate decreed that I
should have to follow such a life regularly, no amount of

money would compensate me, yet I always look forward with pleasure to my duck-shooting trips. I enjoy them while they last, rain or shine—if the ducks are flying.

I am acquainted with a number of the watermen who follow the bay, summer and winter. They are a hardy lot and need to be, or they would not survive. To me, a taste of the hardship that is their daily bread is an inspiration; a little of it would help almost any man to realize that his lot is not so hard after all, and the pleasant memories of these trips add to the enjoyment of a comfortable home on a cold winter's night.

Weather, luck, and skill all have an important influence on the bag. I usually have the luck, and am pleased with any weather that brings a stiff breeze. My bag each day was close enough to the limit to please anyone but a pot hunter. This year the ducks were all broadbills and redheads, with the former predominating, and I got twenty brant also. In former years, there was a greater variety, but broadbills generally outnumbered any other species.

The baymen told me that early in the fall season the hydroplanes and aeroplanes hovering over the bay annoyed the ducks greatly; these contraptions would alight in the midst of a flock of feeding ducks, or chase them in the air and even shoot their rapid-fire guns at them. I did not see any of this myself, and was told that it had been stopped. But planes passing up and down the shore were a frequent sight when I was there.

The baymen and guides are bitter about the new law, especially over not being allowed to sell their game. So far as I can learn, they are not taking any chances and are not selling ducks. They also tell me they will respect the law of seasons, and next spring [1919] will be the first year they will give up spring shooting. Our state law has always permitted it, and last spring the baymen and guides all shot in defiance of any law or regulation to the contrary. No one seemed to have the authority to stop them, or even to attempt it. The slaughter was terrific, and from what I heard, most wanton. Old baymen have told me they never in their lives saw anything to equal the last day of the open season. Everyone had fowl of all kinds to the limit, and many shooters respected no limit but that of their plentiful supply of shells.

### *Editor's Note*

The "new law" referred to by M. H. Ittner was (and is) the Migratory Bird Treaty Act of 1918, by which the federal government prohibited, except as permitted by regulations, the killing, capturing, or selling of any migratory bird included in the terms of a 1916 treaty with the British Commonwealth (Canada). The 1918 Bird Treaty Act was considered by some to be a violation of states' rights, and a constitutional test case, *State of Missouri v. Ray P. Holland, United States Game Warden*, was decided by the United States Supreme Court on 19 April 1920. By a seven to two majority, the court held that "the rights of the several states are not unconstitutionally infringed by the Migratory Bird Treaty of 8 December 1916, and the Migratory Bird Treaty Act of 3 July 1918, enacted to give effect of such treaty, under which the killing, capturing, or selling of any of the migratory birds included in the terms of the treaty are prohibited except as permitted by regulations to be made by the Secretary of Agriculture."

Raymond Prunty Holland (1884–1973) had his fifteen minutes of fame as the nominal defendant in the case, which validated the federal government's constitutional prerogative to control migratory bird hunting. (*Missouri v. Holland* is still read by law students as a leading case on the separation of federal and state police powers.) For many years Holland was a U.S. Game Warden for the Biological Survey, and was a lifelong conservationist who advocated strict game laws. He left government service for a career as a writer, and from 1924 to 1941 was editor of *Field and Stream*.

Holland was a prolific outdoor writer with at least eleven books to his credit from 1929 to 1961, mostly about gun dogs and hunting on uplands and lowlands. His best-known title is probably *Now Listen, Warden* (1946), a compilation of eighteen game warden yarns. He was author of many shooting stories that appeared in the *Saturday Evening Post* and *Collier's*, as well as in *Field and Stream*. He occasionally used the pen name "Bob White." After his retirement from *Field and Stream*, Holland moved to Vermont, where he wrote many of his full-length books, all of which continue to be popular with bibliophiles and sportsmen.

This chapter concludes the annotated anthology portion of *When Ducks Were Plenty*. The old-time duck-shooting chapters are, in effect, pieces of a historical puzzle that assemble and merge into an accurate and interrelated first-person saga of the grand passage of wildfowl. The reader now has a sense of history and can proceed to some facts and opinions that may or may not dovetail nicely with prior preconceptions.

For example, while in the midst of revising this manuscript for the umpteenth time, I was thumbing through the September 1998 issue of *Petersen's Shotguns* magazine. An article about snipe shooting by Tom Davis caught my eye, and I found another one of those "articles of faith" with which shooters continue to abuse our sport. Davis opined the snipe as his most challenging gamebird and gratuitously remarked how it had "finally received permanent protection." Then his zinger: "Sadly, this protection came too late for the passenger pigeon, which was driven to extinction by incessant year-round shooting." After reading chapter 56, "Going the Way of the Passenger Pigeon," the reader may see how Mr. Davis's opinion compares with firsthand observations and investigations by ornithologists and sportsmen who were present when the passenger pigeon suddenly and surprisingly, almost overnight, disappeared from the face of the earth. History and science place the blame on loss of habitat, squab gathering, and the wild pigeon's delicate psyche. Latter-day revisionists find it politically correct to blame the gun.

# Federal Protection of Wildfowl
## by Ed Muderlak

When I studied constitutional law at Northwestern University School of Law in 1970, one of the leading teaching cases was *State of Missouri v. Ray P. Holland, United States Game Warden*, 252 U.S.416 (19 April 1920). From the perspective of a law student, the case upheld the right of the federal government to pass laws, so long as such legislation was necessary and appropriate to implement a valid treaty with a foreign power. But from my view as a duck hunter, *Missouri v. Holland* was really about protecting ducks from the unprecedented firepower then in the hands of average sportsmen, not to mention market hunters.

Until about 1870, the typical fowling piece was a black-powder percussion-cap muzzleloader, with all the limitations implicit in such an arm. By 1902, however,

# Federal Protection of Wildfowl

the state of the art was a gas-operated semiautomatic repeating shotgun, that with modifications could rapidly fire almost a dozen self-contained "nitro" shotshells as fast as one could squeeze the trigger. A number of other factors compounded the need for federal protection and control of migratory wildfowl, even though the Tenth Amendment of the Constitution reserved police powers to the states. William B. Mershon's 1923 book, *Recollections of My Fifty Years Hunting and Fishing*, describes many of the factors that combined to diminish wildfowl numbers at the turn of the century. According to Mershon:

> How times have changed on the Saginaw River. Back from the river's edge in the 1880s stretched great areas of marsh land, tremendous beds of wild rice miles in extent, pond holes with cattails, muskrat houses, pond weed, water lilies, and all the surroundings and inhabitants that an ideal old-fashioned duck marsh ever contained. Of course these tremendous stretches of marsh meant quantities of wildfowl.
>
> The marshes were inaccessible except by boat or canoe. Then a railroad was built from Saginaw to Bay City. Dredges went through the marsh and put up an embankment. Then more railroads followed. An interurban line rattled slappety bang through the very heart of the duck country. Dikes and ditches reclaimed hundreds and hundreds of acres to make so-called prairie farms that were hard to subdue, but when the wild grasses were finally exterminated, some of these reclaimed areas were developed into rich farms. And with all these changes came the lessening of the wildfowl, so that where half a century ago the ducks congregated in hundreds of thousands, today they are few and far between and only steal in at night to feed.

# When Ducks Were Plenty

Mershon was a consummate hunter of all game including passenger pigeons in his youth. (He wrote the definitive book on the subject, *The Passenger Pigeon*, in 1907.) He and his hunting cronies bought a rail car in 1883, and used it as their "shooting box" to roam about the country in pursuit of game. In 1884, Mershon and nine others had a new rail car, City of Saginaw, built for $8,000. According to Mershon:

> It was perfectly plain, but it was a larger, stronger car: six wheel trucks, more convenient and roomy. We had the luxury of a bathroom with tub. We could carry five hundred gallons of water, and there was room for seven hundred fifty pounds of ice, so we were quite independent when side-tracked in places without a good water supply. The car was a great comfort in many ways, for with ample ice and storage facilities we could take care of our game and fish; we had our meals as we wanted them, and some sort of a card game every evening. Those were great old days of the hunting car.

The automobile also played a part in the lessening of wild game numbers, and Mershon cautioned that:

> Before condemning the old-time sportsman for the size of his bag, do not overlook this: There was not one man hunting where there are hundreds today. There were endless hunting and fishing grounds then inaccessible that are now easy of access. Reaching the hunting ground by horse and wagon was quite another thing than going by automobile. In the old days, three-quarters of the marshes, woods, bogs, and prairies never heard a gun. These places maintained the supply. When the forests were lumbered, burned, and cleared for the farm, when the lakes

# Federal Protection of Wildfowl

and marshes were diked and drained, when the roads and Fords both came to the cedar swamp, when the rail fence gave way to the barbed wire, then there had to be a change in what inhabited these regions.

During the Age of Progress from the 1870s to 1890s, the increased firepower of breechloaders and repeating shotguns combined with the speed and comfort of rail travel to accelerate the decrease in wildfowl numbers occasioned by the draining of swamps, leveling of forests, and conversion of wildlife habitat to agricultural and urban uses. The train was in its glory days by 1900, with 193,000 miles of track crisscrossing the United States, and the typical long-distance trip could average fifty miles per hour from point of departure to destination. The advent of Duryea's motor car in the late 1890s so improved mobility and access for the masses that, according to Mershon, "when the roads and Fords both came to the cedar swamp . . . there had to be a change in what inhabited these regions."

## The Lacey Act

The federal government entered the migratory bird protection fray with the Lacey Act of 1900. As reported in the 7 June 1900 issue of *Shooting and Fishing*, the Lacey game bill had just been passed by Congress and signed into law by President McKinley:

> Briefly told, this law will prohibit interstate traffic in animals or birds killed in violation of the laws of a state. The importance of this new law is very great, even though it comes several years too late to save countless animals and birds from extermination that should be alive now. It is not likely that persons who are accustomed to laugh at state laws will act similarly, now that the federal government is to aid each

# When Ducks Were Plenty

state or territory in punishing violations of its laws
by persons living in other states and territories.

Notwithstanding editorial high hopes, the new Lacey law was almost null when it came to controlling the state-by-state slaughter of migratory game birds, and it was mostly ineffective in controlling interstate commerce in game killed for the market. The federal government was not prepared to become the nation's game warden, especially when a federal offense was contingent upon the violation of a state game law—and the laws of every state were different! Suffice it to say that the Lacey Act had some impact on the feather merchants, but from the stand-point of market hunting—whether or not the game crossed state lines—it was mostly business as usual.

*After waterfowl in our hunting automobile.*

# Federal Protection of Wildfowl

## The Shiras Game Bill

By 1904, hunters were at each others' throats. Sporting publications were filled with accusations back and forth, bolstered variously by definitions of sportsmanship and condemnations of market hunting. There were a few feeble attempts to control market hunting on a state-by-state basis, but state legislators were aware that effective control of migratory bird hunting in one's own state, without similar controls up and down the flyway, would be futile, and political suicide to boot. Enter the federal government. According to an editorial in the 10 December 1904 issue of *Forest and Stream*, "the first federal game law was House Bill No. 15601 introduced 5 December 1904 by Hon. George Shiras III, of Pennsylvania, and was referred to the committee on agriculture." After the wherefores and whereases, the bill stated that:

> All wild geese, wild swans, brant, wild ducks, snipe, plover, woodcock, rail, wild pigeons, and all other migratory game birds which in their northern and southern migrations pass through or do not remain permanently in the entire year within the borders of any state or territory, shall hereafter be deemed to be within the custody and protection of the Government of the United States, and shall not be destroyed or taken contrary to regulation hereinafter provided for.

After *Forest and Stream* published the Shiras Bill, there was an avalanche of letters from sportsmen, state game commissioners, wardens, and conservationists supporting federal control. At the same time, some serious questions were put forth by persons for whom the end did not justify the means. A sampling of letters to the editor follows:

# When Ducks Were Plenty

10 December 1904

Editor, *Forest and Stream*

I heartily approve the idea of this measure; though, to be entirely frank, I fear the courts will not hold it to be constitutional.

Signed, *J. H. Acklin*
Game Warden, State of Tennessee

\* \* \* \* \*

16 December 1904

Editor, *Forest and Stream*

I think the Shiras bill should pass in spite of a possible clash of state and federal jurisdiction, as with such a federal law as a guide, it would unquestionably be enacted into statute law in every state interested in the protection of wildfowl. I sincerely hope the bill will pass.

Signed, *Henry Overbeck Jr.*
Wisconsin State Game Warden

\* \* \* \* \*

16 December 1904

Editor, *Forest and Stream*

The question of federal protection of game has been much discussed for several years, mostly by laymen, and such protection urged as the only hope for the game. Lawyers are generally of the opinion that it cannot be done except through a constitutional amendment, to which the consent of Congress cannot be obtained, and that the validity of such an amendment even if secured, would be doubtful. The Shiras Bill, by a number of whereases reciting facts

# Federal Protection of Wildfowl

showing the inefficiency of state laws, undertakes to construct a foundation for federal control. It seems obvious that such a foundation is of sand, and that further inquiry into its merit is scarcely necessary.

Signed, *D. C. Beaman*

## Migratory Bird Law of 1913

The possibility of federal involvement in the protection of migratory birds rattled around in various committees until 1913, when the first Migratory Bird Act (Weeks-McLean Bill) was passed by Congress and signed by President Wilson. Essential provisions of the law were soon held to be unconstitutional for the reason that the federal government could not simply declare migratory birds to be within its "custody and protection" without some grant of powers in the Constitution. All powers not specifically granted to the federal government are reserved to the states and the people by the Tenth Amendment. The Feds attempted to justify the law with the specious claim that migratory birds simply flying from state to state were engaged in "interstate commerce," but the Supreme Court didn't buy the argument. Selling game across state lines was held to be interstate commerce, however, and certain sections of the 1913 law survived the challenge, but enforcement was a problem.

As reported in a short article, "Protection Pays," in the January 1914 issue of *Outing* magazine, the Migratory Bird Act of 1913 was not an immediate success:

> Last fall a New Yorker cruising in Pamlico Sound noticed the low price of ducks offered for sale in the local markets. Something like forty cents apiece was the price asked. The visitor remarked that forty cents would hardly pay

# When Ducks Were Plenty

for the cost of shells at the usual average of hits.
Then he was informed that "they don't pay much
attention to the law down here. Mostly they get
'em by shinin' 'em." Evidently the market hunter
is not yet an extinct species. Shining ducks,
incidentally, is not only unsportsmanlike but
also illegal in every state in the Union. If it were
not so before the first of October [1913], it then
became so by the prohibition in the Weeks-McLean
Law of shooting between sunset and sunrise.

The provisions of the Weeks-McLean Law not directly
related to interstate commerce, such as shooting at night,
were soon held by the courts to be unconstitutional.
Another problem with the 1913 law was that enforcement
often took the path of least resistance. Overzealous state
and federal wardens would seize legally procured game from
a train's baggage-car refrigerator, citing the arguable tech-
nicality that it was "not in possession" of the sportsman,
who was asleep in his Pullman berth. Market hunters, meanwhile, continued to ply their trade, and the standard fare at
every decent restaurant and political fund raiser continued
to be—you guessed it—canvasback duck and terrapin soup.
The federal government then tried another approach.

## Do It by Treaty

By 1914, Wilbur Parker's vision of associations of
state and local sportsmen's clubs had reached fruition
on an international scale, and *Outing* magazine in the
January 1914 issue editorialized that the United States
and Canada should "Do It by Treaty":

> Apropos of bird protection, the American
> Game Protective Association is fostering a treaty
> with Canada, which will clinch the work begun by

# Federal Protection of Wildfowl

the Weeks-McLean Bill. The bulletin of the association declares that such a treaty would:

1. Protect during nearly the complete line of their flight most of the migratory species found in both countries.

2. Set at rest forever any talk as to the constitutionality of the Weeks-McLean law. The regulations that have been promulgated under authority of that law are made part of the proposed treaty. It is, of course, beyond the authority of any court to alter any part of a treaty.

The attorney general of New York is reported to have volunteered the opinion that the bill is unconstitutional. This attitude strains the doctrine of states' rights unduly and is doing serious harm to a worthy movement. Fortunately, the friends of the measure are warned in time.

## Migratory Bird Law of 1918

President Wilson negotiated, at the behest of the American Game Protective Association and other sportsmen's and game conservation groups, the treaty with Canada to cooperate in the protection of migratory birds. Congress ratified the treaty and then enacted the Migratory Bird Treaty Act of 1918 to implement the treaty. The law was immediately challenged by various states claiming usurpation of their states' rights. The United States Supreme Court held in *Missouri v. Holland* that if the treaty with Canada was a valid exercise of federal treaty powers under the constitution, then it would necessarily follow that the law to implement the treaty would be valid, even though identical provisions of the Migratory Bird Act of 1913, enacted absent a treaty, had been declared unconstitutional. The Migratory Bird Treaty Act of 1918 withstood the challenge and was declared reasonable and necessary to implement a valid treaty. As a consequence, ducks, geese, shorebirds, cranes, woodcock, and even doves were brought under federal jurisdiction.

The 1918 law is the basis for all federal regulations having to do with migratory bird hunting, and has provided employment for five generations of federal employees. But the Migratory Bird Treaty Act may be an anachronism, and it has certainly spawned a patchwork quilt of screwy "sudden-death" regulations. Anyone who can figure out the enforcement policies with respect to baiting can use the same intellectual process to pick a winning number in the lottery. And dusting geese with relatively ineffective steel shot from pit-blinds in the middle of cornfields defies logic and symbolizes the triumph of regulatory form over substantive game conservation. With some of these regulations, the tail is wagging the dog! Meanwhile, migratory birds migrate and their numbers and itineraries are primarily controlled by weather and habitat, not treaties.

## *Cause and Effect*

Retired market hunter H. Clay Merritt wrote the swan song for American waterfowl in his 1904 book, *The Shadow of a Gun*:

> American genius and enterprise are scouring the back bays for new railroads and new lines of travel. Cities are planned, new ships come to port, and the rivers are unlocked and their treasures transported away. [Farmers] . . . reclaimed so much waste and flooded land that the ducks eventually avoided it, and their associations were so thoroughly dissipated they never cared to come back.

# Federal Protection of Wildfowl

Multiply and compound the pressures of development and civilization the country over, and it's not surprising that migratory bird numbers are as sparse as their habitat. But sparse does not mean endangered. There are plenty of ducks, geese, snipe, woodcock, and doves to satisfy reasonable bag limits for the ever-decreasing population of sport hunters. "Endangerment" is more likely with the hunters than the hunted, given the complexity of game laws and regulations, restrictions on the ownership and transportation of firearms, and all the incremental nitpicky things that have cropped up over the years to encumber sportsmen.

## Divide and Conquer

Contributing to the decline of sport hunting is the fact that the term "sportsman" seldom goes without a prefix. Well-known gunwriter Stephen Bodio called the modern trend the "Balkanization of shooting sports." Each species of wild game seems to have its own support group, and they aren't necessarily hunters. A general-interest sportsman is a person of the past. The Illinois sportsman's license has places for so many picayune stamps that the sportsman of many interests (both shooting and fishing) carries around a mini art gallery in his wallet.

Meanwhile, those of us who lived vicariously the broad sporting experiences of a young Robert Ruark—as told in his books, *The Old Man and the Boy* and *The Old Man's Boy Grows Older*—are acutely aware that there will never be a next generation of Robert Ruarks. For example, it is against the law in the state of Illinois to go afield or to the marsh (or anywhere else for that matter) with a gun while not in possession a valid Illinois Firearm Owner's Identification card. No young person can have an FOI until age eighteen (with parental consent) or age twenty-one without. I won't belabor the issues of military service and voting at age eighteen vis-à-vis not being legally entitled to hunt alone with a gun until age twenty-one, except to say that Illinois has equated the "evils" of hunting with the deleterious effects of alcohol consumption in regards to legal age.

Young people are allowed to hunt so long as they are in the direct presence of a parent or guardian who possesses a valid FOI; but what about a young person without a sport-hunting mentor? And what about the rural kids who might want to walk up a pheasant or puddle jump a duck after school? The procedures to establish oneself as a legally licensed duck shooter in the state of Illinois are time consuming, complex, stifling, and, for those not of legal drinking age, impossible! How many young people would play baseball, soccer, golf, or tennis if there was more involved than simply showing up? To drive this point home, let's go through what it takes to even begin to scout for a place to duck hunt in Illinois.

## *Catch-22*

I attended Northwestern University School of Law in the late 1960s, and then as now it was a bastion of knee-jerk liberalism. The number of my classmates (class of 1971) who had ever been hunting could have been counted on the fingers of one thumb: my friend Owen. And as luck would have it, Owen's parents owned a farm on the outskirts of Chicago with a private pond, built-in blind, in-place decoys, and a relatively steady supply of ducks. Owen and I got together a couple of times for some early morning duck shooting, and a mutual friend and classmate, Rick, saw fit to spout liberal drivel about

# Federal Protection of Wildfowl

shooting the feathered equivalent of Bambi. Rick had an open mind, however, and we challenged him to try his hand at the sport. He agreed, thinking he would then have the opportunity to condemn it with firsthand knowledge. Rick never made it to the duck blind, however, even though he made a heroic effort.

Duck season was on, and Rick had no Illinois FOI. Although an adult, he could not legally carry a firearm even if he was mentored by two card-carrying fellow hunters on private property. Thus Rick could not even borrow a shotgun without serious legal implications that might impair his ability to become a member of the bar. Assuming Rick had a FOI, he would have then needed a hunting license, which is not usually a problem, but finding an Illinois duck stamp and Federal duck stamp in Chicago during duck season would have been no easy task. Projecting forward a generation, if Rick were a young man of legal age today, he could not even get a hunting license without proof of having taken a firearms safety course (proof being a certificate or previously issued license). The punchline is that in 1999, a person of the age, character, and intellect to be a student at a major law school, soon to be a lawyer, and perhaps ultimately a judge, cannot be initiated into the loop of sport hunters without establishing a game plan at least four months before the season opens.

Considering the Orwellian preliminaries to even starting to look for a place to shoot ducks, it's not surprising that an ever-increasing number of people are more interested in reading about duck shooting than actually going out and doing it. Under proper management, every species of duck has bounced back to huntable numbers (including canvasbacks and wood ducks), but who will step forward to plead the case of the beleaguered sport hunter?

# When Ducks Were Plenty

## Going the Way of the Passenger Pigeon

As will be seen in the next chapter, the passenger pigeon disappeared because it was incapable of surviving in small numbers. Likewise, sport hunting today is being "Balkanized." Small numbers of species-specific lobbyists go about their self-anointed crusades, unable to see the forest for the trees. It seems that every type of fish and game has its own following. Carp Unlimited? Crows Forever? Each focus group is absolutely sure that increased regulation and a special tax stamp to support their agendas will enhance their own narrow interests. But for every fired-up would-be sport hunter who relishes each laborious, sometimes expensive, and often nearly impossible achievement in the compliance process, there are many more who say, "Why bother? I'll take up golf!" The road to hell is often paved with good intentions, and no one could accuse federal and state legislators and regulators, or the various species-specific lobbying groups, of anything but good intentions. It's a little late for *Passenger Pigeons Forever*, but read on anyway.

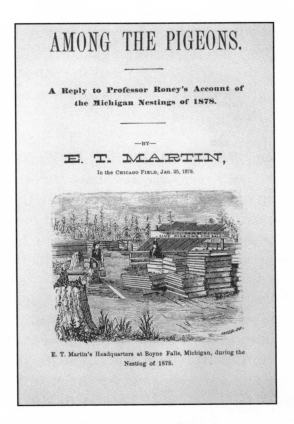

AMONG THE PIGEONS.

A Reply to Professor Roney's Account of
the Michigan Nestings of 1878.

—BY—

E. T. MARTIN,

In the CHICAGO FIELD, Jan. 25, 1879.

E. T. Martin's Headquarters at Boyne Falls, Michigan, during the
Nesting of 1878.

# Going the Way of
the Passenger Pigeon

## Edited by Ed Muderlak

Jacob Pentz, the author of chapter 11, hunted passenger pigeons as a youngster in the 1860s, and wrote in 1896 that "it seemed the thing to do at the time, yet the wild pigeon exists now only in memory of the older generation, and with remembrance comes a pang of sorrow." The passing of the passenger pigeon is probably the single most dramatic consequence of what is now perceived to be the excessive pursuit of wild game in the nineteenth century. For many it is an article of faith that the passenger pigeon was hunted to extinction for sport. I don't think so. Read the following articles, editorials, and letters to editors and see if you agree or disagree with my conclusions.

## *"The Wild Pigeons of Old: 1837 to 1888"*
### *Editorial, Forest and Stream (1909)*

A pigeon roost and nesting place above the headwaters of the Delaware and its tributaries is of historic record, not only for its gigantic dimensions, but for its memorable opportunities and importance in the domestic economy of the region. In 1837, times were very hard in the upper Delaware Valley. That was the year of the great panic. Lumbering was the mainstay of Sullivan County and the neighboring counties of both New York and Pennsylvania. Lumber that year was not selling for enough to

cover the cost of production. To add to the distress, the crops of the year before had been very short.

There were dense beech forests in the region, but beechnuts are an uncertain crop. In the days when they were a factor in the welfare of the backwoods dwellers, a scant beechnut crop meant a corresponding scarcity of wild game. Two years in succession there had been no beechnuts, but a big crop in 1836 had left the forest

*Passenger pigeon.*

# Going the Way of the Passenger Pigeon

floor deep with the food so attractive to wild pigeons. So in the spring of 1837, these birds came to the upper Delaware woods in unprecedented numbers.

An Orange County ancient has personal recollection of that historic pigeon roost, the remarkable and exciting incidents that attended its presence, and the unceasing campaign of slaughter that was carried on against the vast pigeon colony:

When I was a boy of ten, people went by the score from Orange County and from every other county within a hundred miles to get a share of the birds. My father saddled his horse and went too, and took me along with him. It was a two-day journey to the wilderness where the roost was. The time was early April, and we arrived on the scene one afternoon about four o'clock. As far as the eye could see, on every limb of every tree, rested a rude shallow nest of sticks. Above the rim of every nest thrust the heads of two fat squabs, unable yet to fly.

Scattered about in the forest were numerous shacks and shanties built of logs, boughs, or bark. These were occupied by pigeon gatherers who had come from all parts of the country thereabouts. Squabs were continually falling from their insecure nests, and the ground was covered with them, dead and dying. Men, women, and children were gathering, drawing, and curing them over beds of hardwood coals, "jerking" them as it was called. To make the harvest of squabs larger, the squabbers went at the trunks of trees with heavy lengths of timber, using them as battering rams. This would fetch the squabs tumbling from their nests like ripe chestnuts.

The human squab gatherers were not lone sharers in that harvest. At night foxes, raccoons, wildcats, porcupines, skunks, and other four-footed prowlers could be seen sneaking in among the tree trunks, watching for an opportunity to get an easy feast on the squabs as they tumbled from the nest. The howl of an occasional wolf, too wary to venture close to the camp—and the whole forest seemed to be one great camp—was frequently heard. Many of the campers had driven their swine in with them and droves of hogs fed on the young pigeons.

When we arrived at the roost there were only a few scattered pigeons fluttering about their nests, but just before sundown we heard a sound in the distance that rapidly became a roar, and the sky began to darken. The pigeons were returning from their feeding grounds in the bush to their roosts and nests. Immediately following the first rush of returning pigeons, and until long after dark, a closely packed and unbroken flight of birds poured in. They alit in great masses, often one on top of the other upon every spot to which they could cling. Their fluttering calls and the constant breaking and crashing to the ground of boughs giving way produced noise so tremendous that the loudest shouts of men standing side by side could not be heard from one to the other, and the firing of a gun a few yards away would only be known by the flash it made.

The pigeons paid no attention to all the fires that gleamed everywhere, nor to the men who with long poles swept them in heaps from the low-lying branches. Frequently the whole upper part of some brittle and overladen tree would snap off and come down with a crash, carrying with it not only its own mass of living freight, but crushing to death countless numbers of young and old birds on the lower branches. Those of the disturbed pigeons that were unhurt would struggle blindly

# Going the Way of the Passenger Pigeon

upward again, trying to get a foothold somewhere among the trees. If they could not regain a roost in the tree from which they had been hurled, they would huddle together on the ground beneath it and fall victims to the clubs of the slaughterers.

From daylight until nearly midnight, the slaughter of pigeons and squabs was continuous. The old pigeons would be off to the feeding grounds at dawn. The roosts had been there over a month, and thousands of pigeons had been killed before the nesting began. The squabs had just come into condition for gathering. For eight weeks the birds were shot, clubbed, netted, and killed in every known manner and taken by the wagon load to local markets. The spring rafting freshet was on, and every raft that pulled out of the upper Delaware was loaded high with pigeons that were taken to markets along the river, where they found ready and profitable sale. Some pigeon hunters cleared as much as $1,000 during the time the birds were in the woods; besides the pigeon roost saving a great deal of families from trouble and suffering in the valley, it laid the foundation of more than one family fortune. That was the greatest wild pigeon roost and nesting of which there is any record in the east. It was more than fifteen miles long and seven miles wide.

The last flight of pigeons in the east was in 1888. In the spring of that year they filled the forests of western Pennsylvania for miles and miles along the Allegheny River. In 1888 they also nested in the wilds of the Great Michigan Peninsula, in as enormous number as they had ever been, for they occupied an area of forest ten miles long and several miles wide. The usual period of slaughter and netting made inroads upon the colony, but when it rose for departure after the nesting season

# *When Ducks Were Plenty*

was over, it was estimated that there were not less than ten million birds in the flight. From that day to this [1909], however, no eye, so far as is known, has ever seen them again.

\* \* \* \* \*

7 October 1886

Editor, *Forest and Stream*:

How entirely shooting has changed here even in the last ten years. Then the wild pigeons were thick every fall and spring. If a man was too lazy to hunt them in the woods, he could buy them for the trap and thus keep his gun from rusting. Now not a pigeon can be found in all the woods where they used to breed by the millions. Truly, pigeon trap shooting is already a thing of the past. In its place artificial targets bid fair to be more popular than ever at the trap.

Signed, *Penn*

\* \* \* \* \*

26 July 1888

Editor, *Shooting and Fishing*

The sportsmen of Walla Walla, Washington Territory, have just organized a rod and gun club with forty members. The shooting tournament of the Sportsmen's Association of the Northwest will be held at this place beginning 15 August 1888, and will hold for three days. The contest will consist of clay birds, Peoria blackbirds, and live-bird shooting. We expect to have 1,000 or more live birds. We now have to shoot the tame birds as there are no wild pigeons in this part of the territory.

Signed, *Arthur W. du Bray*

# Going the Way of the Passenger Pigeon

## The Passenger Pigeon
### by William B. Mershon

For the last three years [since 1904] I have spent most of my leisure time collecting as much material as possible that might throw light on the oft-repeated query, "What has become of the wild pigeons?" It's hard for the older generation to believe that as recently as 1880, the passenger pigeon was thronging in countless millions through large areas of the middle west. We could find no exaggeration in the record of such earlier observers as Alexander Wilson, the ornithologist, who said that these birds associated in such prodigious numbers as almost to surpass belief. Their numbers had no parallel among any other feathered tribes on the face of the earth, and one of their roosts would kill the trees over thousands of acres as completely as if the whole forest had been girdled with an ax.

Audubon estimated that an average flock of these pigeons contained a billion and a quarter birds, which consumed more than eight and a half million bushels of nuts in a day's feeding. The pigeons, in turn, supplied a means of living for thousands of market hunters, who devastated their flocks with nets and guns, and even with fire. Yet so vast were their numbers that after thirty years of observation, Audubon was able to say that "even in the face of such dreadful havoc nothing but the diminution of our forests can accomplish their decrease."

Many theories have been advanced to account for the disappearance of the wild pigeons, among them that their migration may have been overwhelmed by some cyclonic disturbance of the atmosphere that destroyed their myriads at one blow. The big nesting of 1878 in Michigan was undoubtedly the last large migration, but the pigeons continued to nest infrequently in Michigan and the north for several years after that, and until as late as 1886, they were trapped for the market and for trapshooting. The pigeons did not become extinct in a day, nor did one tremendous catastrophe wipe them from the face of the earth. They gradually became fewer and existed for twenty years or more after the date set as that of their final extermination.

The habits of the birds were such that they could not thrive singly nor in small bodies, but were dependent upon one another. Vast communities were necessary to their very existence, and an enormous quantity of food was necessary for their sustenance. The cutting of the forests and consequent diminished habitat and food supply interfered with their plan of existence and drove them into new localities, and the ever-increasing slaughter could not help but lessen their once vast numbers. The passenger pigeon laid only one egg in its nest, rarely two, and although it bred three or four times a year, it could not replenish the numbers slaughtered by the professional netters. The history of the buffalo is repeated in that of the wild pigeon, the extermination of which was inspired by the same motive: the greed of man and the pursuit of the almighty dollar. We have locked the barn door after the horse was stolen.

### *"Last Passenger Pigeons?"*
#### *Editorial, New York Sun (1919)*

Since the death on 1 September 1914 in the zoological garden at Cincinnati, Ohio, of what was generally believed to be the last surviving passenger pigeon, there have been numerous reports of sightings, but on investigation the birds proved to be mourning doves. An attempt was made

# Going the Way of the Passenger Pigeon

in 1910 to find an undisturbed nest of passenger pigeons. Although more than $3,000 was offered in reward to the discoverer of one, and the offer held good for several years, no reward was ever collected. State rewards of $100 were offered in New York, New Jersey, Massachusetts, Connecticut, Pennsylvania, Illinois, and Michigan where the passenger pigeon once was prolific.

Civilized man was the exterminator of the bird. Millions of birds were brought down by systematic slaughter for the market and pot by the shotguns, clubs, and nets of the earliest American pot hunters. How could a bird, even though its numbers once darkened the skies, stand such slaughter as was involved in a daily shipment of three carloads for forty days? The town of Hartford, Michigan, shipped that amount in 1869. The total number of birds was estimated at 11,883,000. Two years later another Michigan town marketed 15,840,000 passenger pigeons.

Massachusetts passed a law in 1848, protecting the netters of wild pigeons. There was a fine of $10 for damaging nets or frightening pigeons away from them. Pigeon slaughter was a legitimate industry. New York came to the conclusion in 1867 that the wild pigeon needed protection, but the following

*Last of their kind?*

year saw its last great nesting, and the last roosting was in 1875. Michigan gave the birds protection in 1869, but Pennsylvania did not do so until 1878, and in 1870 Massachusetts gave protection to the birds that once were sold for twelve cents a dozen.

The millions of passenger pigeons were so suddenly exterminated that it was hard to believe they became extinct. Assertions were numerous that the birds, which formerly ranged from the Atlantic coast westward to the Rocky Mountains, had taken refuge in South America or Mexico. Alexander Wilson, the pioneer American ornithologist, once estimated the number of passenger pigeons at 2,230,272,000; no wonder wasteful Americans regarded them as food for hogs.

## *Editor's Note*

The 2.23 billion passenger pigeons estimated by Alexander Wilson were in one flock! According to Wilson, he was on his way from Shelbyville to Frankfort, Kentucky, in 1810, when a single flock of pigeons began passing overhead about one o'clock in the afternoon. As he continued on his way, the flock streamed overhead until about six in the evening. Based on his firsthand experience, Wilson sharpened his pencil and started calculating:

> I have taken from the crop of a single wild pigeon a good handful of the kernels of beechnuts, intermixed with acorns and chestnuts. To form a rough estimate of the daily consumption of one of these immense flocks, let us first attempt to calculate the numbers that passed me between Frankfort and the Indiana territory. We suppose this column to have been one mile in breadth (and I believe it to have been much more), and

# *Going the Way of the Passenger Pigeon*

that it moved at the rate of one mile a minute. The time it passed took four hours, which would make its length 240 miles. Again, supposing that each square yard of this moving body comprehended three pigeons, the square yards in the whole space, multiplied by three, would give 2,230,272,000 pigeons!—an almost inconceivable multitude, and yet probably far below the actual amount. Computing each of these to consume half a pint of mast daily, the flock would need 17,424,000 bushels per day! Heaven has wisely and graciously given to these birds rapidity of flight and a disposition to range over vast uncultivated tracts of the earth, otherwise they would perish in the districts where they reside, after devouring the whole production of agriculture as well as that of the forests.

And now the punch line: Wilson computed the amount of mast consumed by the one flock of passenger pigeons observed near Frankfort, Kentucky, in 1810, to be roughly 17.5 million bushels per day. Projecting forward to 1998, a fully loaded semitrailer truck will carry a thousand bushels of corn, or the production of about seven acres at the current national average corn yield. If Wilson's flock should miraculously reappear in the midwest, it would consume 17,500 fully loaded semitrailers of corn each day of the year! And it would take 80,000 square miles of field corn at the average 1998 yield estimated by the USDA to feed that flock of wild pigeons year round! By comparison, the USDA estimates the entire 1998 corn crop will be harvested from approximately 116,000 square miles; according to the *Rand McNally Road Atlas*, the land area of the state of Kentucky is 39,674 square miles. Just how many flocks of passenger pigeons were there?

# When Ducks Were Plenty

In my opinion, the "tragedy" of the passing of the passenger pigeon was no tragedy at all. I for one am glad that flocks of a billion or more birds are no longer cruising the countryside looking for a roost in my woods and intending to depredate my crops. I'm sure other farmers are equally relieved. The fact that flocks of passenger pigeons blackened the sky and had roosts measured by square miles demonstrated their dependence on living in great numbers, like hoards of locusts. Bemoaning the absence of passenger pigeons is tantamount to regretting the absence of earthquakes, floods, forest fires, and tornadoes. The last passenger pigeon reportedly died in 1914 at the Cincinnati Zoo. *C'est la vie.*

# *Epilogue*

I know but one small grove of sizable trees
left in the township, supposed by some to have
been planted by the pigeons that were once baited
with beechnuts nearby. . . . How can you expect
the birds to sing when their groves are cut down?
—Henry David Thoreau (Walden, 1854)

The demise of the passenger pigeon is often cited
by activists as an example of man's inhumanity to
animals, and it is an article of faith that wild pigeons
were hunted to extinction. However, waterfowl and
shorebirds, upland game, deer, elk, and buffalo were

*(Picture: Ed Muderlak, circa 1986, Lake Guerrero, Mexico.)*

also hunted relentlessly; many species had their numbers reduced to levels of rank endangerment, yet still survived. Market hunting went hand-in-hand with westward expansion and the pressures of civilization. Hard-working Americans on the move, building a country, had to eat, and market hunting was simply a division of labor that facilitated the Industrial Revolution and led to the Age of Progress.

My understanding of the passing of the passenger pigeon was gleaned from reading much of what was published on the topic at a time when memories were fresh and experiences firsthand. American ornithologists Alexander Wilson and John James Audubon linked the prosperity of the passenger pigeon to an abundant mast of beechnuts, chestnuts, and acorns on the floors of vast hardwood forests in the upper midwest. Westward expansion and the needs of a growing country for lumber and farmland diminished the forests and, in turn, diminished the flocks of billions of wild pigeons. When numbers were drawn down to scattered flocks of reduced size, the passenger pigeon—unlike the bison, deer, and various species of wildfowl—could not survive due to an inherent inability to adapt to lesser numbers. Thus the passenger pigeon went the way of the dinosaur for reasons totally extraneous to sport hunting.

Meanwhile, most other overhunted species of big and small game bounced back (to varying degrees) under the protection of appropriate game laws and preservation of habitats. There were so few deer in Illinois in 1902 that the season was closed indefinitely, but with closed seasons and the reduction of subsistence hunting, deer numbers bounced back. Fifty-five years later, in 1957, the Department of Conservation in Illinois declared a

# Epilogue

one-day shotgun season. Soon there was a three day season, and then two seasons of three days each. As I write this in 1998, the Illinois deer herd has mushroomed to the point where it's dangerous to drive on country roads at dusk.

The life cycle of the American bison is such that it can exist in small numbers and breed back to herds of controlled size. Few would argue for a renewed migration of millions of buffalo trampling crops and stopping traffic on the interstate. The bison survived wholesale slaughter for buffalo robes and the fencing of the west by farmers. At the dawn of the twentieth century, the entire buffalo (American bison) herd in the United States numbered less than one thousand. Herds are now scattered throughout the United States, with numbers limited only by "habitat"—i.e., the size of the buffalo rancher's fenced-in pasture.

Duck numbers rise and fall with the vagaries of weather and habitat. Canvasbacks and other deep divers feed on bottom grasses that are "out of sight, out of mind," and thus of little concern to land regulators. Wild celery, the favorite food of canvasbacks, has virtually disappeared from large areas of their historic migratory routes as a result of dredging, channelization, pools created by locks, and boat traffic, compounded by runoff pollution from development, industry, and agriculture. Canvasbacks, which became scarce on Wisconsin's Winnebago lakes in the 1950s, are physiologically less able than geese to go ashore and feed regularly on available grains and grasses. Thus their numbers have severely declined since the nineteenth century.

Federal and state restrictions now make duck and goose hunting the least cost-effective of shooting sports, and the ban on lead shot has all but stopped casual waterfowling. Even so, our web-footed friends are not likely to stage another grand passage anytime soon, for not all wildfowl have fared as well as Canada and snow geese. The once scarce Canada goose is now a genuine "hazard" on many golf courses; they have thrived by adapting to feeding on land, grazing winter wheat, gleaning cornfields, and ruining lawns. Snow geese, too, have adjusted to the inroads of civilization and are overrepresented proportionally to other waterfowl.

According to an article in the 29 April 1998 issue of the *Rockford* (Illinois) *Register Star*, a gaggle of snow geese is creating a "botanical desert" above the Arctic Circle. Biologists say the birds are clearing tundra of surface vegetation, which may never recover. The Associated Press blurb states there were fewer than 800,000 snow geese thirty years ago, but that the population today has been estimated as high as six million, growing at the rate of 250,000 birds a year. The article goes on to say:

> Their numbers soaring, millions of snow geese are threatening one of North America's treasured ecosystems with their voracious appetites. And government biologists are grappling with some rather extraordinary suggestions on what to do about the too-fruitful birds. One solution: Kill nearly 3 million of them, about half the population. But how? So far, napalm has been mentioned, and, along with poison, has been ruled out. But by next winter, thousands of shotgun-toting hunters may be let loose on the wily birds that annually migrate from the Gulf Coast to the Canadian Arctic.

Meanwhile, everyone has an opinion. "Their massive numbers put such a high demand on the limited food supplies that vast tracts of the Arctic have been converted to highly saline, bare soil where few plants can grow," says Bruce Batt, the chief biologist of Ducks Unlimited. "The problem is of our own making," says Frank Gill, president of the National Audubon Society, "It goes back to America's agricultural successes." Gill said the Audubon Society's board has endorsed new efforts, including expanded hunting, to reduce the snow goose population. Meanwhile, Congress is debating the issue, and the Fish and Wildlife Service is expected to propose giving hunters open season on the birds by expanding the hunting days, scrapping bag limits, allowing the use of bait, and hunting in areas now off limits. One can only wonder how the Canadian tundra survived since the last Ice Age without the help of the U.S. Congress and Washington bureaucrats.

The decline of American waterfowl from habitat destruction and overhunting has been a hot topic since my teenage years in the 1950s, and the issue is not likely to be resolved during my lifetime. Beginning in 1918, and increasing since the 1960s, federal and state regulators have micromanaged seasons and bag limits to stem the real or imagined statistical decline of wildfowl numbers. But their efforts may have been, for the most part, misdirected; their focus was on gross flyway numbers—increasing, decreasing, or stable—rather than on the ever-decreasing lack of diversity.

Canvasback ducks and their habitat were once excessively abundant, but habitat and, in turn, the ducks have declined as civilization has made irreversible inroads into the wilderness. The ducks, furthermore, have been unable to adapt to other habitats. No matter how abbreviated the season, no matter how high the point score toward the bag limit, and no matter if canvasback hunting is outlawed entirely, their numbers will be limited by lack of habitat. In fact, the pressures and encroachment of civilization act as a stress test to select out those species that can survive in proximity to man. It would seem that Canada and snow geese are passing with flying colors, while the canvasback is getting a barely passing score, and, of course, the passenger pigeon flunked the test.

The extinction of the passenger pigeon is not an example of man's inhumanity to animals. The wild pigeon could not survive in the wild when its habitat declined due to the spread of civilization. Civilization, likewise, would not have tolerated passenger pigeons had they survived. Adult birds scoured crops within hundreds of miles of their roosts to reserve food in the immediate nesting area for their squabs. The flock of 2.23 billion birds observed by ornithologist Alexander Wilson in 1810 would need more than two-thirds of the entire 1998 American corn crop for its sustenance. I think it's fair to say in 1998, when a flock of Canada geese in a neighborhood park is considered to be a threat to domestic tranquillity, and some game biologists have "mentioned" napalming snow geese on the Arctic tundra, that a typical flock of passenger pigeons roosting anywhere would be as welcome as a free-range brontosaurus.

There is always a danger of misinterpreting history by applying current standards to past events, so it's important to keep an open mind and put events into context. The clearing of virgin hardwood forests for farms and cities triggered the decline and ultimate extinction of the passenger pigeon, and there could be no alternative scenario. Likewise, the story of five hundred canvasback ducks killed from one battery in the 1880s contains no lessons for duck shooters or game managers entering the twenty-first century.  Every one of those five hundred ducks would otherwise have died of natural causes within their short life span; it's a false premise to think, given another scenario, that the offspring of hypothetical survivors might have led to an increase in duck numbers today.  Pollution and channelization diminished water celery beds and, in turn, made the canvasback a rare bird.  Canvasbacks will not miraculously reappear in historic numbers on the Winnebago lakes or Susquehanna flats without the equally miraculous reappearance of their historic feeding grounds.  The efforts of Ducks Unlimited are much appreciated by ducks and duck shooters alike, but it is one thing to preserve and restore vacant Canadian marshland, and quite another to undo the impact of civilization in and near American population centers.

Just as I was finishing this manuscript, Colonel Bob Schmidt of Lake Forest, Illinois, loaned me his copy of William B. Mershon's 1923 book, *Recollections of My Fifty Years of Hunting and Fishing*.  In the introduction I found my thesis concisely stated:

> I very much doubt if the bag of the sportsman of old was any cause for the diminishing supply of wildlife.  Environment, and not the gun of the sportsman—I will not exempt the market hunter entirely—must be the explanation.  The wide-ranging buffalo had to go.  Had no wild pigeons been killed, where could they feed in numbers now? [Amen.]

The blinds and brush houses alongside marsh and river are filled every fall with intrepid duck shooters, looking ever skyward, hoping against hope for another grand passage of waterfowl. Some of us have even begrudged being born a hundred years too late. But, alas, history is not likely to repeat itself, so the more we understand the context in which our ancestors fed themselves with canvasback ducks and passenger pigeon squabs, warmed themselves with buffalo robes, cut forests to build our cities, and plowed virgin prairie to plant crops, the less likely we are to be ex post facto judgmental. One thing, though, is certain: In light of civilization's continuing quest for people-friendly habitat, there will never be another golden age of wildfowling as *When Ducks Were Plenty*.

# Bibliography

An Old Sportsman. "Loon Used for Duck Decoy." *The American Field* (7 June 1919).

Askins (the Elder), Charles. "Old-Time Wildfowl Shooting." *The American Rifleman* (December 1934).

Bogardus, Adam H. "Canada Geese on Thin Ice." *Field, Cover, and Trap Shooting.* Rev. ed. New York: Published by author, 1878.

Bumstead, John. "How to Shoot Ducks." *On the Wing—Book for Sportsmen.* New York: Happy Hours Publishing Co., 1869.

Burroughs, Julian. "A Flyer in Geese." *Forest and Stream* (23 January 1909).

C. B. "Spring Goose Shooting on Bay Chaleur." *Shooting and Fishing* (19 September 1889).

Cosmopolitan. "Tame Ducks as Decoys." *The American Sportsman* (18 April 1874).

Crittenden, L. E. [Adirondack, pseud.] "A Comparison: 1844 to 1900." *The Amateur Sportsman* (May 1901).

Crooker, L. B. "Duck Shooting in Illinois." *The American Sportsman* (May 1873).

Colville, W. L. [Dick Swiveller, pseud.] "Duck Shooting on Delaware Bay." *Shooting and Fishing* (20 September 1894).

Don. "On the Kankakee." *The American Sportsman* (May 1873).

Du Bray, Capt. A. W. [Gaucho, pseud.] "Duck Shooting." *Shooting and Fishing* (18 December 1902).

———, et al. "Recent Duck Shooting by Fred Kimble." *Fred Kimble, Master Duck Shot of the World.* Chicago: W. C. Hazelton, 1923.

Fitzgerald, David Bruce. "Shooting the Chesapeake Duck." *Outing* (December 1905).

Forester, Frank [Henry William Herbert]. "Rail Shooting." *Frank Forester's Field Sports of the United States and British Provinces of North America (1848).* New York: W. A. Townsend, 1866.

Friend, Alex. "A Day's Hunt at Lily Lake." *The Amateur Sportsman* (November 1895).

Gasper, Howland. "Market Shooting on Chincoteague Bay." *Shooting and Fishing* (12 April 1900).

———. "Securing a Point." *Shooting and Fishing* (13 October 1904).

Gooseman. "When Wild Geese Were Plenty." *The American Field* (5 April 1913).

Griswold, Sandy. "Days with the Wildfowl." *Forest and Stream* (8 October 1904).

Hazelton, William C. "Timber Mallards on the Illinois River." *The American Field* (15 January 1921).

Hunter, Alex. "No Ducks on Currituck Sound." *Shooting and Fishing* (12 March 1891).

Ittner, Martin Hill. "No Spring Shooting on Barnegat Bay." *The American Field* (4 January 1919).

J. J. B. "Batteries on Sandusky Bay." *Forest and Stream* (9 April 1885).

J. W. G. D. "Close to Home in Minnesota." *Shooting and Fishing* (13 July 1899).

Kansas Chief. "Selfishness Cured." *Shooting and Fishing* (7 January 1904).

Kanuck. "Coot's Revenge." *Forest and Stream* (7 October 1886).

Kendall, Joseph R. "With Powder Flask and Shot Pouch." *Forest and Stream* (13–20 February 1909).

Kimble, Fred, et al. "Among the Geese and Sandhill Cranes in North Dakota." *Fred Kimble, Master Duck Shot of the World.* Chicago: W. C. Hazelton, 1923.

Krider, John. "'Sunk Box' Canvasbacks." *Krider's Sporting Anecdotes.* Edited by H. Milnor Klapp. Philadelphia: A. Hart, 1853.

Leopold, E. A. "Never on Sunday." *Forest and Stream* (5 November 1885).

Lewis, Elisha Jarrett. "Tolling Ducks." *The American Sportsman* (1851–55). Philadelphia: Lippincott, Grambo & Co., 1855.

Long, Joseph W. "Muzzleloader or Breechloader?" *American Wild-Fowl Shooting*. New York: J. B. Ford & Co., 1874.

Marliave, E. T. "Bay Birds on the Orleans Marshes." *The American Sportsman* (7 March 1874).

McLellan, Isaac. "Caught in a Snowstorm on Barnegat Bay." *The American Sportsman* (10 January 1874).

Merritt, H. Clay. "The Shadow of a Gun." Chicago: F. T. Peterson Co., 1904.

Mershon William B. "A Shooting Box Named 'City of Saginaw.'" In *Recollections of My Fifty Years Hunting and Fishing*. Boston: The Stratford Company, 1923.

Muderlak, Ed. "Breechloading Shotguns"; "Dangerous Ducking"; Epilogue; "Federal Protection of Wildfowl"; "Going the Way of the Passenger Pigeon"; "Lacey Interstate Bird Law of 1900"; "Teal Story"; and "Wilbur F. Parker, Conservationist" were written for the purposes of this manuscript.

Mulligan, Frank H. "Memories Are a Siren's Song." *The American Field* (27 December 1919).

Murphy, John Mortimer. "'Piles' of Florida Ducks." In *American Game-Bird Shooting.* New York: Orange Judd Co., 1882.

S

———. "Wild Geese." In *American Game-Bird Shooting.* New York: Orange Judd Co., 1882.

———. "Wild Swans." In *American Game-Bird Shooting.* New York: Orange Judd Co., 1882.

Page, Paul E. "Mallard Shooting in the Alberta Wheatfields." *The American Field* (18 September 1920).

Pastnor, Paul. "Sweeney's Snipe." *Shooting and Fishing* (2 October 1890).

Pentz, Jacob. "Wild Pigeon Shooting—A Memory." *Shooting and Fishing* (10 September 1896).

Pettitt, Ernest. "'Ducking' With Perkins." *The American Field* (14 June 1913).

Purdy, C. R. "Brant Shooting on Great South Bay." *American Duck Shooting.* Edited by George Bird Grinnell. New York: Forest and Stream Publishing Company, 1901.

"R" of Lowell, Massachusetts. "Black Duck Thanksgiving." *Shooting and Fishing* (9 December 1897).

Ross, Robert E. "Duck Shooting in Southern California Years Ago." *The American Field* (4 December 1920).

Shufeldt, R. W. "Slaughter of Wildfowl at Hog Island Light Station." *Shooting and Fishing* (8 March 1900).

Special. "A Shameful Fashion." *Forest and Stream* (7 January 1886).

Stinson, Melvin Oscar [Rambler, pseud.] "Duck Shooting on the St. Lawrence." *Shooting and Fishing* (4 July 1889).

Townsend, Wilmot. "My Three Blackbreasts." *Shooting and Fishing* (17 February 1898).